COUNTER CULTURE
THE SHERIDANS GUIDE TO CHEESE

www.transworldireland.ie

www.transworldbooks.co.uk

COUNTER CULTURE

THE

SHERIDANS

GUIDE TO CHEESE

KEVIN & SEAMUS SHERIDAN
WITH CATHERINE CLEARY

TRANSWORLD IRELAND

TRANSWORLD IRELAND PUBLISHERS
28 Lower Leeson Street, Dublin 2, Ireland
www.transworldireland.ie

Transworld Ireland is part of the Penguin Random House group of companies
whose addresses can be found at global.penguinrandomhouse.com

Penguin
Random House
UK

First published in the UK and Ireland in 2015
by Transworld Ireland
an imprint of Transworld Publishers

A CIP catalogue record for this book
is available from the British Library.

ISBN 9781848272125

Typeset in 12/15.5pt Adobe Jenson Pro by Falcon Oast Graphic Art Ltd.
Printed and bound by Clays Ltd, Bungay, Suffolk.

Penguin Random House is committed to a sustainable
future for our business, our readers and our planet. This book
is made from Forest Stewardship Council® certified paper.

MIX
Paper from
responsible sources
FSC
www.fsc.org
FSC® C018179

1 3 5 7 9 10 8 6 4 2

Seamus and Kevin
For
Our parents, Seamus and Maura Sheridan
Our partners, Miriam and Rachel
The next generation: Shane, Molly, Aoifa, Ian, Freddie,
Manus, Juno, Cass, Donagh and Alexander

Catherine
For Liam, Shane, Peter and Isaac. May you never tire of cheese jokes.

TABLE OF CONTENTS

ACKNOWLEDGEMENTS

For sharing your knowledge, thank you to archaeologists Peter Bogucki, Seamus Caulfield, Pam Crabtree and Jessica Smyth, microbiologist Rachel Dutton and UCC's dairy expert Alan Kelly.

For sharing your story, thank you to Anna L'Eveque, Breda Maher, Eamonn Lonergan, Bill Hogan, Quinlan Steele, Jeffa Gill, Giorgio Cravero, Sarah and Sergio Furno, Jane and Louis Grubb.

Thank you to our friends in cheese who contributed notes on their favourite cheeses.

Thank you to Dan Fennelly and Elisabeth Ryan for advice on cheese and wine notes and to Franck Le Moenner for help with the photography.

Thank you to Catherine Cleary, for putting up with us – it has been a true pleasure sharing thoughts and working with you.

Thank you to our agent, Sharon Bowers, who encouraged us to write this book. Thank you to the team at Transworld: Henry Vines, Eoin McHugh, Micaela Alcaino, Becky Wright, Peter Ward, Katrina Whone, Phil Lord and Alison Martin.

Catherine would also like to thank Ger Siggins for thinking of her when someone said cheese, and her parents Joan and Shane, who provided a much-needed writer's retreat.

The story of Sheridans Cheesemongers is a story of the many wonderful people who have been a part of this small company over the past twenty years. We would like to thank all of the people who have worked with us. It is impossible to mention every one of you but a few we must thank in particular. Fiona Corbett, a partner for many years and a big part of the Sheridans story. Finn O'Sullivan who supported us for many years and sadly passed away. Those in our team who have stayed with us for so long – Mark Booker, Gerry Flynn, Paula le Moenner, Elisabeth Ryan, Sharon Bagnall and John Leverrier.

To those who have supported us down through the years – thank you, John and Sally McKenna, Derek Ryan, Phillip Caswell, Peter Dunne, the Jephson Family, Keith Newman, David Byers, Roisin Coyle, Niall Sweeny and Simon Phelan.

Every cheesemaker we work with in Ireland or abroad has a fascinating story to tell. However, we had space in this book to give a window to only a few. Thank you to all those we have worked with down through the years.

Most of all, thank you to our customers. To those who have supported our shops and market stalls in Galway, Dublin, Ardkeen and Meath. And to the chefs and shopkeepers who have been so loyal.

INTRODUCTION

We love cheese. Chances are you do too. In this book we'd like to share some of what two decades working as cheesemongers has taught us. We've learned patience, determination and respect for the ingenuity of people. We know what makes a great cheese – people working with their landscape and their animals to transform the milk of here and now into a chunk of there and then. Great cheese can't be faked. It is the antithesis of a modern food culture in which the relationship between people and the land and its animals has been destroyed.

When we visit cheesemakers, we're always struck by the sense of rhythm in their lives. They talk to you as they stir, cut and scoop, explaining things but never breaking the rhythm. There's a rhythm to the milking, the cleaning, the cheesemaking, the turning and wiping of the cheeses. Although cheesemakers approach their craft in all kinds of different ways, they all share the same steady tempo, set by the daily rhythm of milking and making. The other surprise that you can't help but notice is the hard physical work of cheesemaking. In warm, humid dairies arms are stretched and backs are bent. There is a weight of dripping curd to be stirred and lifted and turned in the moulds. After the cheesemaking, there is the scouring and scrubbing, washing and mopping of every inch. This is not work carried out in flowery shirts and sandals – cheesemaking requires white coats, rubber boots and tough aprons. When the washing is done, the cheeses of yesterday, last week and sometimes the previous summer need to be looked after, pressed, turned, wiped, washed, packed. This is work done by men and women who get up early and go to bed tired.

We at Sheridans are proud of our role as cheesemongers. We are the bridge between farmers and cheesemakers on one side, and the Michelin-starred chef or the home cook on the other. The quest for the next delicious thing to put in our mouths has taken us from small Irish farms down tiny country roads, to cheese cellars hidden behind kitchens high in the French Alps. We have listened, smelled, tasted and learned. And it is those experiences we want to share in this book.

It is mind-boggling to think that everything in a cheese shop like ours comes from the same simple honest starting point: milk.

Cheeses of every shape and size line our shelves like blocks from a child's shape game. Some of them are wrapped, others have light coatings that feel like human skin. Some are marbled and mouldy, others a pure vibrant colour – the whitest of whites or the creamiest of yellows. There are cheeses you could slide into a matchbox and ones that would need several people to heft on to a table. Some of our cheeses look like they've been hewn out of a landscape, saved from the ashes of a fire or sliced out of the side of a cliff face.

The milk might be yaks' or sheep's or goats', buffaloes' or cows'. But all cheese starts with the same magical white liquid produced by an animal to nourish its offspring. It is the ingenuity of the men and women who make the cheese that gives us the riot of choice. It's food with personality. And yet, cheesemakers aren't all a common 'type'. They have no single set of values. Some come to cheesemaking from tradition – they are born into a way of life. Some are misled entrepreneurs. Some are farmers looking for more than they can get in an anonymous market place. Some are people in search of another way to live, looking for a connection with the land and the thrill that comes from creating something beautiful. Some are restless and creative. Some don't even like cheese that much.

In this book we're going to take you into the dairies, maturing rooms, labs, archaeological digs and cheese shops to explore a fascinating food. By the end you will know a lot about cheese. We might even nudge you away from your old reliable favourites into a host of incredibly delicious alternatives. You'll be able to work your way around a cheeseboard, use cheese to create memorably good meals at any time of the year and negotiate a cheese shop anywhere in the world like an expert.

As well as guiding you through the different types of cheeses and how to buy, use, cook and store them, we also hope to explore the places and the people who have created them. We believe cheese opens up important stories of culture, history, science and agriculture. Yes, we're biased, but we think cheese has a lot to tell us about life. We want to cut through myths, food snobbery and rose-tinted romanticism to show you that not everything from a farmhouse is sensational and not everything from a factory is mediocre.

After two decades in the cheese world, we still have a sense of adventure and the ability to be blown away by something new. Since we sold our first cheese, food production has grown vaster and has become ever more industrialised. The response from people to this phenomenon has been a growing hunger for connection with real food and the people who make it. It's a yearning for nourishment.

The countless variations in cheesemaking do not divide easily into distinct groups, but we have used broad brushstrokes to separate them out into six categories.

By the end of this book we hope you'll love cheese as much as we do. Not only for how it tastes but for what it represents.

PART ONE

OUR HISTORY
OF CHEESE

CHAPTER ONE

THE SHERIDANS STORY

How did two Dublin city kids end up in the beautiful world of cheese? Accidentally, is probably the best answer.

A typical story of cheesemonger brothers might start with early memories of driving around France with their parents in a *deux chevaux*, dipping toddler fingers into ripe cheeses or teething on Parmesan rinds. We didn't have any of that. Food at home was prepared from scratch and on a tight budget. We were lucky to live close enough to school to be able to come home for lunch every day and we grew up in Dublin eating just what other Irish families of the 1970s were eating. There were stews, fish from the local fishmongers and soda bread – still hot out of the oven so that butter melted on it. Soda bread and potatoes were the staples. Cuts of meat coming back into fashion now, like ox tongue, beef shin and lamb shoulder, were stewed alongside whatever vegetables were available, mostly onions, carrots and turnip. A steak was a very rare treat, only cooked on a day when one of us had a big hurling match.

Our mother was reared in Donegal, one of the most remote and rural areas of Ireland, and her style of cooking reflected this upbringing. The fact is we didn't eat much cheese. Most families at the time consumed dairy in the form of fresh milk, butter and buttermilk. We were teenagers when yoghurts first began to become popular – a new exotic treat. What cheese we did eat came from a simple block of Cheddar. Later, as supermarkets started to open, we were introduced to Easy Singles, the orange processed cheese slices individually wrapped under a thin cellophane sheet. They would be melted on some sliced pan bread. They bubbled and burnt under the grill in a very particular way.

In the early years we lived in Portobello, a neighbourhood in Dublin's south inner city. This was the house where our father had grown up: a handsome Victorian building. Eventually, its damp walls and the smog drove our parents into the suburbs. Yet even in the heart of the city, farm life and wildlife were never far away. In Portobello our backyard shared a border with a large slaughterhouse and we would watch cattle, sheep and pigs walking down slatted wooden ramps from the backs of trucks to disappear through the large metal gates.

The back garden, like every other garden around us, had its plot of peas, radishes, potatoes and summer and autumn berries. We lived beside Dublin's Grand Canal and we would fish there, catching rudd and perch with nets for sport. We'd return them to the murky waters after watching them swim around a large white bucket for a few hours.

Every summer we visited our mother's childhood home on the Inishowen Peninsula in Donegal, the most northerly tip of Ireland. We would stay on her school friend's farm and live the country life for several months. We even went to school there one year for the last few weeks before the summer holidays began. Seamus can remember children passing dillisk seaweed like chewing gum around the class behind the teacher's back. The food was much the same as at home, though there did seem to be even more potatoes, or 'purdies' as they are known in that part of the country.

Our days were spent milking cows, turning hay and digging turf. Our favourite activity was picking hedgerow gooseberries and raspberries, and collecting periwinkles by the bucket on the seashore. In the kitchen we learned how to make butter and watched from a

Maura Sheridan.

distance as dangerously hot pots of jam bubbled volcanically on the stove. We queued up at breakfast time for drop scones and pancakes. We drank warm fresh milk from the cows after milking. Help was always needed with digging the potatoes and the rich brown soil would be permanently under our fingernails. Hens were in the farmyard and you might even find a pet hen in the kitchen. Young chicks would be minded beside the stove and older hens that had stopped laying would have their necks skilfully broken and end up plucked over the kitchen sink.

Our father was a true Dubliner, though. Both his parents were from Dublin and his side of the family brought a different perspective. He grew up in the 1930s and 40s in a neighbourhood full of local shops that sold rabbits. Not as fluffy pets – these rabbits were skinned, gutted and ready for stewing. Oysters were sold on all the street corners as the men came home from the pubs. Lots of streets had their own dairy and grocery shop. The area where he lived had a strong

Jewish culture and was not far from the Bretzel Bakery, a Jewish bakery whose gorgeous smells were part of our childhood landscape. On Saturdays, Dad would often cook coddle, a traditional Dublin stew of sausages and rashers. Many years later a TV crew from Rick Stein's food show asked him to name the essential ingredient. He said it didn't exist any more, because the essential ingredient was necessity.

The greatest gift our dad gave to us wasn't culinary, though, it was a connection with nature through his love of hillwalking and the mountains. Our friends might have taken occasional Sunday drives but every weekend we tramped the hills and mountains of Ireland and fished brown trout in mountain streams on long summer evenings, frying the catch with butter and salt over a camping stove for tea. Dad taught us to have huge respect for the farmers' lands we crossed. Long before we had any concept of sustainability, preservation of natural habitats or environmentalism, we had already been taught these lessons and that sense of connection. So, looking back, how could we not have had a respect and love for food and farming?

But something else was happening during our childhood that shifted our relationship with food. In the 1970s Ireland began a headlong rush into the arms of convenience foods and supermarket culture. Over a couple of years we stopped using our local shops and the Friday-night trip to the supermarket became a weekly highlight, opening up a world of synthetic luxuries like Angel Delight, hazelnut yoghurts and, our favourite, small frozen pizzas. Our seven-day porridge regime became a six-day one. Now, our Saturday mornings were marked with a box of cereal.

Wholesome simple foods made from scratch didn't measure up to the shiny, bright packaged foods of the supermarkets. And convenience foods, encountered in better-off and progressive households, often seemed like beacons of a brighter future, symbols of progress and prosperity. It has taken almost 40 years for us to appreciate the value of the food we were nourished with as children and the hard work and care that went into providing it.

Like many of his generation, Seamus went to London as a teenager to look for work. He was lucky enough to return to Ireland in 1989 and the following year, aged 22, he opened an art gallery and coffee shop in Galway with his partner, Sara. There he met two young chefs, Michael Ryan and Claude Gay. They were to change his life for ever. They convinced him to buy two cookers and turn the coffee shop into a restaurant, and so The Blue Raincoat was born. Being young and idealistic, in their first winter they decided to cook only wild meats and fish, and source as much food as they could from local farmers and growers. It was a restaurant trend before its time. But they saw it as just having fun.

Harriet Leander, 1992.

As a teenager Kevin would escape from home and head west to wash dishes in The Blue Raincoat. It was during one of those summers that Harriet Leander arrived in our lives. Harriet is our food mentor, the woman who taught us so much about how to eat. She grew up in Scandinavia and moved to Paris as a teenager. She married a painter and moved to Switzerland. She worked as an archivist and lived a bohemian and cultured life in a world of fine art, music and food. In 1991 she arrived in Ireland after falling in love with the simple pleasures of Galway and the west coast where she had holidayed since the early 1970s.

She arrived into the restaurant kitchen one day during the summer of 1991 with a bag of scallops and cockles and showed us how to cook them. Then she said she'd help out in the kitchen for a few weeks. She ended up staying for the next 15 years. She later took over the restaurant, which became Nimmos. Harriet introduced us to cheese, cured meats, red wine, wine glasses, table settings, and a whole world of food outside our experience. She brought a knowledge of the fine cuisines of Europe but also a passion for the traditional cooking of the women of rural Greece, Morocco, Italy and the many places she had visited over the years. We cooked together and created dishes. We had a food awakening.

In the winter of 1991 Seamus moved to Scotland and Harriet took over the kitchen. Kevin moved to Galway to study fine art and escape Dublin. He spent almost as much time in the kitchen working with Harriet as he did in college completing a degree in sculpture.

In the summer of 1994 Seamus came back to Galway. With his good friend Terry Barman, they decided to open an ethical food shop called Food Nation in The Cornstore on Middle Street. They included a very small fridge with a few cheeses.

Food Nation struggled and stalled. It was Harriet Leander, over a glass of wine, who came up with the brilliant idea of opening a cheese stall at the Saturday market in Galway. Seamus had experienced great food shops while working in London and Edinburgh, and we had an inkling that the small selection of Irish cheeses on offer was the most interesting part of Food Nation. But we needed to find more cheeses. That evening we pulled out the Irish food promotion agency's list of Irish cheesemakers. The list folded out like a wall planner and, displayed beside their name, each cheesemaker had their cheese label, a paragraph about their cheese, their address and phone number. We picked out a selection: some hard, some soft, some goat and some cows' milk cheeses and some that just sounded intriguing.

The first call was to Breda Maher on her Tipperary farm where she makes Cooleeney. Straight away she said she'd send some cheeses in the post. It was a matter-of-fact conversation, like she was used to this kind of call out of the blue. After the first success, we continued down the list (from memory there were not many more than a dozen) and each cheesemaker agreed to send us some cheese. As we made the calls we got a bit more confident and ventured into the occasional chat, trying to picture these people on the other end of the phone line.

A few days later the boxes started to arrive. When we opened them, a delicious, clean dairy smell breezed out of them. It is a smell that is still so clear in our memories. We were taken back to childhood present opening as the beautiful labels, each so unique, somehow matched the voice on the phone line. The handwritten invoices, on various types and sizes of paper, and the different handwriting, continued to build the image of the person behind the cheese. We noticed many things before we even got to the cheese: how they were wrapped – the newspaper, tissue paper, heavy wax paper, plastic vacuum, some just in the cardboard box. The cheeses were so attractive. Their textures and forms were so perfect. There was such a variety of different colours – ochres, greys, pinks and bright yellows. Then came the taste. We opened each cheese with reverence and an open mind. We had little experience and so we didn't come to them with any expectations. We tasted the cheeses for what they were and mostly we were delighted.

The majority of cheese professionals would have started off by travelling through the countryside, sitting at the kitchen table with the cheesemakers and tasting their cheeses, selecting the best ones and learning about the different recipes and methodologies. Had we planned it, we might have done this too. But there was no big plan – it was just something to do that summer. The cheese stall was going to be something we did on the way to doing something else. Kevin thought he might go on to continue his art studies in Belfast or London. Seamus knew he wanted to work in food but was still exploring.

We had to develop brass necks and the ability to get up very early in order to get into the stallholder-run Galway Saturday market. There was a definite wariness towards anyone new trying to set up. We moved from space to space, occupying pitches left vacant by no-show stallholders. Pretty soon we knew the stall was our future but it took at least a year before we were accepted and longer before we found a permanent pitch.

When we laid out our cheeses, we stood behind the stall and invited passers-by to taste them, chatting to customers about where the cheeses came from, tasting them with them. We became the go-betweens – the producers were in the background and the customers in front of us, just beginning to be open to new food experiences. We were learning on our feet.

During that first year, we came across French cheese expert Pierre Androuet's 1971 *Le Guide du Fromage*. The opening chapter, a letter written to his daughter, advises her on how she should shop for cheese. Androuet tells her to find a good cheesemonger, one who would always allow her to taste the cheese before she bought it. This

Kevin, Galway Market, 1995

resonated with us. It was what we had been doing instinctively, though in many ways it was revolutionary at the time in Ireland. This is what we were: cheesemongers.

The stall became more successful than Food Nation, so we closed the shop. Our first instinct was to open a smaller shop where we could sell our cheese during the week. We found a small kiosk in the Galway City shopping centre and mimicked the layout of the Saturday stall. We managed to get a couple of second-hand fridges and the most basic equipment. This shop was in the wrong place, though – the heavily air-conditioned atmosphere of the shopping centre did our cheeses no good and the smell emanating from our little kiosk was not appreciated by our shopkeeper neighbours. We did, however, learn a lot during that time and we gathered more loyal customers. We also began to sell a few other foods apart from cheese.

Shortly after we opened, our mam, Maura, travelled down with our young nephew from Dublin to see her sons' new shop for the first

Shane, Maura and Kevin.

time. Kevin has a clear memory of standing behind the counter, hands on his hips, watching her looking through the glass at our various cheeses, cured Italian meats and a large Parma ham. Growing up we saw the home-cooked food our mother made as plain, functional food, rather than anything of gastronomic value. We were jealous of the packed pizzas and other processed foods that we'd seen in the houses of friends. They were rarely, if ever, eaten in our house. So, with all the swagger of a newly born cultural tour guide, Kevin began talking her through the cheese display. She pointed to the Parma ham and asked what it was. He explained that it was a very special cured ham from Italy.

'It's very like the ham we used to have hanging over the chimney up at home,' she said, interrupting the explanation. 'Up at home' was the small village of Carndonagh where she had grown up in the 1940s.

Hers was one of the few families in the area that kept a pig, she explained. And every year Paddy Reid would arrive at the house with a mallet and his knives to butcher the pig. She never witnessed the act. She was the youngest in the family. Every year she fell in love with the weanling. She hated the arrival of Paddy Reid and would go to a neighbour's house for the day or down the fields to play.

Not all the meat from the pig was easily preserved, so neighbours and friends would get some and Paddy was paid with his own share. The blood went to a man in the village who made pudding, the cheeks to Fanny, a family friend, and the crubeens, or pigs' feet, to another friend. Food was shared and neighbours helped each other when they could. The bacon and the hams were salted and hung in the kitchen above the fire, where the turf smoke kept the meat preserved. Mam remembers her brother Barney had a special knife for cutting slices from the hanging bacon. The preserved pig's meat would keep them through the winter.

As our mother told Kevin this story, it dawned on him that

preserving food was part of every culture and these preserved foods, anachronistic and out of their time, are now the foundation for almost all of what we consider speciality or gourmet foods. We saw that we would find the foods we were looking for not necessarily on the high tables of Europe but hidden in ordinary food cultures, including our own.

We needed somewhere we could store and sell our cheese properly, and a shopping centre was not it. We found a small stone shop in Kirwan's Lane, a back street in medieval Galway. The shop looked like a cave.

Kevin's grounding in sculpture and design and our feeling for food created a unique place in Kirwan's Lane. We went to Coillte, the Irish forestry service, and bought timber planks with the bark still on the edges. We went to a plumbing salvage shop and found some ancient cistern brackets. Kevin used an angle grinder to shave the tops off them so they could hold up our new shelves. We sculpted the shop out of the cave-like space, built every inch, and painted it. Our tiler and plumber were paid in cheese. Now, we had a weekly market stall and our gorgeous cheese shop on Kirwan's Lane, and that's the essence of where it all started. We weren't daunted by being newbies in the cheese world. It felt like walking on to a blank page. There was a great freedom in making it up as we went along. We weren't tied into complicated distribution chains. We could go directly to England to discover the best people in the English cheese world, or to France to find the best Comté.

As we searched for cheeses from outside Ireland, Sheridans Cheesemongers became one of the few places in Ireland you could get Parmesan that didn't come ready-grated in a cardboard tub and smell like old damp socks. People arrived to buy our Irish farm cheeses, Brie de Meaux, fresh mozzarella, Keen's Cheddar or just to look at this crazy little shop. We had turned the whole space into a fridge by putting a chill unit on the ceiling so that we could keep the wheels of cheese on the counters and not have to pack them into small fridges where they could dry out. As we continued to source cheeses from around Ireland and Europe, the shop became more and more packed with wheels piled on the counters and shelves. We not only loved the cheeses themselves but the space itself was very important and still is: the whole sensory experience of a space dominated by the colours and shapes of cheeses, their aromas, the boards and tables that held them, the damp walls that housed them; the way our customers could interact with the cheeses. There was no consideration of conventional retail practice or business models. The whole endeavour was shaped by the joy of working with the cheeses and bringing them to our customers.

Dotted amongst these were other foods that we came across: local honey, salamis and cured meats, olive oils, anything that we found and

Kevin, Kirwan's Lane, 1996.

loved and thought our customers would love too. Local chefs began to call in, delighted that they could get cheeses outside of the normal range.

At that time the general understanding of a delicatessen was that it took something from far away, whether it was good or not, and put it on to the shelves, hoping customers would want it because it was new and exotic. Our concept was different: we just wanted to sell good food. It didn't matter whether it was from the Loire or West Cork, the criteria were the same. It all came back to the same questions: does this taste really good and is it produced by people with whom we can connect? This was not a marketing strategy or business concept, it just reflected what we valued and what excited us.

FIRST GENERATIONERS

In those early days of the mid 1990s it felt like starting from zero. We were first generationers in a new food culture, coming to it with a blank slate. There had always been a culinary culture in small wealthy pockets of Ireland, particularly in areas of the cities like Cork and Dublin. The capital had a restaurant boom between the wars when French and Belgian chefs came to cook in kitchens like Jammet's and the Café Belge opened by Bob Geldof's grandfather Zenon Geldof. There had been a culinary tradition around the big houses of the aristocracy where cooks worked with game and fish and vegetables from the surrounding estate. But by the time wealth was spread more evenly in Ireland, supermarkets had gained a firm grip on household spending.

The flipside to rising wealth, though, was that people were travelling more and seeing a different way of eating and shopping. A food market was something they might have visited in France or Spain, so what we were trying to do was starting to be more familiar. Our first regular customers were people who had returned from holidays in Europe and had experienced the culture of buying and eating good cheese as part of daily life.

One of the real difficulties with a specialty food shop in Ireland at that time, though, and to some extent still now, was that people were nervous of coming into a shop like ours. They knew how to shop in a supermarket – they were free to pick up things that were clearly priced from a shelf. They didn't need to talk to anyone, much less a cheese 'expert'. When they entered our shop, many of them felt intimidated. They were afraid to pronounce a name wrong or ask a silly question. One of the elements of our success was that we never thought of ourselves as experts, because we weren't. We learned with our customers, never correcting a pronunciation mistake and always speaking about the cheese in a way that suited the customer we were serving.

If we had a customer who was well travelled and a bit of a gourmet, we could talk in depth about the cheeses, their origins and the flavours. But we were happier introducing new cheeses and flavours to people who'd never had the opportunity to experience much more than processed cheese. The best way to break the perceived barrier of knowledge and expertise was to say little and allow the customer to taste. Then we could explain where the cheese came from and could focus on the families, farmers, crafts and people who produced them. We have never been comfortable with the idea that Sheridans is a 'posh' food shop. The cost of quality food has meant that a large proportion of our customers are from well-off households, but we would be as happy selling cheese on a market stall in a country town or housing estate as in a gourmet shop. We want our cheese to be available to everyone.

Sarah Murphy and Ross McGuinness, Dun Laoghaire Market.

SHERIDANS CHEESEMONGERS BEGINS TO GROW

After just two years, our Galway shop was reasonably busy, the Saturday market was a great success and more chefs had started to come to us for their cheeses. None of these business elements would have been sustainable on their own but together they were enough to pay us a wage and employ some part-time staff to help on Saturdays. It might have been enough to stop at that point – to be happy with that quite comfortable existence. We often look back and wonder whether it would have been better, more fulfilling, to have stayed there. However, we were young and excited and hungry for new experiences.

The Galway market was successful for Sheridans but it also

provided a thriving business for Toby Simmonds, who owned The Real Olive Company and travelled up from Cork every Saturday to sell a groundbreaking selection of olives. This made us look to Dublin, where the market scene hadn't really happened. Together with a few other producers we set up a food market in the new cultural centre of Dublin, Temple Bar. The city-centre district had been earmarked to be turned into a bus depot until Taoiseach Charlie Haughey designated it a cultural quarter in 1991 and it was dubbed Dublin's Left Bank. His successor Bertie Ahern would later refer to it mistakenly as 'Dublin's West Bank'.

Seamus drove up to Dublin every Friday night, the boot of his car stuffed with cheese. His friend Fiona Corbett began helping out at the stall and soon became a full-time member of staff and later a director in the business. Mam provided a freshly ironed white linen tablecloth every Saturday morning for the stall. The Temple Bar market was a success and Seamus's itchy feet took him to the streets of Dublin looking for a location for a new Sheridans shop. He found the worst shop on the best street, a tiny premises on South Anne Street, and we decided to go for it. The decision was made a lot easier as Kevin's soon-to-be-wife Rachel had just moved back up to Dublin and he was keen to follow. We used the same principles to fit out the new Dublin shop as we'd used in Kirwan's Lane. We built shelves and tables to display the cheese and installed an overhead chill unit to turn the whole shop into a fridge. Seamus and Kevin moved between the two locations. One of us was always in Galway or Dublin on a Saturday – in one of the shops or behind one of the market stalls.

Our growth as a company was helped by the expanding and maturing Irish food culture. More and more independent retailers and small deli owners were opening their doors in the cities and towns across Ireland. The new shopkeepers were looking to source good cheeses and other foods. We were happy to supply anyone who asked and the increased volume allowed us to buy more directly from farms and producers across Europe. We became wholesalers.

Travelling abroad we met up with other companies and began to sell Irish cheeses into the UK and Europe. For the first few years after opening the Dublin shop we ran the business from a cramped office in the basement. We also held all the stock for wholesale and export in the tiny shop. We would load and unload articulated lorries that had to park on tight city streets, carrying boxes up and down the narrow stairway to the basement.

Eventually, we just couldn't fit it all in any more and we had to search for a warehouse. Although we were doing well enough, the business model never allowed us to do much more than pay our wages, so we had to be creative in our search. We found a creamery that had just closed down in Co. Meath, just north of Dublin. It already had a number of cold rooms and a little office section and the rent was cheap. We operated from there until 2007 when the lease ran out and again we found we had outgrown the building. We had been based in rural Co. Meath for eight years by then, with many great staff from the area, so we didn't want to go too far. We resisted the easy option of moving into a ready-built unit in an industrial estate. Instead we found a derelict and crumbling old railway station in the very north of Co. Meath in the heart of a gentle and beautiful part of rural Ireland.

All the sensible people we showed it to thought we were mad but we could see that this was the place for us. We spent two years cleaning it up, building on and restoring it. Kevin and his family bought the old station house and restored it as a home. We opened a shop and started a market for local food producers. We now have the space to run an annual food festival attracting thousands of visitors and showcasing the foods of our producers from all around Ireland.

Although Sheridans has expanded, the core of what we do has changed little in the 20 years since we set up that first stall. The

Our shop in Co. Meath.

greatest change has been the increased focus on foods produced in Ireland. As the awareness and demand for artisan-produced food has grown, creative people have stepped up and turned the wonderful natural resources of Ireland into new innovative foods, as well as rediscovering traditional foods and methods. We have worked as closely with many of these producers as we have with our cheese-makers. Unhappy with the crackers we were importing to sell alongside our cheeses, and realising there were none at all produced in Ireland at the time, in 2012 we approached a wonderful baker of sweet biscuits in West Cork, Richard Graham-Leigh, to work with us on developing Sheridans crackers. The result has been a huge success.

Not only did we manage to replace the imported crackers but have ended up exporting our new ones around the world. They are simple crackers, but they fully reflect our food ethos. Our brown bread crackers are made with just three ingredients, all sourced locally to the bakery in West Cork. The recipe is inspired by the brown soda bread we baked with our mother at home and their flavour is subtle and balanced.

As brothers, working together in Sheridans and growing a business from a market stall to an international food wholesaler meant getting to know each other better. The six-year age gap between us made it feel like we'd almost grown up in different families. We were like chalk and cheese, one of us restless and spontaneous, the other shyer and more cautious. The blend of our two personalities is probably what makes things work. We have always learned from each other, first as big brother and little brother, and then as equals. There is a depth of trust and flexibility that exists between brothers that could never be matched by friends or business partners. No matter what mistakes are made, arguments had or faults exposed, we are always brothers, always connected at a deeper level. This has allowed us to work together and support each other through all the things that have happened in our lives, each stepping up when the other fell back.

As much as the Sheridans story is about cheese and cheesemakers, it is also about the people who have worked with Sheridans down through the years. Perhaps because of our lack of management experience or just our personalities, we have always worked with our employees in a very unstructured and fluid manner. We have been lucky enough to have attracted many creative and passionate people over the years and we always encourage them to be themselves and bring their individual talents with them, rather than asking them to slot into a tight system. The result has been that the direction of our company has been shaped as much by the talents of these wonderful people as it has by our own vision. They have brought so many skills, which on our own we lacked. Some stayed for only a short time, working while in college or while establishing careers in the arts or food, many have gone on to work in and set up their own great food businesses around the world. Thankfully, some have stayed with us for the long haul. Each has had their part in our history and will shape our future.

Kevin, Fiona, Seamus, 2005.

CHAPTER TWO

THE WORLD'S OLDEST CHEESE

DIGGING UP THE ORIGINS OF OUR DAIRYING CULTURE

We've never met Peter Bogucki but he's a big man in the cheese world. As an archaeologist and an Ivy League academic, his day job has nothing to do with cheese but he's a regular visitor to Ireland, a big fan of Gubbeen and the man who found evidence of the world's oldest cheese.

We love the story of how a mystery buried for thousands of years in Polish soil was unlocked by one man's hunch and how it changed the history of cheese. It starts on a rainy night as Peter Bogucki (pronounced Bowgoodski) was driving home to Boston in the summer of 1980. It was quiet. He and his wife were tired from the long journey back from a cousin's wedding in Canada. They had stopped off in Grafton, Vermont, to visit his wife's friend. The young archaeologist was turning an idea over in his mind on that drive home. He was thinking about sieves and cattle bones and a new part of the puzzle he had just seen in his friend's living room.

The sieves were curious bits of 7,000-year-old clay pottery. Bogucki had dug them out of Polish soil the previous summer.

Bogucki was a Polish speaker, the grandson of Polish immigrants to America, whose mother kept the language alive at home. He had got himself a summer posting at the Neolithic site at Brześć Kujawski in the lowlands of north-central Poland. The site was first excavated in the 1920s and 30s. The man leading the dig was a Polish archaeologist not much older than Bogucki and the two men became friends. Over that summer of 1979, among many fragments of pottery buried in the mud, they found several puzzling pieces of clay pot, with holes deliberately baked into them. It was obvious they were used for straining something; the question was what?

The sieves and other pottery pieces were clues to the lives of pioneer farmers in the forests of lowland Europe, the people of the linear pottery culture. They are believed to have originated in western Hungary around 5,600 BC, moving from there into Germany, eastern

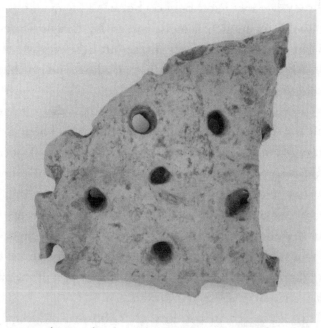

A piece of pottery found at Brześć Kujawski.

France, Ukraine and Poland. They were Europe's first migrating farmers.

Alongside the pottery, the archaeologists kept finding cattle bones. All the theories about Neolithic animal husbandry suggested that early farm animals were killed for their meat. But cattle bones didn't make a lot of sense for pioneer farmers in dense forests. Farming cattle for meat took 42 months to get the animal to a point where it was worth slaughtering. If early farmers wanted meat, they kept pigs.

So the niggling mystery of cattle bones and sieves remained. Until Bogucki walked into his friend's living room and saw on a table there a redware perforated clay pot. It bore no resemblance in shape to the Neolithic sieves but something struck him as being similar.

'What was that used for?' he asked.

'Cheesemaking,' she told him. 'It was designed to drain the whey from the curds.'

On that drive home to Boston, Bogucki formulated a hunch about his ancient sieves – they were cheese strainers and these Neolithic first farmers were making cheese. The theory was not based on any smoking gun of evidence; it was a leap of faith from fact to conjecture that archaeologists take. His cheese-strainer theory, published in 1984 in the *Oxford Journal of Archaeology** met with a lukewarm response. Some people started treating it as fact. Others just dismissed it as 'something that a US archaeologist believes'. The idea sat in a quiet backwater of academic literature gathering virtual dust.

Nearly 30 years later, Richard Evershed, a biochemist at Bristol University, discovered that lightly fired ancient pottery has an interesting ability. It holds on to traces of whatever has passed through it, giving the object a kind of 'material memory'. Evershed discovered

---

* Peter I. Bogucki, 'Ceramic Sieves of the Linear Pottery Culture and Their Economic Implications', *Oxford Journal of Archaeology* 3(1), 1984: 15–30.

that lipids or fats penetrate into the body of the pottery. It can be washed and scrubbed, or buried in soil for thousands of years, but the lipid residues remain. Evershed's team was soon able to identify the different kinds of fats trapped in ancient artefacts from their chemical signature. Bogucki's fragments of Polish pottery – potsherds – were perfect test material. They were shipped to Bristol and tests confirmed the presence of milk lipids. The 7,000-year-old clay strainers were the tools of the world's earliest-known cheesemakers.*

Bogucki's cheese strainers tipped long-held beliefs about the world's first farmers on their heads. They were known to have

* Mélanie Salque, Peter I. Bogucki, Joanna Pyzel, Iwona Sobkowiak-Tabaka, Ryszard Grygiel, Marzena Szmyt and Richard P. Evershed, 'Earliest Evidence for Cheese Making in the Sixth Millennium BC in Northern Europe', *Nature* 493, 522–525, 24 January 2013.

domesticated plants and animals, grown wheat and farmed cattle, but Neolithic farming was assumed to have been a primitive everything-they-grew-they-ate form of farming. Archaeologists believed that a 'secondary production revolution' using the products of the animals, rather than just the animals themselves, happened much later, around 3,000 BC. It was at this stage, the theory went, that farmers began dairying, shearing sheep for their wool and using animals for traction to pull ploughs. Bogucki's discovery proved that these early farmers were doing something much more sophisticated than archaeologists had ever imagined. Not only were these first farmers milking cows but they were also turning that milk into a form of cheese.

HE WHO DAIRIES, WINS

It has only been possible in recent years to unlock one possible reason why people were making cheese at least 7,000 years ago. Why did they go to all the trouble and bother? Why didn't they just drink the milk?

The answer has come from analysing the DNA of ancient bodies found in glaciers and bogs. Scientists have proof that our early ancestors were lactose intolerant. Early humans could drink milk as children but they lacked the enzyme, lactase, needed to digest lactose in milk in adulthood. If you gave early man a drink of milk he would have had a violent dysentery-like reaction to the liquid.

Over millennia humans mutated to develop lactase in order to enable them to drink milk, and mapping when and where humans developed the ability to drink milk is a growing area of study for scientists who believe it unlocks part of a map of human evolution. Slowly, over thousands of years, human biology adapted to avail of the plentiful nutrients in a dairying world. But none of this slow, steady evolution was going to help our 7,000-year-old farmers drink milk. They couldn't wait for biological evolution, so they started a cultural one. They needed a way to unlock the nutrients in milk and they did that by draining the lactose-rich whey and leaving the curds, which could be digested more easily.

These Neolithic cheesemakers, who pierced holes in clay pots to drain the whey, were accessing a superfood. They were farmers who could preserve a solid source of nutrition to give them an advantage over other farmers or hunter-gatherers. Crops could fail or falter but milk was reliable and could be preserved in the form of cheese. It was a case of he who dairies, wins. Milk and dairy products got early farmers through the hungry gap when the previous year's crop of wheat was eaten and the next crop was still at the growing stage.

Cheese was evidence of human ingenuity and appetite. Cheese was early man's way of turning milk into a digestible food. It's a fact that puts milk and cheese at the heart of human evolution.

EUROPE'S OLDEST DAIRY PASTURES

One fascinating aspect of Bogucki's fieldwork is that it helps to unlock a mystery closer to home of the ancient field system known as the Céide Fields on the west coast of Mayo. Three years after Peter Bogucki first pulled broken pot fragments out of Polish soil, Irish archaeologist, Seamus Caulfield, was pushing iron probes into a bog on one of the most western edges of Europe. Seamus is the son of the local schoolteacher Patrick Caulfield. His father began writing to the head of the National Museum in 1934 about prehistoric artefacts he was uncovering on his nearby farm and bogland.

Inspired by his father's fascination with what lay under their feet in North Mayo, Seamus Caulfield became an archaeologist.

It was 1983 when Caulfield had his eureka moment, when the probes kept striking rock through the layers of bog, confirming metre after metre of ancient wall, stretching under the peat for over a kilometre. 'It was like putting a skewer through butter and hitting a plate,' says Caulfield, who's now retired.

Caulfield was investigating a stretch of bogland rising up from the coast of North Mayo midway between Broadhaven and Killala Bay. Turf cutters had exposed ancient walls long buried under thick layers of bog close to the crashing Atlantic waves. Caulfield believed the walls stretched much further under the bog and the steel probes confirmed that first wall at Glenulra stretched back from the sea and travelled inland for a significant distance. The length of that first wall confirmed the huge extent of the site, which is now known as the Céide Fields.

The probe was a surprisingly precise search tool and where the bog was lighter they found a wall with a probe of a metre and a half. At the top of the hill and the bottom of valleys, the bog could be four metres deep before they hit a wall. But that first wall they tracked in 1983 indicated that the Céide Fields covered a huge organised area.

Under their feet was the monumental evidence of one of Europe's oldest surviving farms, 'a landscape fossilised', as the poet Seamus Heaney put it. No animal bones survived the acidic conditions of the bog but the walls only made sense as enclosures for animals. Despite the fact that Peter Bogucki's theory that Neolithic people may have been a dairying culture entered academic literature a year after Seamus Caulfield confirmed the extent of the walls, for almost 30 years they were thought to have been a system of fields designed for beef cattle.

When news of the Bristol study broke, the Céide Fields made a new kind of sense. Dairying was a much more efficient use of resources,

Caulfield explains. An animal could produce dramatically more calories through a lifetime of milking than the one-shot calorie hit of their meat post-mortem. The ante-mortem food provided valuable calories that could be taken from an animal throughout its lifetime in the form of milk. 'There was no ante-mortem value in a beef economy. And the farmer had nothing to do with the animal from the day it calved until the day you have to kill it.' The only possible ante-mortem product of a beef animal was to bleed it for blood pudding – a practice carried on in some African farms today. But even that couldn't explain the elaborate system of walls at Céide.

Caulfield concluded that the Céide Fields were a pattern for dairy farming that farmers still use today. 'Current research on Irish Neolithic pottery has established that these vessels also show evidence of having been used to hold milk. Céide Fields now fits much more readily into a dairying economy with the fields functioning as herd management, with drystock separated from milch cows, weaned animals confined to other fields, and milch cows in direct contact with farmers at least once a day.'*

It is still a theory but one that is backed up by Peter Bogucki's and Richard Evershed's joint discovery. We have evidence of the world's oldest cheese in a Neolithic site in Poland, and the Céide Fields in Mayo may be able to claim to be the home of Europe's oldest surviving dairy farm.

DÚN AILINNE

Another piece of prehistoric research into Irish dairying came over a decade before Seamus Caulfield's probe excavation. It was 1972 and Pam Crabtree, a young American archaeologist, was on her way to Lebanon when funding for the project she was going to join suddenly fell through. 'I was looking at spending a summer at home teaching swimming and living with my mom.' Instead, the archaeologist Bernard Wailes asked her if she'd like to go to Ireland. For Crabtree it was like being asked, 'Is the Pope Catholic?'

She arrived at Wailes's excavation in Kildare in the summer of 1972. The 13-hectare oval site sat on top of a low hill. From the air, Dún Ailinne looks like an eye in the centre of a patchwork of green – square or rectangular fields surrounding it on all sides.

Crabtree arrived with one idea and left with another. Her PhD had been a study of the changes in rural settlements over time. But during those late-season digs at Dún Ailinne, she kept pulling animal bones, lots of cow bones, from the earth, some 18,000 samples in

---

* Seamus Caulfield, 'Céide Fields: Europe's oldest surviving dairy fields?', in Matthew Jebb, Derek Mooney and Colin Crowley, *Secrets of the Landscape* (Cork: Atrium, 2013).

total. That got her thinking and set her in the direction of zooarchaeology. Working at the Archaeology and Anthropology Museum at the University of Pennsylvania, she decided to pull together all the bone work she had done in Dún Ailinne and work through it.

It turned out that Dún Ailinne was a ceremonial site, where feasts and rituals were held, rather than a settlement where everyday foods were being consumed, but Crabtree has no doubt that dairying was part of life in Iron Age Ireland.

'Do I think they were dairying and cheesemaking at that time? Absolutely.'

A final piece of the jigsaw of Ireland's ancient dairy history was found recently. Dr Jessica Smyth, a young Irish archaeologist, is doing post-doctoral research at Bristol University. She took hundreds of potsherds from early Neolithic sites around Ireland and subjected them to organic residue analysis, the Evershed tests for the presence of animal lipids. More than half the samples from seven sites showed appreciable traces of animal fats. The vast majority of these were found to be milk fats.*

The results point to evidence of a migrating wave of dairy farmers, moving east to west across Europe, who reached Ireland with their herds after perilous sea crossings. They brought new building methods, pots and animals, which were not part of the native culture or ecology. Organic residue analysis is a tool that can unlock information that sits in storage boxes in museums all over the world. It has the potential for an exciting new school of cold-case archaeology, breathing new life into materials that were thought to have yielded all their

---

* Jessica Smyth, Richard P. Evershed, 'Milking the Megafauna: Using Organic Residue Analysis to Understand Early Farming Practice', *Environmental Archaeology*, 2015.

secrets. We expect to learn much more about ancient diets and the importance of foods like milk and cheese.

The Smyth and Evershed research dates Ireland's dairy history back more than 6,000 years. The close relationship between humans and cattle, sheep and goats, has long been known. The new information is that cheese was at the heart of that relationship and central to what separated human farmers from other mammals. Harvard anthropologist Richard Wrangham famously argued that cooking made us human. It now seems clear that we could add cheesemaking to that too.

Kerry cattle.

CHAPTER THREE

HAIRY PROTEINS AND LEGO BLOCKS

THE SCIENCE OF CHEESE

There's a great story in the 'when' of cheese. But the 'how' of cheese is just as intriguing. The science of food is suddenly sexy. There is a new wave of thinking in the food world that embraces the men and women in white coats, inviting scientists out of their labs and into the kitchen to share the stage with chefs. And the science of cheese is as beautiful and brilliant as any other discipline. If the phrase 'molecular science' makes your eyes glaze over, bear with us. With the help of some hairy particles and a couple of simple tricks, you can amaze your friends and families at home, and we think you'll start to enjoy the science of cheese.

No one knows how the first cheese was made but a happy accident is the most widely accepted theory. Here's how it might have happened:

A woman is walking with a bag of milk. It's warm and she is pleased to find a shady cave in which to rest. But something strange has happened. The bag feels different. The liquid doesn't slosh around any more. She peers in and finds her drink has turned to jelly surrounded by a watery substance. She pokes the wobbly white stuff with her finger, picks up a handful and drops it back in. Then she shakes the bag and throws it in disgust into the dry corner of the cave, where it lodges between two stones. The liquid leaks away.

Some time later, hunger or curiosity or coincidence brings her back. She opens the bag and falls back awestruck. The spirits of the cave have taken pity on her. They have transformed her spoiled milk into something different, something she can break off in chunks and gnaw like meat. A delicious magic has happened.

That first cheesemaker's carrier bag would have been a calf's, lamb's or kid goat's stomach. It was perfect for carrying liquids – a stretchy pouch of silken muscle that was light and watertight. The invisible element inside that stretchy pouch that turned it into a cheesemaking tool was its natural lining of rennet. In a live animal, the

enzymes in this substance would be used to unlock the nutrients in its mother's milk. Millennia after those first cheeses appeared like gifts from the gods, dairy scientists would figure out what was happening.

Cheese is made by separating milk into curds and whey, then draining the liquid whey and pressing the curds into soft shapes or harder blocks that can be matured. Cheese can be made from the milk of any mammal. In different parts of the world different cultures have domesticated many species for milk production, including sheep, goats, cows, buffaloes, reindeer and yaks. And within these species there are many different breeds. Each breed produces cheese with different flavours and varying protein and fat contents. Cows' milk is almost 90 per cent water, with protein, fat and lactose making up the remaining proportion. Different breeds of cow will have different proportions of these three nutrients: Friesian cows' milk has more lactose than fat or protein. Jersey cows' milk is higher in fat and lactose than protein. These levels all vary depending on the season and the feed the animal is receiving. Sheep's milk is much more concentrated than cows' milk, with almost double the fat. Goats' milk is more similar to cows'. All share the same basic characteristic, though: they can all be split into curds and whey.

There are an infinite number of different cheeses that could be made from the milk, each distinguished by small decisions the cheesemaker makes and nature imposes. The first decision is which animal's milk to use. Each has its own particular physical structure, giving slightly different results during cheesemaking. The local environment together with the cultures the cheesemaker adds, or removes through pasteurisation, will decide the microbiological make-up of the cheese. The microflora of the milk will impact on the way the cheese develops, not only during the first change from milk to curds and whey but right through the maturation of the cheese.

The catalyst for the miraculous change from liquid to solid is a combination of the right temperature and acidity, which can be helped greatly by the use of rennet, of which there are several types. Already we have many different computations and the cheesemaking process has hardly begun. The amount of moisture removed from the curd will determine not only the texture of the finished cheese but also how the cheese interacts with the microflora within the curds as it matures. Moisture can be removed to different degrees at various stages in production. The first is when the newly formed mass is cut by the cheesemaker. To keep lots of moisture in, the curd is left in larger chunks. The more it is cut, the more moisture, in the form of whey, is taken out. This curd can then be removed gently to form moisture-laden cheeses or warmed, scalded, kneaded, cooked, stacked, milled and pressed gently or pressed using massive force. Any combination of these moisture-removing methodologies changes the structure of the cheese.

Before the curd is shaped into cheese, the cheesemaker will also vary acidity levels using time and temperature. The acidity of the curd is a result of the controlled action of the bacteria operating in the milk and the curd. The resulting acidity levels will also influence the later activity of bacteria within the maturing curd. Salt is almost always added but there are several ways to introduce it and different amounts give different results. Some cheeses have salt added directly into the curd while the cheese is being made, some have it rubbed on the fresh rind, and others are set afloat in baths of brine.

The resulting solid forms of curd can be eaten straightaway or allowed to develop for days or even years. How the cheesemaker treats the rind of the cheese and where and how the cheeses are stored allows for many, many more different flavours and textures. Fungi already in the new cheese can be encouraged to grow and develop inside or on the surface of the cheese. More can be introduced by the cheesemaker in the maturing room or they can colonise the cheese from the local

environment. The rinds can be sealed in plastic, smoked, bandaged in cloth and lard, washed with various concoctions, brushed, rubbed or just left alone.

The myriad ways milk can be transformed into cheese was worked out by cheesemakers before the science behind them was fully understood. They are the legacy of thousands of years of tradition, culture, necessity and a desire for sensory pleasure. Science has followed the art of cheesemaking like a butterfly catcher with a net. We now have a much better understanding of the non-human players in the cheesemaking process, the communities of microbes that digest parts of the milk to produce the flavours, textures and aromas in the preserved milk to make what we know as cheese. The invisible series of events happening silently inside the curd can now be magnified 10,000-fold with electron microscopes. Yet the butterfly is still fluttering above our heads. Recent DNA tests on cheese rinds have revealed how much is still to be learned about the complex microbial communities that give cheeses their unique set of textures and flavours.

Science has revealed strangely beautiful images. There's a

honeycomb coral reef of interlinked chains that form when the structure of milk collapses. Less beautiful but more fascinating are the casein micelles that form the links in these chains. The clumps of protein are depicted in line drawings like a fibrous dustball or magnified like a grey raspberry with a hairy halo. Casein, the main protein in milk, has the same Latin root as the word cheese. This hairy clump is the cheese particle, the part of the milk at the heart of it all.

Professor Alan Kelly of the School of Food and Nutritional Sciences at University College Cork has helped us look at cheese from the perspective of the curious scientist. UCC has a long and proud tradition in dairy science. Cork is a city surrounded by lush Munster farmland and its university has been training people for careers in Irish creameries since the 1920s. Alan Kelly loves his subject. A city boy raised in Dublin's Glasnevin, his friends and family tease him over his choice of discipline. This professor of cheese was a PhD student before he first got up close and personal with a cow. One of the things Professor Kelly loves about food science is how humans did things for a long time before fully understanding what they were doing and why they were doing it. Cheese is a perfect example of that, he says. It was an art long before it was a science.

FROM MILK TO CURD

Alan Kelly opens his lectures to new students with the same simple statement each year: Milk is an amazing material. Eighty seven per cent of it is water. Under a low-power microscope you'll see large bubbles floating around in it. These are fat globules. They account for around 4 per cent of the milk. But the fat globules are not the secret to cheese. An electron microscope is needed to see those. They are the protein clumps, smaller, hairy spheres called casein micelles, which make up just 3.5 per cent of milk's total content. Scientists have argued for years over the structure of these clumps. The consensus is that they are made up of four types of protein molecules that hold almost 80 per cent of the protein content of milk.

Microscopes can show how milk is made up of a universe of fat planets floating in a liquid sky surrounded by smaller stars of protein clumps. It doesn't take a lot to destabilise everything so that the planets collide. There are two forces that keep them stable and separate. The first is the four casein proteins' feelings towards water. Three of the four proteins hate water so much that they huddle together to try to stay dry, clumped like a tangled ball of wool. The fourth casein protein (called Kappa-casein) has a split personality. It wraps around the outside of these tangled casein clumps waving its water-loving ends in the water solution and keeping the rest of the proteins comfortable in their clump.

The first step in cheesemaking is to send in an agent with one specific mission – it must shave the Kappa-casein of its protective hairs. That single-mission agent is rennet. It contains an enzyme called chymosin that swiftly eats one part of the Kappa-casein, turning micelles from hairy spheres into clean-shaven ones. Without protection from their liquid environment, panic ensues and the micelles clump even closer together for protection. They become protein-rich clumps of curds. The milk splits and the solids separate from the whey.

All young mammals have rennet containing the chymosin enzyme in their stomachs; so what benefit does the unweaned youngster derive from using rennet to help digest its food? Calcium is not simply dissolved in milk; it is actually trapped within the proteins. So the casein micelle is effectively a delivery mechanism for calcium, a way of carrying a lot of calcium to the newborn. The rennet in the young mammal's stomach enables it to unlock this vital nutrient.

You may be familiar with the term vegetarian rennet, which is often displayed on the label of cheeses. This almost always refers to a microbial rennet substitute. Microbial rennet is produced by a fungi grown and fermented in a lab setting. This type of rennet works quite well and is cheaper than traditional rennet but can produce a bitter taste in mature cheeses. However this pure microbial rennet has almost entirely been replaced by a more modern version, FPC – Fermentation Produced Chymosin rennet. This version of microbial rennet is made by taking the enzyme-producing gene out of the mammal's cell's DNA string and introducing it into a host fungi's DNA string. This enables the fungi to produce the chymosin enzyme. This fungi can then be cultivated in a lab and fermented, ready to be used as rennet. This genetically modified rennet does not give the bitter flavour in mature cheeses and it is even cheaper to produce. The use of vegetarian rennet is not always advertised on the labels of cheese. The ingredients often just say rennet but, because of its cost effectiveness, genetically modified rennet is used in the production of almost all industrial cheeses. It is important to distinguish this genetically modified organism from genetically engineered foods. When the DNA from the animal is inserted into the fungi, it is not altered, whereas in genetically engineered products the DNA is altered to change its function, altering completely the nature of the gene.

There is a third version of vegetarian rennet called thistle rennet. This is the only true vegetable rennet produced from the cardoon thistle (*Cynara cardunculus*), a species of artichoke. This plant contains an enzyme called cardosin which acts to coagulate the milk in a similar way to the chymosin enzyme. Coagulation takes longer and works better in milk with high levels of protein and fat, so sheep's milk is perfect. It is most commonly used in Portuguese sheep's milk cheeses but has also been used for centuries in areas of Spain, Italy and France. Jewish communities were using it to make kosher cheese before the invention of modern rennet substitutes. It gives a particular citrusy and slightly bitter flavour and a more fudgy texture. Some of the most interesting and delicious cheeses are made using this gift of nature.

If you do choose not to eat meat but love cheese, it is important to remember that no young animals are slaughtered in order to produce rennet. The nature of dairy farming means that there are many male calves born and they cannot be raised to produce milk so are instead slaughtered for meat. It makes sense to use this animal as efficiently as possible, and so they are also used in the production of natural rennet.

Rennet is the one-shot agent that begins to turn milk to cheese but there is another substance that can also start the process. This substance is acid. The second stabilising force keeping fresh milk in its coherent liquid form is the electrical charge all particles have. Particles with the same charge repel each other. The casein clumps are all negatively charged, so when they float too close to each other they bounce away in normal conditions.

Even ambitious home cooks don't normally have access to their own rennet but there's an easy home experiment that will quickly turn milk from a coherent liquid into a lumpy mess. Pour some milk into a glass and drop in some vinegar. The milk will curdle before your eyes. Swirl the glass and it will coat the sides with spindly tendrils, fragile solids that are separating from the rest of the liquid. The vinegar has acidified the milk down from its natural pH 6.7 neutral state, eliminating the electrical charge on the casein micelles. Tiny particles that used to repel each other now crash together and form visible lumps.

But if you manage to achieve a slower increase in acidity over

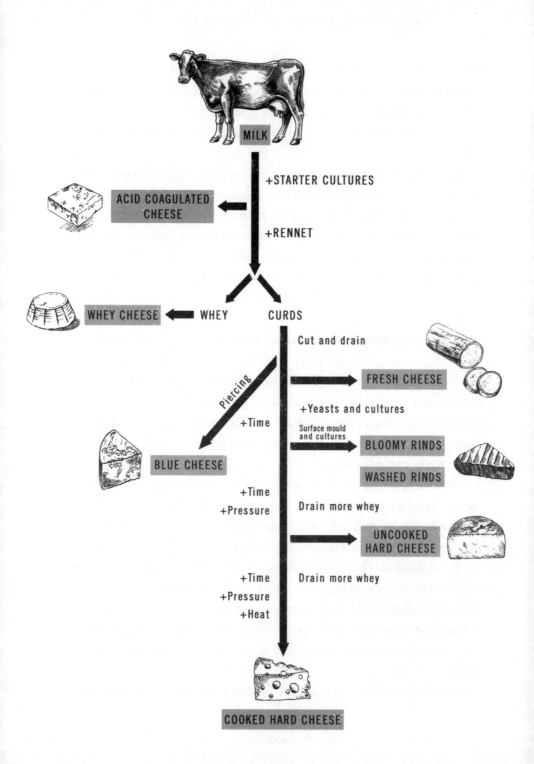

MILK

+STARTER CULTURES

ACID COAGULATED CHEESE

+RENNET

WHEY CHEESE ← WHEY   CURDS

Cut and drain

Piercing

+Time

FRESH CHEESE

+Yeasts and cultures

Surface mould and cultures

BLOOMY RINDS

WASHED RINDS

BLUE CHEESE

+Time
+Pressure   Drain more whey

UNCOOKED HARD CHEESE

+Time
+Pressure
+Heat   Drain more whey

COOKED HARD CHEESE

hours rather than seconds, the casein micelles assemble more calmly, forming an orderly queue. This slower increase happens during natural fermentation when bacteria digests the lactose, or sugar in milk, turning it into lactic acid. This does the job of slowly acidifying the milk over several hours, allowing the proteins to gently thicken into a gel rather than splitting violently from the whey and, at the end of that process, you have yoghurt.

Many cheesemakers use a combination of acid and rennet to coagulate milk and start the cheesemaking process. They add a starter culture (some lactic-acid-producing bacteria) and rennet (those protein-shaving enzymes) to milk. Some fresh and soft cheeses, like paneer, cottage cheese and queso blanco, are made using only acid coagulation without rennet. But the majority of cheeses start with three basic ingredients: milk, bacteria and enzymes.

FROM CURD TO CHEESE

When the milk is coagulated, it turns into a weak, jelly-like blancmange. To begin to separate the more solid curds from the liquid whey the cheesemaker simply cuts the curd. Stirring the resulting soup of curds and whey bashes the curds against each other, releasing more moisture. The essence of cheese is its ability to last and the more moisture that is taken out of the curd, the longer the cheese will remain edible and keep its nutritional value. People have developed many ways of squeezing the whey out of curd while making cheese. The more the curd is cut, the more whey is released. It can also be extracted through heating the curd. Gently raising the temperature of the curds causes them to contract and expel more moisture. The degree to which this is done also determines what type of bacteria survive in the curd, which has a significant effect on flavour development in maturing cheeses. Curds can also be stacked and milled to extract more whey. When the new cheese is formed, pressure can be applied to push moisture from the cheese; again, the more pressure applied the drier the cheese will be.

The use of salt is fundamental to the preservation process in many foods. Salt has several functions in cheesemaking, some immediate and some more long term. When salt is applied directly to the cut curds, it pulls moisture out into the whey, adding to the drying of the curd. At this early stage the salt also temporarily slows the acidification of the curd by inhibiting the action of the acid-producing bacteria. When added to the rind of a cheese, through brining or dry salting, moisture is diffused out of the curd's surface and evaporates. The surface of the cheese becomes drier and a rind is formed. In addition to the surface of the cheese drying out, salting also gives a rind high in salt, which controls the microbiological activity on the rind. The amount of salt absorbed within the cheese also controls internal microorganisms. The cheesemaker must get the proportions right so as to not inhibit the action of important microbes which help develop flavour during the ripening of the cheese. We cannot ignore the flavour-enhancing effect of salt as a seasoning as well. The correct amount will enhance the taste. Too much will override the subtle flavours.

In essence, you separate your milk, stir, dry, salt and press your curd and you get cheese. Technically, yes, but this kind of fresh cheese will be very mild, only exhibiting basic milk and yoghurt flavours and aromas. The fresh cheese is an ecosystem and it will get its flavours and textures over time from the biology within that system, as invisible agents break down the fats, proteins and sugars from the original milk. The first stage starts when enzymes from the rennet and from the milk get to work on the proteins, chewing up the long chains of amino acids into smaller chains. The smaller chunks they produce are perfect food for the starter bacteria enzymes to step in and start to break down. It's a beautiful ballet and each player gets its time on stage. At the beginning, cheese is full of starter bacteria that grow for the first few weeks and months and then run out of food. At that stage they burst and release a lot of enzymes into the cheese. This happens just when the cheese has produced lots of material for those enzymes to act on, so there's a constant supply of food for each stage.

During ripening, the fats and proteins break down to soften the

cheese. It's the digestion of the lactose that leads to a burst of flavour compounds. Although humans control the environment in which this happens, it's another form of life that is doing the work.

Not very long ago, cheese scientists hunted specific flavour molecules. There was once a lot of talk about finding the 'Cheddar molecule' – a single entity that gave Cheddar its distinctive flavour. Now it's better understood that Cheddar flavour doesn't come from a single molecule. It's the end result of the work of a colony of teeming bacterial activity along with the enzymes in the milk and the rennet. Cheddar gets its rind from the air around it and is largely untouched during ageing. Bloomy-rind cheeses, like Brie and Camembert, get their fluffy rinds from fungi with which they are inoculated. Washed-rind cheeses, like Taleggio and Époisses, are treated like bloomy or natural rind cheeses but are also washed with a salt solution as they mature.

A recent Harvard study carried out DNA tests on cheese rinds and they discovered bacteria that had never been identified before. Although science has developed a huge understanding of what goes on inside and on the surface of the cheese, there is still a huge amount that is a mystery. The most mysterious microbes in the process arrive in the cheese without anyone knowing where they originated. Dairy scientists have given these uninvited visitors their own name: NSLABs or non-starter lactic acid bacteria. These are bacteria that have not been added by humans to the milk but end up colonising the cheese and playing a large role in how it will taste when it's mature.

In effect, every dairy has its own environmental fog of bacteria and they just colonise the cheese and add to its character. They are in the air, swimming in the brine baths or clustered on the shelves in a ripening room. Even in the most controlled cheesemaking environments, NSLABs have an impact and in the maturing rooms of farmhouse cheesemakers where they are encouraged, they are integral to the nature of the finished cheese.

Research has highlighted exactly how much is still unknown about the cheesemaking process. Precise scientific explanations for how milk becomes cheese end somewhere around the door of the ripening room. Theories get more broad-brush and vague. The cheesemaker's role is to gently control and manipulate the rot and decide at which point decay has become delicious. We're almost back with the spirits of the cave from that story of the first accidental cheese, who are not spirits after all, but microbes.

Dick Willems, Coolea.

DO TRY THIS AT HOME: SIMPLE RECIPES FOR MAKING YOUR OWN CHEESE

A lot of the cheeses you'll learn about in this book seem very complex and specialised, using ingredients that you wouldn't find in domestic kitchens. But, at its heart, making cheese is simple. Irish cheeses like Milleens, Coolea and Cashel Blue started in people's kitchens before they moved into specialised dairies with lots of stainless steel and white rubber aprons.

It's surprisingly simple and fun to make your own cheese at home. Making cottage cheese is brilliant for that moment when you'd like something luscious to jazz up a salad or stir into a pasta dish but the nice shop with its tubs of artisan cheese is closed.

Forget expensive cheesemaking kits, these recipes use store-cupboard ingredients. There's nothing more satisfying than a bit of kitchen magic. And if you have children, they'll love the idea of an edible science experiment.

Labneh

A strained yoghurt, labneh is eaten throughout the Middle East, India and parts of Asia. It makes a beautiful, creamy fresh dip, keeping the flavour tang of yoghurt but giving you a thicker consistency. It's perfect for the start of a meal when everyone can dip in vegetables, crispbreads or toasted pitta fingers.

SERVES 6

500ml natural Greek yoghurt
1 teaspoon smoked paprika

a good pinch of salt flakes or table salt

1 tablespoon olive oil

200g mixture of pine nuts, sunflower and pumpkin seeds

50g hazelnuts

juice of 1 lemon or lime

a handful of fresh flat-leaf parsley, roughly chopped

a handful of fresh coriander, roughly chopped

The night before you want to serve the labneh, place the yoghurt in a sieve lined with a muslin or a clean, cotton tea towel and strain over a bowl. The liquid that drains from the yoghurt is the whey and you can throw this away (although it makes a wonderful skin toner if you bottle it and keep it in the fridge).

The next day, mix the smoked paprika and salt into the olive oil and then drizzle lightly over the seeds and nuts. Place them in a dry frying pan over a medium heat and toast until they are brown and fragrant. Watch them carefully to prevent burning.

Stir the lemon or lime juice into the strained curds (it should have the consistency of cream cheese) and spoon on to a large serving plate.

Just before serving, sprinkle your citrus-flavoured labneh with the toasted nuts and seeds, as well as the parsley and coriander leaves, and serve with celery and carrot sticks or toasted pitta fingers.

Paneer (Cottage Cheese)

Paneer comes from southern Asia, where it's made in kitchens by heating the milk and adding an acid. The difference between paneer and cottage cheese is that paneer is pressed into a more solid cheese than the crumblier cottage cheese. Heating the milk speeds up the acid coagulation and the curds appear in minutes. These curds are then strained and pressed into a block, but if you'd prefer not to wait, you can eat the cheese immediately as a crumblier cottage cheese. Cottage cheese is extremely versatile, used in a recipe or simply spread on toast or a cracker. You can easily add in flavourings such as fresh herbs. Paneer has very little flavour and won't last long but is a useful way of adding protein into vegetable dishes. It's a simple cheese you can make beautifully at home. You can fry it or bake it in slices to make a delicious addition to a salad.

MAKES 100G

1 litre whole milk
2 tablespoons lemon juice
a good pinch of salt

Heat the milk in a saucepan to a gentle simmer over a medium heat, stirring occasionally to prevent burning.

When the milk is steaming and frothy, remove it from the heat and stir in the lemon juice. Let this curdled mixture sit for 10 minutes.

Line a sieve with cheesecloth or a clean, cotton tea towel and place this over a mixing bowl. Pour the curdled mixture into the strainer and gather the edges of the cloth together like a purse. Squeeze the curds gently to remove the whey.

Open the cloth and sprinkle with salt.

You can transfer the cheese to a clean jar at this point or use it immediately as a fresh cottage cheese. If you prefer paneer, lift the cloth with the curds on to a plate and flatten them into a square. Fold the cloth over the top of the cheese. Then put another plate on top. Put a few tins of beans or any other heavy weight you have to hand on top of this plate to add more pressure to the cheese. Remove the bottom plate and replace it with a draining board so the last of the whey can drain away. After about an hour, the weave of the cloth will be pressed into the cheese and you can use it or put it in the fridge, where it will become less crumbly as it dries out. It will keep for up to a week.

PART TWO

THE CHEESES

CHAPTER FOUR

FRESH CHEESES

FROM MOZZARELLA TO THE LOIRE
CHÈVRES – LOCAL OR AUTHENTIC
AND A LIVELIHOOD IN CHEESE

When I first started shopping in Sheridans, Sainte-Maure de Touraine was the cheese that really made me realise cheese was a living entity and it changes constantly. The difference between a young fresh log and an oozing mature one is amazing.

Chef Enda McEvoy, Loam Restaurant, Galway

As a simple rule, fresh cheeses are younger, wetter and less influenced by their rinds than other types of cheese. The cheese-maker keeps more whey in the curd than in a harder cheese and this makes for a softer, moister cheese, which is made to be sold and eaten quite quickly. Like fresh fish, vegetables and fruit, fresh cheeses are best eaten relatively soon after they are produced. But (and this is not the first 'but' you'll come across in the complex and sometimes contradictory cheese world) some fresh cheeses, like brined cheeses, keep for long stretches depending on how they're stored and aged.

Lots of fresh cheeses, like mozzarella, mascarpone and cream cheese, don't have any rinds. There are also fresh cheeses with rinds but these rinds are not the dominant influence on flavour and texture.

These would include fresh cheeses with naturally developing rinds, like many fresh goats' cheeses. So fresh cheeses can be broken into two groups: those without any rind and those with a naturally formed rind. As soon as a cheese is made and exposed to air, it will begin to form a rind naturally as the cheese reacts to its environment or the microorganisms within the cheese make their presence visible on its outside layer. If a cheese is not to develop a rind, it needs to be stored in a way that keeps oxygen away from the surface of the cheese. Traditional methods to achieve this are storing in sealed vessels such as earthenware jars or immersing cheeses in brine. Modern methods include vacuum packing, gas-flushed packaging using nitrogen, or sealing cheese in plastic tubs.

If fresh cheeses are not sealed off from the air, a light rind will start to form within a couple of days of production. This rind could form as a delicate dusting of mould or yeast that has barely any influence on the cheese. Or it might be in the form of a stronger growth, which wrinkles the surface of the cheese and changes its texture underneath. The effect of these robust rinds is to develop more intense flavours than a purely fresh cheese will have at the start of its life. It also causes the cheese just beneath the rind (called the paste in the cheese world) to soften. A more purist view of fresh cheese might exclude any cheese with a rind from this category but in the shops we would consider any young cheese where the rind is not the dominant feature to be fresh. The nature of artisan cheeses and the great variation you find within them means that defining a group is never perfect and many fresh cheeses with active natural rinds could sit happily alongside bloomy-rind cheeses (see Chapter Five).

But, as a rule, fresh cheeses are just that – fresh. The flavour of these fresh cheeses tends to be mild and comes almost entirely from the milk and the transformation of the lactose into lactic acid during the cheese production. They have not had the benefit of the production of flavour compounds that are released during ripening, either by the action of microorganisms on the rind or within the cheese as it ages. This does not mean that fresh cheeses are bland, though. The best have complex flavours and aromas, and an appealing luscious and velvety texture. Their subtlety comes with the advantage of delivering the flavours and aromas of the feed and landscape where the animals grazed directly to the cheese eater. Their spectrum can range from acid and citrus tartness, to floral and herby tastes, where you can taste the animal's diet in the cheese. Some fresh cheeses can be mushroomy or buttery and sweet. All of the aromas tend to be raw and unfermented, such as fresh mushroom, grass and herbs, along with the dairy flavours of yoghurt, sweet milk and butter.

When we first started selling cheese, our nearest and dearest cheese producers were Meg and Derrick Gordon's St Tola goat farm

on the Burren in Co. Clare. We got dripping wet trays of cheese, with the cardboard leaking tangy whey because the cheese was so fresh. That set the standard for the kind of fresh cheese we wanted to sell. It was one of those lucky influences where you realise the difference between cheese that has just been brought from the dairy and the long shelf life, easily transportable supermarket versions.

Fresh cheeses are probably the most commonly used in cooking across the cheese-producing cultures. The mild flavour means that they can work with almost any other ingredients and offer the cook texture as well as a valuable source of nutrients. Their moist creamy texture means that they easily break down in sauces and bakes.

If we believe the practical purpose of cheese is to preserve a plentiful milk supply for times when it is scarce, then fresh cheeses are not very useful. Their lifespan cannot compare to the harder cheeses that can last for months or years. Maybe fresh cheeses began as a means of producing a more digestible food than fresh milk and later grew to be loved for their delightful fleeting flavours, luscious textures and just-made freshness.

BRINED CHEESES

THE ANCIENT SOCIETIES around the eastern Mediterranean and the Black Sea have been farming and dairying for many thousands of years. The hot climate where Europe meets Asia and Africa brought about the sturdy method of preserving cheese curds by storing them in salted water. Dairying in this part of the world is dominated by sheep and goats. These are the animals suited to this climate and terrain. Feta is of course by far the most famous cheese from this region. It's exported to and copied by countries across the globe. Feta is like Cheddar on the world cheese stage in that its ubiquity has taken away its specialness. Just as Cheddar is known as a bland block of yellow cheese, overshadowing the rich array of cloth-bound cheeses, feta's similar popularity overlooks the diverse and rich range of brined cheeses from this region. Each country from Ukraine to Turkey, Bulgaria to Eygpt has its own different sheep's and goats' cheeses stored and fermented in barrels, animal skins and various containers of salted water. We may think of these cheeses as simply fresh pressed curd preserved in brine but most of them have the influence of moulds and yeasts grown at some stage during maturation on their rind. The Bulgarian goats' cheese Tcherni Vit is matured in wooden barrels for two years but then allowed to form a blue rind that penetrates the cheese. Before Greek feta is packed into barrels it is cured in dry salt for up to two weeks. During this period, a layer of bacteria and yeast form on the cheese, developing the flavour and texture.

A LIVELIHOOD IN CHEESE

A hush has fallen in Anna L'Eveque's dairy. The young French woman is scooping soft curds out of a plastic half barrel with a silver ice-cream scoop. She packs the cloudy mousse into plastic cups about the size of a large takeaway coffee cup. Beads of milky whey press their way through the holes in these cups or moulds as if the curd is swelling and breathing it out. Close by, an occasional bleat from one of Anna's herd of 24 calm, friendly goats, whose milk she is turning into cheese, can be heard. It is a beautiful, golden, sunlit September morning. Around her in the rich Waterford farmland near Piltown, the orchards that her partner Phil farms are bursting with sweet apples. A crate of them lies outside waiting to be transported for sale. Here in the south-east of Ireland is a family who are taking the best of what the local land and climate have to offer and adding to it in a simple way, but the result is quite extraordinary.

Anna L'Eveque is small framed, studious and very young looking, and when she first presented us with examples of her goats' cheese a few years ago we were instantly enchanted. The delicacy and meticulousness of her craft came through in the small, ashed and white cheeses she brought to us. Her cheeses nailed a need that, up to that point, we had only been able to satisfy by bringing in some of the wonderful traditional French chèvre from the Loire. We were much happier to find a local source.

So far so wonderful. Anna is an artisan cheesemaker making roughly €100 worth of Triskel goats' cheese every day. But that is where the romantic, rose-tinted world view ends. She is an unsentimental Breton who tells it like it is. After subtracting her costs, her cheese business is barely a living. She is earning significantly less than the minimum hourly wage and working a seven-day week. The dairy is a small building made with plastic, prefabricated walls. Her goats

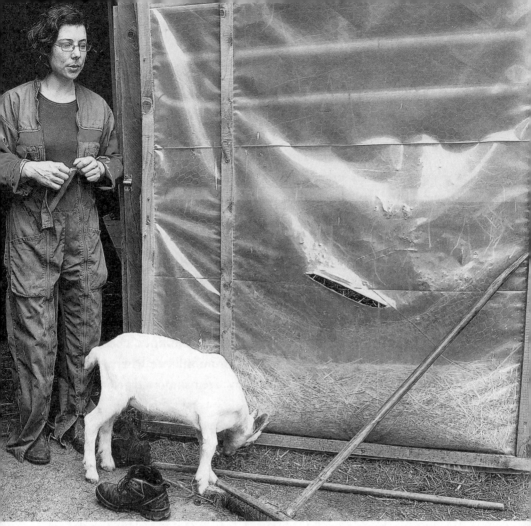

Anna L'Eveque.

are lying or standing in clean-smelling straw in a shed nearby. When some potential customers hear that Anna's herd lives indoors, they say they don't want to buy her cheese, preferring to imagine goats wandering up the side of a craggy mountain. But she doesn't have enough land or money to farm them outdoors. Both she and her Irish partner are tenant farmers, renting their dairy and orchard from larger farmers. On another farm Anna has a further 35 younger goats who move between an old stone shed and a pasture where they graze. The costs of putting a dairy into these old stone sheds was too high, so Anna assembled her plastic-walled dairy at a different site and moves between the two farms every day.

Anna is a purist and a pragmatist. She doesn't want to be a cheese-maker who uses other farmers' milk. She sees the raising of the animals and the daily milking as an integral part of cheesemaking. In France her cheese would be classified as *fermier* – made on the farm from a herd that lives on the same farm. France has strict definitions when it comes to certain marketing terms, such as *fermier*, as well as rigorous classification of traditional foods and wines under their AOC system. AOC stands for Appellation d'Origine Contrôlée, a strict set of rules on how and where cheeses must be made in order to call themselves by certain names. In other countries, cheese can be termed farmhouse even if it is made from milk or frozen curd that comes from hundreds of miles away, even imported from another country. Happily here in Ireland a new system of classification has been introduced for marketing terms including Artisan and Farmhouse. These are quite loose but are a welcome step in the right direction. This type of regulation protects genuine producers from unfair competition from those who take short cuts while giving a different impression to their customers. It's not that we believe there's a right or wrong way to produce food, but we believe customers should be able to make informed decisions.

One of the wonderful attributes of artisan fresh cheeses is that they depend so much on the milk and the environment for their flavour, rather than the maturing process. Customers often ask us whether one of our goats' cheeses has thyme or lemon balm in it. But those herbs haven't been added – they were eaten by the goats on the hillsides and their flavour compounds made it smoothly into the finished cheese. Goats' cheese has an astonishing ability to take on the taste of what the animals have eaten. This ability to translate environment directly into taste can occasionally have a nasty side effect and is to blame for the negative feelings some people have towards goats' milk and cheeses. If you leave a pail of goat milk within 30 metres of a Billy goat, his high, musty smell will be absorbed by the milk. It's all down to the kind of fatty acids in goats' milk. The short-chain caproic, caprylic and capric acids trap and concentrate odours into flavours. (These fatty acids are also found in cows' milk but at much lower levels.) This is what makes fresh cheese, especially fresh goats' cheese, taste of a place, an animal and a time.

The difference between Anna L'Eveque's Triskel Ash Log and a cheaper supermarket goat log exemplifies so many of the contradictions and complexities of modern food production. In order to meet

the huge demand for goats' cheese, frozen goats' curd is shipped across Europe to be made into the ubiquitous goat log, combining the cheapest source of raw material with the cheapest industrialised production. As cheesemongers we see mass-produced goat log as something less honest than industrial Cheddars or Emmentals. It comes wrapped in a vaguely artisan halo, so shoppers are led to believe they are buying something of quality. It is the cheese equivalent of pulled pork made from the meat of battery-farmed pigs. It gets put on to menus and shoved into recipes as a box-ticking trend, rather than for reasons of flavour or authenticity.

Anna loves the animal part of the working day even more than the cheesemaking, she says. In the early days it took her nearly three hours a day to milk the gentle white nanny goats, as they learned to stand on the raised wooden platform. Now they line up happily and the whole thing is done much more quickly. Anna milks them once a day. It is all she has time to do. The milk flows directly into stainless steel churns which she wheels the few metres from the parlour to the dairy to turn into cheese.

On this September Saturday morning, the goats have produced around 40 litres of milk. She will add some whey from a previous batch and a little rennet. The fresh milk will sit and rest for the remainder of the day and night, curdling slowly thanks to the acidity that develops in the milk, nudged into action by the whey from the previous batch.

The use of whey as a 'starter' culture in cheese is quite unusual in modern cheesemaking but it is the method by which all cheese would have been made originally. The process is very similar to the way yoghurt can be made by adding some live yoghurt to fresh milk. The bacteria in the live yoghurt under the right temperature will multiply and colonise the fresh milk, consuming the sugars and creating lactic acid until the milk is turned into yoghurt.

This process can be repeated indefinitely, passing the cultures from one batch to the next. In both modern cheesemaking and modern yoghurt-making a more consistent result is achieved when a freeze-dried culture is added to every new batch. It eliminates the risk of unwanted cultures invading from the environment. However, some traditional cheesemakers feel that they get a better and more unique result using their own cultures.

By allowing the cultures to work slowly over a long period, Anna gets her milk to coagulate with the use of very little rennet. This is called acid coagulation and is quite common in traditional French goats' cheeses and some other fresh cheeses.

This morning, the previous day's milk is already in curds and is draining in a cheesecloth bag. The milk from the day before that has become the 6kg of curds she is moulding now. Before pressing the curds into moulds she has salted them, adding around 60g of salt to 6kg of curds. There is no weight or other pressure applied to the curd, ensuring it retains a lot of moisture.

Her dairy is very small scale. It is just her and a kind neighbour who 'helps for the sake of helping'. Her companion is her two-year-old daughter Lucy. She's been here since babyhood, when she first joined her mother in a backpack as Anna worked. Lucy sometimes behaves more like a goat than a child, Anna says. One of her favourite games is to run headlong into your legs and butt you.

Anna's grandparents were farmers but her parents weren't. She went to Clermont-Ferrand in the Auvergne to study agriculture. It was a place where her home region of Brittany was the butt of French jokes for its reputation as the home of industrial farming, processed food and potatoes you would only feed to pigs. She has seen the unlovely side of French agriculture: poultry farms where a small shed houses 50,000 chickens. Food is lorried in to them and when the farmer presses a button, eggs come out. It's an experience that has left

her wary of the marketing phrase 'fresh from the farm'. Anna would ideally like to sell most of her cheeses directly to customers at a local market – getting the full retail price might make the business more viable – but the nearest one already has a cheese stall and doesn't want another cheese seller. So she sells her cheese to us at Sheridans and our customers are delighted.

In a perfect world we would probably only eat a fresh cheese made less than 20 miles away. For this to be possible we would have to imagine a world where every town and village, city and suburb had producer markets where we could buy from the people who made food in our locality. Municipal markets, where the cost of trading is minimal, would allow producers of every size the opportunity to sell their products directly to their customers and receive the full retail price. It's such a win-win scenario it is difficult to understand what stands in its way. Then you consider the marketing budgets of the major food retailers which persuade us that big supermarkets are better, cheaper and more convenient than small local markets. A well-structured system of local food markets could put the best artisan cheeses back where they belong: on the family table. A busy market close to their dairy would allow a small-scale cheese producer to make a decent living from their cheesemaking. This is particularly true for the producer of fresher cheeses, like Anna L'Eveque.

Because she does not vacuum pack or seal her cheeses in any way, as soon as the cheeses are left to drain a rind begins to form. Naturally occurring yeasts and moulds find their way on to the nutritious surface and begin to colonise. Many of these microorganisms are close relatives of those introduced intentionally on to the surface of Camembert and Brie to create their trademark bloomy rind. After just a few days, the surface flora will begin to interact with the paste nearest the rind, causing new flavours to be produced and releasing moisture, turning it semi-liquid. On some of her cheeses Anna uses charcoal to cover the rinds. The story goes that the tradition of putting ash on goats' cheeses originated when cheesemakers sprinkled wood ash from their fires on the surface of the newly made cheeses to

protect them from flies. It was another happy accident of the materials to hand being perfectly suited to a purpose. Charcoal is alkaline and it absorbs moisture. When it's put on a fresh cheese, it dries the rind and lowers the acidity, making it attractive for the growth of delicate moulds and yeasts like *Penicillium candidum* and *Geotrichum candidum*. Both these fungi help ripen the cheese. The subtle fur of naturally occurring fungi on the black charcoal gives that distinctive, lovely, soft, grey rind we see on ashed goats' cheeses.

Anna's cheese is a fresh cheese in the purest sense. It is made from milk that is still warm from the goat. The flavours of the grass and hay make their way into the finished cheese because nothing happens to it between udder and dairy. It travels metres rather than miles. The gentle acid fermentation with whey and a small amount of rennet

gives it a firm but incredibly delicate texture. The delicate rind that develops in the few days between the cheese being made and eaten adds another dimension but its influence is subtle and never overpowers the cheese. It is a perfect example of fresh cheese.

In a sad postscript, a few weeks after this visit to Anna's dairy she rang to tell us she was giving up cheesemaking. She had decided that it was better for her family if she focused her energy on her husband's apple business and their many beehives, rather than trying to raise their soon-to-be two children and juggle two demanding separate food businesses. It is sad that her wonderful cheeses were not valued enough to make the business a more viable concern. However, we cannot have all the advantages of people-centred crafts without acknowledging that sometimes those people need to make the right choices for their own lives. For us and our customers we are thankful for the pleasure that Anna's cheeses gave us, however fleeting. Thankfully, there are other cheesemakers in Ireland and in many other countries who have managed to continue to produce wonderful fresh cheeses and succeed in making a sustainable living. There are also new cheeses and cheesemakers appearing, full of promise and vitality. Some will be with us for a short time and others we will enjoy for generations.

MATCHING WINE AND CHEESE

FINDING WINES THAT pair reasonably well with cheese is a fairly simple exercise if you stick to a few basic rules. Finding a match that elevates the flavours and textures of both the wine and the cheese is a little trickier. This should not be an academic exercise; it is about enjoying the pinnacle of human culinary endeavours and the fun is in the trying.

As a rule of thumb, white wines tend to have more versatility and pair better with cheeses overall. Reds have over the years become a traditional pairing more because cheese is so often served at the end of a meal, by which stage, maybe after a meat course, everyone has already switched over to red wine. Choose a wine you like and a cheese you like. Look at the 'weight' and flavour profile of the cheese and try to stick to something similar: so a light, delicate mild cheese would go with a lighter style of wine, whereas a stronger hard cheese can match with a heartier or richer style of wine.

CHEESE AND MARKETS MAKE THE PERFECT MATCH

Sheridans Cheesemongers would not exist without the Galway City Market. This Saturday market evolved from a poultry market, one of many markets that were thriving a hundred years ago. As in most other towns and cities, the other Galway markets died off as supermarkets arrived. However, the City Market was kept alive by some vegetable sellers and the odd craft stall who traded from spring to Christmas.

We are social beings. We like to chat and to have a relationship with the people who sell and produce our food. We love to hear the stories, get advice and learn about new things. At a small market, producers get a good price. Customers get good locally produced food and receive maximum value for money.

The retail structure of a market offers independence for consumers and producers from the power of large retailers and food companies. It's inherently built on a short supply chain that can do more for food safety than all the regulations that a food safety authority could imagine. It also means that perishable freshly made cheeses can go from a dairy to where they belong, quickly and deliciously. Market food does not have to be expensive and markets don't have to be exclusive. A massive proportion of food costs are currently spent on packaging, transport and marketing.

When they have the back-up of a solid market, the cheesemaker can focus on producing cheese for which they will get a good price and not have to worry about extended shelf life, long credit terms, industry audits, price pressure and the mountain of paperwork that comes with dealing with a big industry supply chain. For the most delicate cheeses ripened with natural rinds, every additional step in the supply chain reduces the quality and viability of the product. Warehousing these cheeses robs them of their inherent freshness. They are lesser versions of themselves when they're finally unwrapped and eaten, far from their best.

PASTA FILATA

Pasta filata cheeses are in a category of their own – a particular way of making cheese, which originated in Italy. The term translates from Italian as 'spun paste' and they are referred to in English as stretched curd cheeses. Getting elasticity into the curd isn't easy. It has to be left to ripen for a relatively long time until it has reached a high level of acidity thanks to the lactic acid produced by bacterial fermentation. The curd is then re-cut in a similar process to cheddaring; this removes more moisture and allows the acidity to continue to rise. Next the curd is 'scalded' in very hot whey or water, about 85°C. The curds are then kneaded until they are soft and stretchy, then pulled apart into the desired shape before being cooled in cold water. The most famous pasta filata cheese is of course mozzeralla. This super fresh cheese is best eaten as soon as possible; however, this type of cheese can also be aged and preserved. Provolone is aged for at least one month and the giant Provolone Valpadana 'pancettone', which weigh up to 100kg, can be aged for more than four months. In order for the cheese to last this long the curds are well kneaded to expel air and moisture, and the finished cheese is soaked in brine to help form a protective rind. Other well-known pasta filata cheeses are Caciocavallo Silano, Pallone di Gravina and Scamorza. These cheeses also undergo further processing – brining, ageing and sometimes smoking.

CREAM CHEESE

Despite what we are often told, cream cheese was not invented in the United States in the late nineteenth century. That was when it was popularised by the brand Philadelphia.

Cream cheese is simply fresh cheese which has a reasonably high fat and moisture content, has not been allowed to develop any sort of rind and has very little added salt. Soft cheese was often stored in sealed ceramic pots in the millennia before refrigeration but the lack of salt, along with the high fat and high moisture content, means it has little use as a means of preserving milk nutrients for any length of time.

Many different variations of cream cheese exist in different cultures, including quark, cottage cheese, queso fresco, fromage frais and fromage blanc. The recipes tend to differ in relation to the fat content of the milk, the method of coagulation and whether the cheese has been strained or pressed. Clotted cream, mascarpone and crème fraîche are varieties of cream cheeses made with cream. For English clotted cream and French crème fraîche, the cream is coagulated using acidification from the action of bacteria. With mascarpone the acidification is brought about by the addition of an acid such as lemon juice.

SYNTHETIC MILK AND CHEESE – THE GASTRONOMY OF THE FUTURE?

THERE ARE WONDERFUL and exciting groups of young scientists currently pushing the envelope of genetic engineering and synthetic biology. This science is sometimes labelled as 'frankenfood' and seen as a symbol of large food corporations rushing to control all we farm and eat. However, if you scratch the surface you will find quite the opposite. Groups of researchers motivated by veganism, environmental concerns and solving global hunger are on the cusp of synthetically creating milk and, more interestingly, curd. If and when they succeed, they could halt our planet's unsustainable march of increased meat and dairy consumption and in doing so go some way to halting global warming and the unnecessary use of arable land for animal feed. We can't wait to taste a synthetic curd ripened in the traditional way. Will this science develop and end up being part of the gastronomy of the future, bringing pleasure to generations to come? There is no reason why this technology cannot exist alongside traditional farming practices to create a more balanced food-production system.

AUTHENTIC OR LOCAL

Most people who are familiar with cheese are so familiar with the term buffalo mozzarella or Mozzarella di Bufala that it now sounds ordinary. Over the past ten or fifteen years it has changed from being a delicacy only found outside Italy in the most serious Italian delis who flew the cheese in once or twice a week; now every supermarket across Europe has little tubs of it on their shelves. This is a great success story in one way. To preserve this traditional regional product from an increasing number of imitators both in Italy and overseas, the Italian government made Mozzarella di Bufala Campana a DOC cheese in 1993. Three years later the European Union granted it Protected Designation of Origin status (or PDO). Most of those tubs or bags have the words 'Mozzarella di Bufala Campana' always accompanied by a little green and red label printed on them. This protected cheese must be made following particular production steps and using buffalo milk within a specific geographical area. This protection means more economic activity in this relatively deprived area of Italy. Yet to produce the quantity of 'Mozzarella di Bufala Campana' needed for all the gourmet pizzas and vine tomato and mozzarella salads we consume in the Western world, both the farming and the production have become extremely intensive and mechanised. We stock it in Sheridans because we love it and our customers love it. We select the best one we can, given that we need to have a couple of weeks' shelf life, but it does not come close to comparing with the real thing eaten in its place. Having eaten it on holidays in the south of Italy, we are not satisfied with this unique culinary experience but instead want to have it available in our local stores. Why do we always want to take these experiences home with us, demanding they be something we should have every week of the year? Is it greed or just natural desire?

There are several accounts as to how water buffalo were intro-duced into central southern Italy. The most likely is that they arrived through Arabian settlements in Sicily in the seventh century. Their strength and large hooves made them perfect draft animals and it wasn't until much later and long after the first mozzarella were made that buffalo milk began to be used to make this cheese in Italy. Buffalo don't give as much milk as cows but what they do give is an amazing milk, extremely high in protein and fat solids, making it creamy and concentrated. Its structure is also suited to the 'pasta filata' method of producing cheese.

As a result of the increasing popularity of buffalo mozzarella in the rest of Europe, Australia and America, small herds of water buf-falo have appeared across these continents and artisan producers of buffalo mozzarella are no longer rare. Of course this cheese can't be

Macroom buffalo.

called 'Mozzarella di Bufala Campana' but it is probably the best way to deliver fresh mozzarella to the ever-growing market. Here in Ireland we have Macroom Buffalo Farm, an excellent farm in Co. Cork that was set up only a few years ago. It is up to customers to decide whether they want to seek out the original cheese made in its original location or have the taste and flavour experience of eating a locally produced version. Our desire to have buffalo mozzarella can be seen as a success of this cheese and the cheesemaking process, and instead of extinction we have a world-conquering cheese, but what are the consequences? From a culinary diversity perspective, is it survival of the fittest? Will the rapid spread of knowledge and the speed and efficiency of modern transport result in a cheese world inhabited by the top twenty cheeses? Should we be choosing our local buffalo mozzarella, supporting local production, or should we support the original culture and food-producing communities and look for the authentic?

FROZEN MILK

FREEZING MILK OR curd preserves the flavour at the point of freezing and may destroy some of the enzymes and microbes which would otherwise develop stronger flavours during the ripening of the cheese. The biggest issue with freezing milk is the damage that ice crystals do to the structure and texture of the curd. Ice crystals can damage the casein network, leading to a softer cheese. The faster the milk, curd or cheese is frozen the less damage is done, as there is less time for bigger, more damaging, ice crystals to form.

HOW TO CHOOSE FRESH CHEESE

There are two broad categories of fresh cheese. The first is the rindless fresh cheese normally bought in a tub or pack like mascarpone, cream cheese and mozzarella. These should look and smell clean, be pure white and without discolouration. We would liken it to buying fresh fish. Use your nose. If it smells strongly, don't buy it. This is why these cheeses are sold in packaging. Exposed to the air they will start to develop rinds and they were not made to benefit from a rind or the flavours that might be added by a rind. The second broad category is fresh cheese that has developed a gentle natural rind, like Anna L'Eveque's Triskel goats' cheese or Sainte-Maure. A rind will begin to develop on any cheese left for a couple of days that hasn't been sealed. If these smaller, moist cheeses have no visible rind or just a light powdery dusting of mould or yeast, then they are young and will taste delicate and mild. Fresh cheese tends to attract natural or wild *candidum* moulds and yeasts, along with common blue and black moulds. If the maturing environment is not too humid and warm then these rinds tend to grow slowly and have only a very subtle effect on the cheese paste. These cheeses will lose moisture slowly and the flavours will become more concentrated. As cheeses with a slow-growing rind, they will have smooth rinds with a light covering of mould or yeast. If the conditions are more humid and allow the fungi on the rind to grow more aggressively then the rind will have a stronger impact on how the cheese develops. You will recognise these cheeses by the raised knobbly rind and sometimes seeping paste. When this happens, the paste just beneath the rind is broken down, often becoming semi-liquid and, as the cheese matures, they can gain more pungent flavours associated with bloomy-rind cheeses. We continue to define these as fresh cheeses, though, because the dominant characteristics still come from the fresh curd, despite some influence from the rind.

HOW TO STORE FRESH CHEESE

Cold is generally best, and your domestic fridge temperature is fine.

Many fresh cheeses, especially goats', have a barely perceivable rind. These rinds are very delicate and if you smother them in a non-breathable covering, like plastic wrap, they will lose their ability to breathe and quickly take on a rancidity that dominates the delicate cheese. If fresh cheeses are left unwrapped, moisture will evaporate quickly and these fresh cheeses will dry out. This might be preferable to the cheese getting a slimy rind and taking on undesirable flavours but, for the best results, you should wrap fresh cheeses loosely in waxed paper or some baking parchment, which is breathable but stops the cheese drying out in the fridge.

For fresh cheeses with no active rind, such as cream cheese, wrap them in an airtight covering or airtight container. For cheeses sold in whey, water or brine, such as feta or mozzarella, store them submerged in a tub of lightly salted water.

Freezing is fine, but the texture of a fresh cheese will not survive the freezing process. If you have to freeze your fresh cheese, it's best to use it in cooking. Defrost it overnight in the fridge before using.

FOOD WE LIKE WITH FRESH CHEESE

○ Fresh cheeses range hugely in their culinary uses and flavours. Many can be used as an ingredient in cooking, perhaps stirred into a pasta dish, but the best fresh cheeses can sit proudly on a cheeseboard and bring a delicate texture and flavour to the mix.

Kevin, Galway market, *c.* 1996.

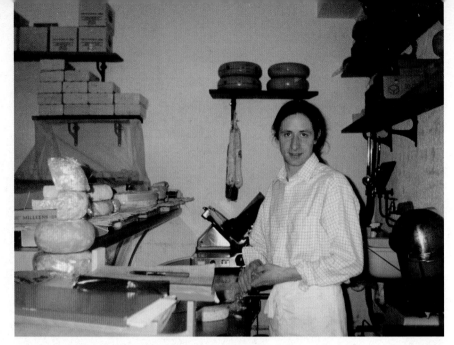

ABOVE: Seamus in the Kirwan's Lane shop, Galway, *c.* 1996.

BELOW: Kevin in the Church Yard Street shop, Galway, *c.* 2002.

ABOVE: Gerry Flynn, Galway wine bar.

BELOW: The staff outside the Galway shop on Church Yard Street. Seamus (*right*).

Kevin Jephson and Seamus in the Ardkeen Quality Food Store, Waterford.

LEFT: The Galway shop.

BELOW: John Leverrier in the South Anne Street shop, Dublin.

○ Because fresh cheeses tend to be light and fluffy in texture, they go well with crunchy foods, like crisp crackers, toasted seeds and roasted nuts. Firm fruits and vegetables, like crisp, green apples, snap-fresh celery and raw slivers of fennel, kohlrabi and crisp carrots, are also brilliant accompaniments. Crumbling fresh cheese over a salad of mandolined crisp fruits and vegetables finishes off a supremely healthy plate with some creamy decadence.

○ Fresh cheeses don't tend to have strong flavours, so they can play with strongly flavoured fresh herbs. Lovage, a herb that looks like flat-leaf parsley but comes with an intense celery sweetness, is a great one to team with a delicate fresh sheep's cheese.

○ Fresh greens are great partners to fresh cheeses. Crumble a delicate goats' cheese over a sorrel and spinach salad lightly dressed with walnut oil and lemon juice, or use a combination of young Swiss chard leaves and rocket. You can even layer in some fresh mint and coriander leaves too.

○ In winter, when it's difficult to find tasty fresh fruit, compotes or pastes, such as quince or fig, can sit deliciously with fresh cheese on a cracker.

○ A good hunk of light, yeasty bread with a generous wedge of fresh goats' cheese or good cream cheese is a pretty perfect light lunch. Little else is needed.

DRINKS WE LIKE WITH FRESH CHEESE

○ A good match with any fresh cheese would be a Sauvignon Blanc or an unoaked lighter white wine. Fresh goats' cheeses are popular in the Loire Valley in France and there's a saying that if it grows together, it goes together. This is true then of the Sauvignon Blanc wines of this region, from the more basic up to the Pouilly-Fumé and Sancerre wines. When goats' cheese has been aged it can suit a light, fruity Pinot Noir such as Sancerre rouge.

○ Semi-sweet cider where the apple flavour is still strong makes a great partner to a stronger, fresh goats' cheese.

○ For a non-alcoholic option there are some great Irish apple juices available. Con Traas's Tipperary apple farm is where they make the Apple Farm Sparkling Irish Apple Juice, an unusual and delicious cloudy, sparkling apple juice.

SOME OF OUR FAVOURITE FRESH CHEESES

BRIN D'AMOUR

PRODUCER: various
MADE: Corsica, France
PRODUCTION: small dairies and farms
MILK: sheep's
RENNET: traditional
TYPE: fresh
RIND: natural with herbs and developing natural moulds with age

RIPENING: 3 to 16 weeks
APPEARANCE: 300g to 400g square
TEXTURE: firm and moist
TASTE: rich, salty yoghurt, developing a nuttiness and slight sharpness with age – also strong flavour of aromatic herbs from the rind

BRIN D'AMOUR is a rich, soft sheep's milk cheese from the Mediterranean island of Corsica. The sheep's milk produces a lovely fatty, rich, fresh cheese. The milk (and with it the cheese) reflects the salty air and herby landscape where the sheep graze. These flavours are emphasised by the cheese being coated in a mix of dried herbs, such as juniper, rosemary and savory (a rosemary-like herb). These herbs are typical of those found in the Corsican scrub. When very fresh it is almost like a salty sheep's milk yoghurt with a sprinkling of herbs. If it matures for a few weeks, it develops some spots of blue mould and becomes more meaty and nutty as the flavours on the rind penetrate the paste.

CROTTIN DE CHAVIGNOL, FERMIER, DUBOIS-BOULAY

PRODUCER: Affineur Dubois-Boulay
MADE: Chavignol, France
PRODUCTION: farms, using their own milk
MILK: raw goats'
NAME PROTECTION: AOC, PDO
RENNET: acid coagulation with small amount of rennet

TYPE: fresh
RIND: natural yeast and moulds
RIPENING: 2 to 12 weeks in cool, damp cellars
APPEARANCE: 60g flattened sphere
TEXTURE: soft but compact
TASTE: fresh, acidic, nutty and herbal to sharp

THE TRANSLATION of this delicate-sounding goats' cheese's name is 'horse shit of Chavignol'. Traditionally, this cheese is aged for several months and the ageing turns it from a pale, bloomy little cheese into a firm, blue-black orb, not unlike a spherical horse dropping. The Crottin de Chavignol most of us love, though, bears no resemblance to horse manure, as we tend to like it aged for only about one month. At a couple of weeks old, the crottin hasn't developed a complexity of flavour and the rind is a faint fuzz of white mould. A couple of weeks later the cheese is covered in a downy white *Penicillium* rind and a speckle of blue mould has appeared on it. Inside, the paste remains white but the flavour has become more robust and complex. By two months the downy rind is covered in blue mould. As the cheese ages it dries further and the mould dies off, leaving a bluey-black rind. The paste protected by this hard exterior remains white and firm but the flavour is deeper, still sweet but a little sharp. All of the nutrition of the fresh goats' milk has been trapped in this little ball and can be released in leaner winter months.

LEAF-WRAPPED ROBIOLA, CORA

PRODUCER: Cora
MADE: Piedmont, Italy
PRODUCTION: seasonal, single
  herd
MILK: raw goats'
RENNET: acid coagulation with
  some traditional rennet
TYPE: fresh

RIND: natural, wrapped in leaves
RIPENING: 2 to 3 weeks
APPEARANCE: 250g wheels
  wrapped in leaves
TEXTURE: soft, sometimes liquid
  under the rind
TASTE: lactic, floral, gentle
  sharpness

ROBIOLA IS a soft, ripened, seasonal cheese from Piedmont with either no rind or a very thin rind. It is often made with cows', goats' and sheep's milk. The Cora family make their cheeses with the raw milk from their own goat herd between February and November. The curd is hung in muslin cloths and allowed to set slowly with help of lactic acid and a very small amount of rennet. When the cheeses are less than two days old, they are wrapped in locally sourced chestnut, cherry, fig, grape, walnut or even cabbage leaves collected during the summer months and stored for use as needed. The cheeses are then ripened in the leaves for two to three weeks. The cheese develops some mild yeasts on the rind, encouraged by the humid conditions created by the leaf wrapping. In turn, this yeast rind causes the cheese to soften under the rind and the flavour intensifies slightly. But creating this micro-atmosphere is not the only benefit of wrapping the cheeses – these delicate fresh goats' cheeses take on flavour from the leaves. It is subtle but you can really taste the difference between each leaf.

SAINTE-MAURE DE TOURAINE FERMIER, JACQUIN

PRODUCER: P. Jacquin & Fils
MADE: La Vernelle, France
PRODUCTION: farms, using their own milk
MILK: raw goats'
NAME PROTECTION: AOC, PDO
RENNET: acid coagulation with small amount of rennet
TYPE: fresh

RIND: ash with natural yeast and moulds
RIPENING: 3 to 6 weeks in cool damp cellars
APPEARANCE: 250g tapered cylinder with straw running through the centre
TEXTURE: soft but compact
TASTE: fresh and acidic with hints of raw nuts and delicate herbs

WE HAVE BEEN selling Jacquin's Fermier Sainte-Maure for many years. It changes from season to season but is always a favourite. Sainte-Maure de Touraine is probably the most famous of the Loire goats' cheeses. Coagulation is mainly through lactic fermentation, although a small amount of rennet is still used to ensure that the curd sets. The young logs are lightly dusted with salt and ash, which helps develop the greyish white and blue moulds on the surface. A piece of straw runs along the length of the chalk-white interior, helping the delicate fresh cheese to stay intact. It also allows air into the centre of the cheese, which helps ripening. The cheeses are normally aged for 3 to 6 weeks. Young Sainte-Maure has a floral and hay aroma and a clean, acidic taste with a nutty finish. Depending on the humidity during maturation, the cheese can develop an almost liquid paste under the skin; these cheeses tend to have a slight pungency and a little sharpness. If matured in drier conditions, the cheese will turn more compact and the flavour will become more intensely nutty.

ST TOLA LOG RAW

PRODUCER: McDonald Family
MADE: Clare, Ireland
PRODUCTION: single farm, using
their own milk
MILK: raw goats'
RENNET: vegetarian
TYPE: fresh

RIND: natural with some natural
moulds and yeast; an ashed
version
RIPENING: 2 to 8 weeks
APPEARANCE: 1kg log or 500g
ashed log
TEXTURE: soft, flaky
TASTE: sweet lactic, floral, vanilla

MEG AND DERRICK Gordon began making St Tola in the Burren in 1978, primarily as a means of making a living out of their 25-acre holding. Meg had picked up cheesemaking skills during her time in Normandy, whilst Derrick, as a former tea-plantation manager, was no stranger to hard agricultural work. This formidable combination allowed the couple to make a success of their business. Some 20 years later, their neighbour, Siobhan Ni Ghairbhith, became interested in learning the cheesemaker's art and began to take lessons from Meg. A year later Meg handed over the running of the business to Siobhan, who took charge of the herd and relocated production to a purpose-built cheesemaking facility on her parent's family farm, a short distance away. When young, St Tola is mild, very delicate with a floral aroma. As it develops, the paste becomes a little firmer and the rind attracts some natural yeasts. The flavour becomes a little sharper with a hint of pungency. When ash is used on the rind, it attracts a more even spread of yeast and the cheese can become quite creamy under the skin.

ROVES DES GARRIGUES

PRODUCER: Fromagerie Cigaloise
MADE: Provence, France
PRODUCTION: small dairy
MILK: goats'
RENNET: acid coagulation, small amount of traditional rennet
TYPE: fresh

RIND: none
RIPENING: 2 days
APPEARANCE: 70g small sphere
TEXTURE: thick, creamy
TASTE: sweet, slight acidity, fresh herb aroma

ROVES DES GARRIGUES takes its name from the brown, long-horned goats used to produce the milk and the garrigue, or scrub on which they graze. Roves are bred for both their milk and their meat, making them a popular choice in this sparse landscape. Roves des Garrigues is made at Saint-Hippolyte-du-Fort by the Fromagerie Cigaloise, although two or three *fermier* versions are also available in the area. Summer curd is frozen and used to produce cheeses during the winter months; they are never quite as good as the summer cheeses but still a treat. The cheese has a definite flavour of lemon and thyme, which is a result of the Provençal flora on which the animals graze. The cheeses are packed in little Styrofoam boxes and vacuum packed to keep them from developing any rind.

And here are some favourites from our friends around the world.

ZINGERMAN'S FRESH CREAM CHEESE

PRODUCER: Zingerman's Creamery
MADE: Ann Arbor, Michigan, USA
PRODUCTION: artisan hand production using milk from a single herd
MILK: cows'
RENNET: traditional
TYPE: fresh
RIND: none
RIPENING: none
APPEARANCE: served in a tub
TEXTURE: firm, smooth
TASTE: fresh, creamy, lactic

ONE OF MY favourite cheeses in the world is one that we make right here at Zingerman's Creamery – it's old-school, handmade, traditional cream cheese. Most of the world has come to believe that 'cream cheese' is a mass-market product that comes in sealed foil packages. But that's akin to believing that Cheddar comes as plastic-wrapped slices. There was a day, a century or so ago, when cream cheese was a handmade fresh product, made with active cultures and without the vegetable gum or extrusion that are typical of large-scale factory production. The flavour is fresh and creamy ... and because it has active cultures it has far more flavour. Without the vegetable gum used as a thickener, it has a much creamier, softer mouth feel. Having become accustomed to this artisan offering, it's nearly impossible to eat the commercial version! *Ari Weinzweig, Zingerman's, Michigan, USA*

SHAW RIVER MOZZARELLA

PRODUCER: Roger and Sue Haldane
MADE: Victoria, Australia
PRODUCTION: single farm, using their own milk
MILK: buffaloes'
RENNET: vegetable
TYPE: fresh, pasta filata
RIND: none

RIPENING: fresh, packed in lightly salted brine
APPEARANCE: 100g pure white balls
TEXTURE: slightly rubbery on the outside, dense and fleshy interior
TASTE: fresh, clean, lactic flavour profile

I LOVE A commitment to product excellence so driven that a family will import buffalo from Italy and Bulgaria to Australia in order to produce cheese as close to authentic as possible. Ahead of their time, the Haldanes pioneered Australia's water buffalo milk industry and I salute their hardship and dedication whenever I eat or serve their magnificent handmade mozzarella to cheese enthusiasts. There is a significant and pleasurable difference in quality compared to the majority of machine-manufactured cows' milk mozzarella more readily available throughout Australia. This clean, dense, milky ball of fresh cheese is a snack in the Bowman household – eaten like an apple. The messy, juicy whey of these mozzarella balls is enjoyed just as passionately as we would a messy mango. *Claudia Bowman, McIntosh & Bowman Cheesemongers, Sydney, Australia*

BEN'S CHEESE PLANET CREAM CHEESE

PRODUCER: Ben's Cheese Planet
MADE: New York, USA
PRODUCTION: small dairy
MILK: cows'
RENNET: acid coagulation
TYPE: fresh

RIND: none
RIPENING: 2 days
APPEARANCE: tubs
TEXTURE: thick, creamy
TASTE: sweet, slight tang

COMPLEXITY MUST be balanced. There is something to be said for the simpler joys, the fundamentals. Ben's Cream Cheese is always in my refrigerator – it's my favourite cheese. I can't get enough of it. You will find a plain ball of salted mozzarella in my fridge. I keep cheese curds on hand so I can fry them up myself. These are essential cheeses in my life, that go nicely with more complex treasures like Montgomery's Cheddar or Harbison. Diversity is crucial. I love fresh goats' cheese too. *Rob Kaufelt, Murray's Cheese, New York, USA*

REBCHÄSLI

PRODUCER: Ruedi Tritten
MADE: Canton of Thurgau, Switzerland
PRODUCTION: farmhouse, using milk from their own herd
MILK: cows'
RENNET: traditional

TYPE: fresh
RIND: none
RIPENING: 14 days
APPEARANCE: 150 to 200g
TEXTURE: smooth, little curdy
TASTE: slightly sour, milky

THE KARTAUSE Ittingen is a former monastery that was transformed into a foundation some years back. Now you can find a hotel there, a restaurant and a shop that sells products produced within the monastery compound, including cheeses from the little dairy that uses milk from the monastery-farm. My favourite is Rebchäsli, a little cheese of about 200g. The cheese is made in a special way with starter cultures that give it a slightly sour taste and a brine wash that contains some annatto, adding a special colour to it. After two weeks of ageing the cheese is ready to bring to the table. It's very refreshing to eat with a light white wine and fresh bread. *Konrad Heusser, Mundig Cheese, Switzerland*

HOLY GOAT MATURED SKYLA

PRODUCER: Sutton Grange Organic Farm
MADE: Victoria, Australia
PRODUCTION: farmhouse, own herd
MILK: goats'
RENNET: vegetarian
TYPE: fresh with natural bloom
RIND: gentle *candidum* bloom

RIPENING: 2 to 6 weeks
APPEARANCE: 100g log
TEXTURE: dense centre, fuzzy, wrinkled rind atop a fudge-like, sometimes molten layer of cheese
TASTE: the rich, dense centre and initial citrus tones give way to a long, lingering, clean mousse, crème fraîche mouth feel

THIS IS THE closest thing Australia produces to the more traditional goats' milk cheeses of the Loire Valley in France. This award-winning, bio-dynamic, organic, *Geotrichum*-rinded cheese is everything you want from a goats' milk cheese. It has a rich flavour whilst being clean and light and somewhat delicate. Fudgy under the rind but still chalky in the centre is my preference in order to best experience the delicate, floral profiles of both flavour and aroma of this beauty and national treasure in Australia's artisan cheese movement. On top of a slice of Pastilla Nash, a caramelised prune and walnut log, it is a match made in heaven. *Claudia Bowman, McIntosh & Bowman Cheesemongers, Sydney, Australia*

RECIPES

SPRING

Harriet Leander's
Warm Fresh Cheese Salad

*Harriet was our food mother in The Blue Raincoat
restaurant in Galway nearly 20 years ago. She is a master of
combining food flavours and textures, just as in this salad.*

SERVES 4

4 rashers unsmoked bacon
80ml Port
salt and freshly ground black pepper
150g fresh goats' cheese
1 head lollo rosso lettuce
1 tablespoon good olive oil

Fry the bacon rashers over a medium heat until crispy and
then put to one side. Pour the fat from the frying pan into a
small saucepan.

Add the Port to the bacon fat and heat it gently until warm.
Season with a little salt and pepper.

Place the cheese in a bowl and pour the warm Port and bacon
fat over the top.

Shred the lettuce into a bowl, tear the cheese into small
chunks, chop the crispy bacon into slivers and scatter both
over the lettuce.

Stir any remaining Port and bacon liquor into the olive oil and
pour over the salad as a warm dressing. Serve immediately.

SUMMER

Seamus's Wilted Greens and Fresh Cheese

*This is a perfect side dish or can be used as a pie filling for a
more robust main course. You could also top it with some
fried chorizo for a simple supper. A tray of oven-roasted
chorizo is a must in a household like mine where a meat-
eater and a vegetarian live. The two can be combined when
serving for a communal meal to suit everyone.*

SERVES 2

a knob of butter
1 onion, chopped
a handful of button mushrooms
100g fresh cheese of your choice
50ml double cream
2 large handfuls of fresh spinach, chard or kale
freshly ground black pepper

Melt the butter in a large frying pan over a medium heat and
cook the onion gently until it is soft and almost melting.

Chop the mushrooms in half and add them to the buttery onion.

Crumble in your favourite fresh cheese and pour in the cream.

Reduce the heat and let this mixture cook down gently.

Just before you are ready to serve, stir in the spinach or chard.
(If you're using kale you should blanch it in boiling water to
soften first.)

Season the cheesy, wilted greens with black pepper before serving.

AUTUMN

Salad of Mozzarella, Poached Pears, Air-dried Lamb and Hazelnuts

A beautiful salad that bridges the gap between summer and winter. The secret to this recipe is a good balsamic vinegar and fresh mozzarella. We are lucky to have buffalo mozzarella from Toby Simmonds's Toons Bridge Dairy in Co. Cork delivered fresh to our shops.

SERVES 6

2 or 3 pears, peeled, halved and cored

750ml water

½ vanilla pod

100g sugar

½ cinnamon stick

1 large buffalo mozzarella, torn into shreds or chopped

150g Connemara air-dried lamb, thinly sliced and cut into small shreds (if you can't find air-dried lamb you could use a good prosciutto)

100g mixed leaf salad

50g hazelnuts, toasted and chopped

For the vinaigrette

2 tablespoons olive oil

2 tablespoons balsamic vinegar

1 teaspoon honey

1 teaspoon mustard

Place the pears in a large saucepan with the water, the seeds from the vanilla pod, the sugar and the cinnamon. Poach the pears over a medium heat until soft. Leave to cool in the syrup.

Once cooled, slice the pears and combine on a large serving plate with the mozzarella, lamb and leaves.

Whisk the vinaigrette ingredients together in small bowl and, just before serving, drizzle over the salad and then sprinkle with the toasted hazelnuts.

WINTER

Seamus's Grilled Halloumi with Lemon

Fried, roasted or gilled, halloumi is one of the best comfort food snacks imaginable. I never buy halloumi for a specific occasion — because of its long shelf life, I leave it in the fridge and forget about it. Then one day or evening it comes to the rescue as a late-night supper, a vegetarian option or to help out an impoverished potato dish. Halloumi should always be cooked and eaten warm. It is usually fried or grilled but I love topping any roast vegetable dish with thin slices and letting it brown and crisp up in the oven.

SERVES 4

1 packet halloumi (usually 250g)
1 tablespoon olive oil
the juice of 1 lemon

Cut the halloumi into slices roughly 1.5cm thick and brush with olive oil. You can do this with a pastry brush or rub the oil on with your hands and gently massage it into the cheese slices.

Place the slices under a medium to hot grill and cook for 3 to 4 minutes on each side, or until slightly brown. (If you wish to fry the cheese, cook for the same amount of time in a medium to hot pan.)

Remove from the grill or pan, brush with lemon juice and serve immediately with a crisp kale salad or a hearty potato gratin — or both!

CHAPTER FIVE

BLOOMY RINDS

FROM BRIE TO TRIPLE CRÈMES – RAW MILK CHEESE, THE CAMEMBERT WARS AND THE WOMAN BEHIND THE CHEESE

Raw milk cheese is more than a wonderful food; it is a deeply embedded expression of our finest traditions. It is both an art and a way of life. It is a culture, a heritage and a cherished landscape.

Slow Food Manifesto in Defense of Raw Milk Cheeses

When we talk about bloomy rinds, we mean soft cheeses with distinctive, white, downy coatings or rinds. It can be a shock to people who have happily been munching Brie and Camembert for years to learn that the velvety rind is a growing, living mould. The pure white coat goes against our idea of moulds. We think of them as grey-blue fuzzy invaders that spoil our food and squat in the dank corners of our houses.

Say 'fungi' and most of us think of mushrooms, but moulds and yeasts are also fungi. Two of them are responsible for the velvety whiteness on bloomy-rind cheeses: *Penicillium candidum*, a mould, and *Geotrichum candidum*, a yeast. These fungi don't just wrap a protective coating around the cheese (like nature's clingfilm), they also change the texture and flavour of the cheese inside.

The fungi can be introduced to bloomy-rind cheeses in three ways. First, the spores can be added to the milk early in the cheese-making process as part of the starter culture. They will begin to grow on the rind of the cheese when it is exposed to oxygen. The second way is to spray the spores on to the surface of the cheese after it is produced. Sometimes both steps are taken. Lastly, the cheesemaker can allow the mould spores to land on the cheese from the air or surfaces in the maturing room and naturally colonise its rind.

When the moulds and yeasts start growing on the surface of the cheese, they form a thick coat which begins to break down the proteins in the cheese into peptides and amino acids, and the fats into fatty acids. This changes the flavour and takes the cheese from a firm, chalky texture to a more sumptuous ooze. Some of this softening in the texture comes from the action of the fungal coating lowering the acidity of the cheese. Bloomy rinds start off quite acidic but as the

Cooleeny ripening.

moulds grow they lower the acidity of the curd. You can see the effect of the rind on these cheeses by looking at a section of Brie or Camembert which hasn't ripened right to the middle. The outer part of the cheese, or the part closest to the rind, will be glistening and creamy, but as you move to the innermost part of the cheese it will still be white and chalky.

Most bloomy-rind cheeses are shaped as flat disks in order to let the effect of the rind work its way to the middle more quickly. If the cheeses were any thicker, it would take too long for this to happen, by which time the cheese closest to the rind would have matured past its best into an unpleasant smelly liquid. Although the action is similar in all bloomy-rind cheeses, the time it takes for the curd to mature and the flavours to develop will vary from cheese to cheese. This is dependent on lots of factors – from the fat content of the milk, to the bacterial landscape of the milk, the cheese and the environment, and the moisture content of the cheese.

The most famous bloomy rinds are Brie and Camembert. The success of these northern French cheeses has resulted in similar cheeses being produced around the world.

Given their fungal beginnings, it's no surprise that the word mushroomy is often used to describe the flavours of bloomy-rind cheeses. The mouth feel of the rind also has a similar downy, fresh mushroom texture. These cheeses tend to taste floral and of raw veg-etable, and have a distinctively creamy soft texture. Because they are relatively high in moisture and have such active rinds, bloomy rinds don't last very long. They are generally best eaten within 12 weeks. Like the fresh cheeses in the last chapter, bloomy rinds are produced more for the pleasure of eating than the practicality of preservation.

DAIRY ANIMALS

ALTHOUGH EVERY MAMMAL produces milk, only some have combined this with an ability to be domesticated and produce enough milk to be worth farming. Here is a little information on the world's main dairy animals, although milk from donkeys, elk and camels, amongst others, is also used in different cultures and places.

WORLD MILK PRODUCTION

Species	Tonnes	Per cent of total
Cow	625,754,261	83.0
Buffalo	97,417,135	12.9
Goat	17,846,118	2.4
Sheep	10,122,522	1.3

Constituents	unit	Cow	Goat	Buffalo	Sheep
Water	g	87.8	88.9	81.1	83.0
Protein	g	3.2	3.1	4.5	5.4
Fat	g	3.9	3.5	8.0	6.0
Carbohydrate	g	4.8	4.4	4.9	5.1
Energy	kcal	66	60	110	95
	kJ	275	253	463	396
Sugars (Lactose)	g	4.8	4.4	5.1	4.9
Saturated	g	2.4	2.3	4.2	3.8
Mono-unsaturated	g	1.1	0.8	1.7	1.5
Polyunsaturated	g	0.1	0.1	0.2	0.3
Cholesterol	mg	14	10	8	11
Calcium	IU	120	100	195	170

Source: FAO of United Nations, 2012

THE WOMAN BEHIND THE CHEESE

Breda Maher has very fond memories of her early years as a cheese-maker. Her proudest moment was standing in an English shop, 'still quite shy and bashful', waiting to talk to the cheese buyer. A customer walked in and said to the shopkeeper, 'Can I have another piece of that wonderful Cooleeney you gave me?'

Breda began making her bloomy-rind cheese Cooleeney in 1986 as a way to make a better living from the family dairy farm outside Thurles in Co. Tipperary. Cheese seemed like a good way to increase the value of the Maher family milk. In the 1970s and early 1980s the European Union bought up excess supply from European farmers in order to keep milk prices stable. Faced with growing milk lakes and butter mountains, in 1984 the European Union introduced its milk

Breda Maher.

quota system under the Common Agricultural Policy. This put a limit on the quantity of milk farmers were permitted to produce. Farmers were able to receive extra quota in order to produce their own products such as farmhouse cheese.

Breda had trained in hotel management and had a great interest in food, so cheese seemed like a good idea. The early years were more exciting than she could have imagined. She visited other cheesemakers and went to cheesemaking night classes at University College Cork. In September 1986 she made her first batch of bloomy-rind cheese in her kitchen using fresh raw milk from the family herd. She started selling it to the Irish-owned supermarket Superquinn and to a small wholesaler in Dublin. In the spring of 1987 Cooleeney won an international cheese award in London. Breda didn't appreciate the full economic potential of the award at the time but it wasn't long until demand grew and she moved the cheesemaking out of her house and built a cheese production plant on the farm.

Cooleeney was among the first cheeses we sold on our market stall in Galway. From the first phone call when we asked Breda to send us some cheese, she stood out as an impressive woman. She has always been very straight, never prone to over-romanticising her role as a cheesemaker. She has had a clear focus on the need to get the sales to keep her family business going. She combines this with a genuine kindness and an altruistic streak. She's always willing to help other cheesemakers and she has a genuine aspiration for co-operation and shared success. Her husband, Jim, is the third generation to run their dairy farm and has been awarded for his voluntary work within the co-operative and dairy industry in Ireland at the highest level. They are a strong team who will pass on a farm much strengthened to the next generation and a local and national dairy industry much better for their contribution.

Cooleeney is often referred to as an Irish Camembert. We believe this narrow interpretation of the cheese does not do it justice and can even hamper enjoyment of it. It is similar to Camembert in that it has the same thick, white, downy rind and it is of a similar shape and size. However, it really is quite a different cheese. This distinction comes from many small variations in the cheesemaking process, including the origin of the milk, the starter cultures used, the handling of the curd and the environment in which it is ripened.

Camembert de Normandie has a much more earthy flavour and aroma spectrum, reminiscent of damp woods, cooked green vegetables and rich cream. Cooleeney is lighter and more floral, bringing flavours and aromas of fresh mushrooms, raw cauliflower and grass. The texture, too, is quite different. A genuine Camembert really is not at its best until the paste has softened right through to the centre and the whole flesh of the cheese is bulging. Cooleeney is often best when it still has a small amount of chalky paste at the centre and is a little more liquid under the rind than the paste of a Camembert.

There are many fantastic farmhouse bloomy-rind cheeses made in Ireland and around the world, each sharing the heritage of Camembert but each with its own individual characteristics shaped by the place in which they are made and the people who make them. If we expect these cheeses to have the classic characteristics of Camembert, then we will be mostly disappointed. If, however, we taste the cheese for itself, it is easier to enjoy the wonderful differences in taste and texture.

Having learned to make bloomy-rind cheese, Breda had to learn to be a businesswoman. But this came naturally to her. It was an exciting time, getting organised, going to food fairs and meeting people who were fascinated by her cheese.

'I loved those years,' she says. 'It's a totally different world now.'

Success as a businesswoman is one of the reasons Breda's world changed so dramatically. Cooleeney is now sold around the world.

Dubai is one of her more recent new markets, selling into the food service industry and specialist shops there. The price of that success has been a mountain of paperwork. Traceability and supermarket-friendly supply systems rule the bigger-scale artisan production. Breda employs two people to manage the paperwork needed to supply her cheese into the supermarkets. Every step of the cheesemaking process is documented in the tiniest detail every day. Each of the supermarkets she supplies sends its own auditor to her farm to carry out their own checks.

'You put the systems in place and you do it. You just get on with it,' she says. But it doesn't take away from the fact that making cheese is more fun than maintaining a paper trail. 'It's three hundred and sixty-five days a year, twice a day. You've got to be there for a couple of hours in the morning and a couple of hours in the evening. It's not a job; it's a lifestyle, with six o'clock starts. It's a good lifestyle but you have to like it and be prepared for the long days.'

Breda began, like most other cheesemakers in Ireland, using only raw milk. As the 'food safety' demands of the large retailers increased, Breda saw that it made commercial sense to introduce a pasteurised version of her cheese to overcome the retail industry's phobia of raw milk cheese, particularly soft cheeses. Did she notice a difference between the raw and pasteurised cheeses? She says she can tell just by touch the difference between curds made with raw milk and those made with pasteurised milk.

'It's a stronger curd with raw milk. You can tell by the feel of it. It feels entirely different.' And the taste of the cheese? 'There's a huge difference. The raw milk cheese is much more earthy. It has a deeper flavour.' For us, the flavours of fresh white mushroom, raw cauliflower and yoghurt come in single file like separate notes in the pasteurised cheese. The flavours in the raw milk cheese are harder to define and more knitted together. They play out in a more complex, nuanced

Cooleeney Farmhouse.

melody, filling the mouth with flavour and more complex aromas.

Breda continued to produce both raw and pasteurised cheese up until the spring of 2015, when she decided to stop making the raw milk version. Chatting to Breda over the previous couple of years, we knew that she was coming under increased pressure from auditors representing large retailers to stop making raw milk cheese. There has never been a case in which Cooleeney cheese, raw or pasteurised, has been implicated in any food safety incident. The concerns of the auditors were based purely on a theoretical risk because there was the possibility of cross-contamination between the raw and pasteurised cheeses. Breda had to make a decision to protect her business and her employees, and we fully respect this. We continue to sell pasteurised Cooleeney and it remains a really good cheese. We do feel, however, that we have been denied the enjoyment of eating raw milk Cooleeney for no good reason.

Breda Maher's decision to stop using raw milk is part of a wider picture where raw milk cheeses are becoming the exception rather than the norm. It is not that long since we started selling cheese – 20 years is only a moment in the history of food – and yet so much has changed in two decades. When we started out, farmhouse and traditional cheeses were made with raw milk. In our very short time there has been a fundamental shift. Even in the rarefied French cheese world, where they have what looks to an outsider like enviable levels of protection and respect for traditional methods, raw milk cheese is under threat.

In the mid 1990s we sold 23 different French cheeses. Back then just one of these was made with pasteurised milk. Today eight of those same cheeses are made with pasteurised milk, an eight-fold increase, with only 15 still made with raw milk. It is a massive shift when you consider how traditional the range is and the fact that many of the remaining cheeses must be made with raw milk as part of their AOC regulations. The change in the raw milk profile of Irish cheeses is even more dramatic. Eleven of the Irish cheesemakers who we worked with when we first began selling cheese are still in business now. Twenty years ago nine of them were making cheese with raw milk; the remaining two were using pasteurised milk. Now the picture has almost reversed. Seven of the eleven cheesemakers use pasteurised milk, with just four continuing to use raw milk. And of those four, only two cheesemakers, Eamonn Lonergan of Knockanore and Silke Croppe of Corleggy, continue to make all of their cheese with raw milk.

During these 20 years, there has been no food scare relating to raw milk cheese in Ireland and there has been no increase in illness due to the consumption of raw milk cheese. If it were not for the huge pressure the cheesemakers are put under by the state regulators and larger retail operators, most of them would have preferred to use raw milk. We can see no reasonable explanation except the relentless application of a narrow-minded view of the risks of producing and eating natural foods, and the lack of value attributed to the inherent quality of the food we eat. Wouldn't it be easier to use pasteurised milk in all cheeses, you could ask? What difference does it make? Raw milk doesn't guarantee a great cheese. That, at least, is true. We have tasted many terrible cheeses made from raw milk and there are many really good cheeses made from pasteurised milk. However, with raw milk we have the possibility of creating a great cheese, a cheese with more complexity and depth of flavour than can ever be achieved with pasteurised milk.

If we look to France, the home of bloomy-rind cheeses, there are two that dominate this category – Brie and Camembert. The names of these cheeses are not protected by French or international law in the way that Roquefort or Comté are. In fact, you can find a 'Camembert' or 'Brie' made in every cheesemaking country in the world, both industrial and farmhouse. However, the original cheeses defined as Camembert de Normandie and Brie de Meaux are protected by AOC and PDO and can only be made in certain geographical areas within France following specific production guidelines, including the use of raw milk. You don't need a book or flowery language to discover the difference in flavour and aroma that raw milk cheese can give us. Simply taste a Camembert AOC or Brie de Meaux AOC alongside a pasteurised version. You may prefer the pasteurised version but you will be left in no doubt that there is a difference: a difference that we believe should be valued and available for customers if they choose it.

At the heart of the debate around the use of raw milk are a clash of cultures and a clash of values. If we hold the belief that the eradication of all food-borne illness takes precedence over any other consideration then we cannot make cheese with raw milk. However, if we believe that reducing the risk of food-borne illness in a manner that is proportional to other values of society, such as food culture, the pleasure of flavour and the rights of people to choose what they want to eat, then we can continue to make cheese with raw milk.

We would have more respect for the argument that the food safety industry is putting forward – that they are interested in public health – if they were consistent. The most persistent cause of food-borne illness in the Western world is a pathogen called *Campylobacter*, which is carried in poultry. It is the single biggest source of food poisoning, with around 2,500 reported cases in Ireland every year. Experts estimate the unreported levels could be five times those reported. The bacterium is killed by properly cooking the meat but it is very easily spread in the kitchen when the meat is being prepared or through contaminated packaging. Cross-contamination is made more likely because of the bacteria's ability to survive in water, which means a damp cloth or the splash from a tap can spread the infection around the kitchen. The prevalence of *Campylobacter* is a direct result of industrial farming practices brought about because of the pressure from large retailers for cheaper and cheaper food. In a modern poultry 'factory' *Campylobacter* can spread from one bird to an entire shed of 40,000 birds within 48 hours.

Even if the root cause of the problem were not tackled, there is a control method that it would be possible to introduce – *Campylobacter* is destroyed by freezing. If large retailers and government food safety authorities truly prioritised the eradication of food-borne illness, why isn't it mandatory to freeze all poultry carcasses before sale? The huge industry that is responsible for the production and sale of poultry meat argues, of course, that there would be an extra cost and that some consumers would notice a difference in the quality of the meat. How is this different to the case for the production of raw milk cheese? The difference is that one is a tiny industry made up of micro-enterprises with little commercial value and the other is one of the largest food industries in the world made up of massive, often multinational companies.

Softer cheeses, like the bloomy-rind cheeses we are looking at in this chapter, have a higher moisture content and generally lower acidity than hard cheeses, which puts them in a higher risk category in terms of food safety, so their producers have been under more pressure to pasteurise their cheeses. In France in the spring of 2007 the two largest Camembert manufacturers, Lactalis and the *co-opérative* Isigny Sainte-Mère, started making their Camembert with pasteurised milk. The move followed a health scare involving six children who got sick after eating raw milk Camembert. The two companies sacrificed the AOC status on the bulk of their Camembert de Normandie production in order to eliminate raw milk from the process. Later that year they lobbied the French government to change the Camembert Charter, the AOC rules on how Camembert is produced, to allow their non-raw milk Camembert to retain its Camembert de Normandie certificate. Traditional Camembert makers said the move would destroy the magic of this hand-ladled cheese. The French media exploded with indignation and rage, accusing the large companies of attempting to kill tradition. Lactalis fought a bitter PR battle for almost two years. The companies' request to the government was rejected. The Camembert Charter remained in its original version. Under AOC rules Camembert de Normandie must still be made using raw milk. The victory was hailed in France as a triumph of a small traditional production method against the might of a globalised giant.

The victory of the small producers in the Camembert wars is a story that says so much about the iconic status of Camembert in French culture. The AOC rules had been changed to allow pasteurised milk to be used in the manufacture of Pont l'Évêque, Reblochon and Livarot cheeses, without any of the same controversy. Camembert, it seems, is closer to the French heart and ideas about food culture and tradition. The cheesemaking world at large, particularly those who value the choice to eat raw milk cheese, owes a huge debt to the

French for their stand on this issue. Large retailers continue to stock raw milk Camembert because their customers demand it and it is this demand that, in the end, is the only thing that will save raw milk cheese from extinction.

I AM LACTOSE INTOLERANT, CAN I EAT CHEESE?

MOST OF THE lactose present in fresh milk used to make hard cheeses is converted into lactic acid and removed in the whey, making them virtually lactose free. The lactose content of most cheeses can be checked by looking at the nutritional facts on the label, as any carbohydrate in natural cheese – those with no additives – comes from the lactose. Most hard cheeses, such as Cheddar, contain as little as 0.1g per 100g, which makes them suitable for many of those who are lactose intolerant. Generally, the softer and fresher the cheese, the more lactose it will contain. For sufferers of severe lactose intolerance, even very small quantities can cause illness.

AMERICAN CAMEMBERT

America has struggled with Camembert for more than a century. In 1909 a government official called Charles Thom wrote a pamphlet called 'Camembert Cheese Problems in the United States'. It was a fascinating account of the struggles American cheesemakers were having in making this French cheese on US soil. The damp, mild conditions around San Francisco proved to be one of the few locations where Camembert could be made successfully, because these are good conditions for mould growth. Drier, hotter conditions elsewhere in the US meant that Camembert didn't mature in the same way that it did in Normandy.

By 1909, most cheese in America was being made in factories rather than farmsteads, like the traditional farm and ripening rooms mentioned by Thom:

> Ripening rooms built for climactic conditions found in France have failed to give success in America. Either domestic manufacture of Camembert must be abandoned in most sections or the construction of the rooms for cheese ripening must be so modified as to obtain the conditions desired.*

The Camemberts those American cheesemakers were making (many of them immigrants from Europe) were made with raw milk. In 1949 the US Food and Drug Administration (FDA) introduced its standards of identity, which banned any cheese made from raw milk that

* Thom, Charles, *Camembert Cheese Problems in the United States* (Washington: The Bureau of Animal Industry, 1909).

Eamon Kiely in the Cooleeney maturing rooms.

had not been aged for at least 60 days – a rule that remains in force today. Camembert, which is aged between 21 and 30 days, is now only available in the US as a pasteurised cheese under the FDA regulations. American Camembert eaters are getting a blander experience compared to their French counterparts.

PREGNANCY AND CHEESE

ONE OF THE most common questions we get asked about eating raw milk cheese is from worried pregnant women or their partners. The chance of getting food poisoning is small if you prepare your food properly and in particular avoid contaminating ready-to-eat food with raw meat, especially chicken. Getting food poisoning from cheese is extremely rare. However, it makes sense for pregnant women to be extra careful for two reasons. First, their immune system is compromised and so some bugs that a healthy adult would easily fight off could make them sick; second, the implications of getting food poisoning are much more serious and could harm the unborn baby. In order to keep risks at an absolute minimum it is advised that pregnant women avoid soft, particularly mould- or bacteria-ripened, cheeses. These cheeses contain more moisture and their rinds are developed to encourage bacteria growth, so they have a higher risk of harbouring unwanted, harmful bacteria. Harder, drier cheeses are much less hospitable to these bacteria and so are much safer to eat. Quite often advice is given to pregnant women to just avoid cheeses made from raw milk; however, this is dangerous, as whether a cheese is made from raw or pasteurised milk, if it has an active rind it can harbour Listeria, which can have a particularly detrimental effect on an unborn baby. So the best advice is to stick with mature harder cheeses and don't forget to avoid paté, raw eggs, shellfish, cured meats and liver products, and thoroughly wash all fruit and vegetables.

BLOOMY RINDS WITH EXTRA CREAM

The addition of extra cream to the milk before cheesemaking is counter-intuitive if we only view cheesemaking as a means of preserving milk. The extra fat shortens the life of the cheese, after all. The practice of adding extra cream is a relatively recent one and is done purely to create a particularly rich, creamy flavour and texture.

Double or triple crème cheeses originated in France and are mostly made with a bloomy rind. (Cream cheeses with a butterfat content of more than 75 per cent are referred to as triple crème; those with a fat content of 60–74 per cent are known as double crème.) Brillat-Savarin is probably the most famous and the original extra cream bloomy-rind cheese. It was created by a French cheesemaker in the nineteenth century and was originally called Délice des Gourmets. It was renamed Brillat-Savarin by Henri Androuët in the 1930s as a homage to eighteenth-century French gastronome Jean Anthelme Brillat-Savarin. Although these cheeses have a bloomy rind, the high fat content slows down the action of the rind. Together with a typically thicker shape to the cheese, the rind of extra creams rarely breaks down the structure of the cheese. If a long ripening is allowed, the cheeses develop an unpleasant sharp flavour, as opposed to the more subtle, sweet, butter flavour of younger extra cream cheeses.

HOW TO CHOOSE BLOOMY RINDS

Like customers in a fruit and veg shop squeezing a peach or pear to check for ripeness, you will often see a customer squeeze a Camembert to see if it is ripe. For small, wrapped bloomies, like

Camemberts, you can give them a little squeeze but it's often hard to tell much. A decent rule, if you like them nice and ripe, is to look for cheeses in the last week of their shelf life. With cut pieces many customers look for a running Brie. But beware – a Brie should bulge, not run. A bloomy cheese with a very pure white rind is either very young or industrially made. But a cheese with a rind that has a good amount of browning around the edge is probably over ripe. A nice ivory tone is probably the happiest colour you can find in a bloomy-rind cheese and a speckle of red or orange can mean you have discovered a gem.

HOW TO STORE BLOOMY RINDS

We find these cheeses prefer a low temperature, about 5°C, which also happens to be the temperature of most domestic fridges. The moulds and yeasts work at a nice slow pace in this environment. If you have a Camembert- or Brie-type cheese that you want to ripen up a little more, just leave it alone in the original wrapper in your fridge and it will do the work itself; a couple of weeks will transform a chalky paste into a soft, bulging one. Even a cut wedge of Brie will continue to ripen in your fridge. You will sometimes notice the bloomy mould begin to colonise the cut face of the cheese, wrapping it in a velvety layer, which is perfectly edible. If bloomy rinds are kept too warm for too long, the rind can become overactive, creating a really runny paste just under the rind, a lot of ammonia and some off flavours.

These cheeses have living rinds, so it's really important to let them breathe and not smother them – so keep them away from clingfilm and use a breathable paper to wrap them. This is particularly important for cheeses that have a delicate natural bloom. It is often suggested to keep cheeses in a sealed plastic box or Tupperware in the fridge, but if you keep any type of living-rind cheese in a sealed box there will be condensation and a lack of oxygen. To allow for a small amount of air exchange, punch some holes in the lid before you use it. Your fridge might smell of cheese but, as people who work all day surrounded by the smell of cheese, we don't see that as a bad thing! For some it is a problem and if you share your home with someone who is not as keen on big cheese aromas as you are, get a Styrofoam box and an ice pack and create a cheese hideaway in a shed or other out-building.

FOOD WE LIKE WITH BLOOMY RINDS

○ So many foods and flavours complement and can be enjoyed with bloomy-rind cheeses, but there are some great partnerships that bring an extra dimension to both the cheese and the accompanying food. With cheeses as soft and yielding as bloomy rinds, you need a partner with a bit of crunch and bite.

○ Toasted sourdough bread with a ripe Brie is hard to beat, particularly with toasted pumpkin and sunflower seeds sprinkled over the top for some nutty crunch.

○ We are very keen on Sheridans crispy, mixed-seed Irish butter crackers with bloomy rinds. They give a crunchy foil to the luscious paste and the hint of toasted seeds works very well with the soft vegetable flavours.

○ A ripe Camembert with a zingy apple is a simple combination but unbeatable. The contrasting textures and juxtaposition of fresh, tangy apple with fatty, pungent cheese is perfect. For the same reason, Highbank Orchard Syrup from Highbank's Kilkenny Orchards can be dripped stickily and sparingly over a ripe Camembert.

○ For an outstandingly decadent dessert, try slices of triple crème Camembert layered with slices of really ripe peach. There is a wonderful play of sweetness, with the juice of the peach washing over the thick, creamy texture of the cheese.

○ Brie and ham are a perfect match in a toastie or just on a plate; especially moist, pink, home-cooked ham that pulls in threads rather than plasticky round slices.

○ Butternut squash or pumpkin cut into crescents drizzled with

olive oil, roasted and topped with slices of Cooleeney for their last five minutes in the oven make a delicious light meal or side dish to a roast.

DRINKS WE LIKE WITH BLOOMY RINDS

○ Bloomy rinds go well with many wines, particularly fruity, floral whites and sparkling whites. Try with an unoaked Chardonnay or, for a bit of luxury, Champagne. Light, young juicy styles of red can also work well, such as Valpolicella, Pinot Noir or Beaujolais.

○ Most beers don't match well with the delicate flavour of bloomy-rind cheeses and tend to bring out the bitterness of the rind. However, a dry cider works almost as well as a simple apple.

○ A good non-alcoholic partner is cranberry juice mixed with soda, or sparkling water finished with a slice of lime.

SOME OF OUR FAVOURITE BLOOMY-RIND CHEESES

CAMEMBERT DE NORMANDIE, GILLOT

PRODUCER: Gillot
MADE: Normandy, France
PRODUCTION: dairy, using milk from local farms
MILK: raw cows'
NAME PROTECTION: AOC, PDO
RENNET: traditional

TYPE: bloomy, soft
RIND: thick *Penicillium candidum*
APPEARANCE: 250g wheel in wooden box
TEXTURE: soft, bulging
TASTE: raw mushroom, cauliflower, light pungency

THIS IS THE real Camembert, made with raw Normandy milk from Normandy cattle and always made in 250g discs packed in little wooden boxes. Gillot have been producing Camembert in Orne since 1912. Although production is relatively large scale, they follow the strict criteria laid down for the production of Camembert de Normandie AOC. It is a unique cheese that has never been replicated despite the thousands of attempts. The fully ripe paste never runs, it just bulges out from between its rind. The skin is a deep white with sometimes reddish blotches or streaks. The aroma is of fresh mushrooms, butter, grass and steamed green vegetables. Although the flavour fills your mouth, it is never overly pungent, sharp or bitter.

ST KILLIAN

PRODUCER: Berridge family
MADE: Co. Wexford, Ireland
PRODUCTION: farmhouse, using
  their own milk
MILK: cows'
RENNET: vegetarian
TYPE: bloomy, soft

RIND: *Penicillium candidum*
RIPENING: 2 to 4 weeks
APPEARANCE: 150g discs
TEXTURE: soft to runny
TASTE: raw mushroom, creamy
  yoghurt

PADDY AND JULIET Berridge began making Camembert-style cheeses on the family's farm near Adamstown in Co. Wexford in 1982. All their cheeses are made exclusively from the milk of their own herd of Friesian, Jersey, Angus and Montbéliarde cattle. This is quite a small little cheese and the mould rind works quite fast, creating a really runny, semi-liquid interior. When you cut it open, the paste spills from between the rind and releases a really pleasant sweet mushroom and hay aroma. It is quite mild for a farmhouse Camembert-style cheese but unlike most pasteurised bloomy cheeses it has much more in flavour than just raw mushrooms and yoghurt.

CHAOURCE FERMIER, GAEC DES TOURELLES

PRODUCER: Gaec des Tourelles
MADE: Reims, France
PRODUCTION: farmhouse, using their own milk
MILK: raw cows'
NAME PROTECTION: AOC, PDO
RENNET: acid coagulation, some traditional rennet
TYPE: bloomy, added cream

RIND: *Penicillium candidum*
RIPENING: 2 to 6 weeks
APPEARANCE: 250g and 450g cylinders
TEXTURE: soft to runny under the rind, chalky centre
TASTE: sweet, lactic, raw mushroom

CHAOURCE IS named after a small town in the Champagne region. Generally mould-rind cheeses are made in discs in order to maximise surface area, thus ensuring that there is sufficient action by the rind's fungi to convert the interior from a chalky, under-ripe texture into a softer, runnier paste. However, Chaource's cylindrical shape means that the rind softens the paste just beneath but leaves the centre chalky. You could ripen a Chaource until it is soft through, but by the time the whole paste has broken down, the flavour will have become over sharp and off. There is a little extra cream added to the milk when making this cheese but not enough to define it as a double crème cheese. This *fermier* cheese has complex but gentle flavours. After cutting the small cylinder in half, the paste just under the rind will flow down on to the plate and a mild aroma of fresh mushrooms and cream will be released. The flavour is creamy, lactic and slightly acidic. It is hard not to eat the whole cheese in one sitting.

BRIE DE MEAUX, DONGÉ

PRODUCER: Dongé
MADE: Île-de France, France
PRODUCTION: dairy
MILK: raw cows'
NAME PROTECTION: AOC, PDO
RENNET: traditional
TYPE: bloomy

RIND: thick *Penicillium candidum*
RIPENING: 5 to 9 weeks
APPEARANCE: 3kg disk
TEXTURE: bulging
TASTE: raw cauliflower and mushroom, sweet milk

BRIE HAS BECOME a word, like Camembert and Cheddar, to describe a type of cheese that can vary hugely in quality. Brie de Meaux is the real Brie and, for us, Dongé are by far the best producers. There are some very good *fermier* Bries made in France with raw milk but they tend to have a different, more aggressive, flavour. Great Brie de Meaux is full of flavour and has a big aroma but is very balanced, almost restrained. It is made in a large, cylindrical disk approximately 35–40cm across and 5cm high. This gives the cheese a high surface area to paste ratio, which it needs if the bloom on the exterior is to break down the interior curd, transforming the texture of the paste from chalky to a soft bulge.

The *candidum* rind gives off the typical raw mushroom aroma and, when ripe, there is a slight sharpness. The flavour is steamed salty vegetables and cream.

SAINT-MARCELLIN

PRODUCER: various small dairies
MADE: Rhône-Alpes, France
PRODUCTION: small dairies
MILK: raw and pasteurised cows'
NAME PROTECTION: PGI
RENNET: traditional
TYPE: natural bloomy

RIND: natural yeast and mould bloom
RIPENING: 2 to 4 weeks
APPEARANCE: 80g disk
TEXTURE: chalky but often liquid under the rind
TASTE: delicate with light pungency, raw vegetable and floral

SAINT-MARCELLIN is a soft cows' milk cheese named after the village of Saint-Marcellin in the Dauphiné region of the Rhône-Alpes. Traditionally made from goats' milk, it looks like many small farm goats' cheeses. More recently Saint-Marcellin is nearly always made from cows' milk. The small disc of fresh cheese attracts natural moulds and yeasts similar to those introduced to Camembert-style cheeses; however, they are gentler and are of a more complex variety. You could say that this is a wild Camembert. Because of the small size of the cheese, if the mould on the surface grows well, it can turn the paste semi-liquid in a short time. Sometimes you will get quite a pungent cheese bursting from the rind. Other times it will be more delicate and acidic with a slightly chalky paste.

BRILLAT-SAVARIN

PRODUCER: several large dairies
MADE: Île-de-France, France
PRODUCTION: large dairies
MILK: cows'
RENNET: traditional
TYPE: triple crème, bloomy
RIND: thick *Penicillium candidum*

RIPENING: 4 to 6 weeks
APPEARANCE: 200g disk
TEXTURE: thick cream, softer just under the rind
TASTE: rich and buttery with some mushroom and a hint of lemon

BRILLAT-SAVARIN is a classic, mould-rind, triple-crème cheese, renamed by the great *fromagier* Androuët after the eighteenth-century gourmet Jean Anthelme Brillat-Savarin. Under a bloomy *candidum* rind is a solid, thick paste of cheese almost like a mix of whipped cream and butter. The taste is quite like clotted cream with a more savoury dimension, and the mushroomy influence of the rind comes through in the nose. A very fresh rindless version is also sold and Robert Rouzaire of Rouzaire Cheese created Pierre Robert, which is Brillat-Savarin that has been left to ripen for longer in their cellars. This extra ageing makes the paste more liquid and the flavour sharper. These cheeses are lovely as a part of a cheeseboard but also make a great dessert served with fresh fruit such as peaches.

WICKLOW BÁN

PRODUCER: John and Bernie Hempenstall
MADE: Co. Wicklow, Ireland
PRODUCTION: farmhouse, using their own milk
MILK: cows'
RENNET: vegetarian

TYPE: bloomy, soft with added cream
RIND: *Penicillium candidum*
RIPENING: 2 to 8 weeks
APPEARANCE: 150g and 1kg discs
TEXTURE: soft
TASTE: raw mushroom, creamy yoghurt

WICKLOW BÁN is a double crème cheese with a fat content of 65–70 per cent, meaning that additional cream is added to the milk to ensure a fuller flavour. The paste is more dense than a traditional Camembert and the bloomy rind does not soften the paste in the same way. The Hempenstalls also make Wicklow Blue, which is a similar cheese but the rind is pierced and *Penicillium roqueforti* is encouraged to grow through the cheese. This type of hybrid blue Brie cheese has become very popular in modern times and is a great introduction for those who find the traditional blue cheeses a little too strong. Cambozola and Bresse Bleu would be the most popular versions.

*And here's a favourite from our friends
around the world.*

TELEEKA

PRODUCER: Tomales Farmstead
  Creamery
MADE: California, USA
PRODUCTION: own herds of sheep
  and goats, cows from neigh-
  bouring farm
MILK: mixed
RENNET: vegetable
TYPE: bloomy, soft

RIND: thick *Penicillium candidum*
RIPENING: 2 to 3 weeks
APPEARANCE: soft, ripened
  square, about 8 oz (225g)
TEXTURE: soft, gooey, lightly
  crumbly
TASTE: cream and lemon, light,
  grassy, green notes

AS DEMONSTRATED by the fact that they restored the farm's native plants and waterways and named their cheese in the local Native American Miwok language, Tomales Farmstead is as well known for their devotion to their region as their cheese. Teleeka, meaning 'three', is their most recent creation. A combination of their own sheep's and goats' milk, with cows' milk from down the road, Teleeka is a soft, surface-ripened cheese reminiscent of Italian Robiola with wrinkly, rippled rinds. Perfect for bubbles, preserves and introducing people to the goats' and sheep's cheese world. *Kirstin Jackson, It's Not You, It's Brie, California*

RECIPES

SPRING

Cheese and Onion Pie

This is as simple as it is traditional and tasty. We have replaced Lancashire cheese with Brie and added a few herbs to the traditional English recipe. For those of you with cold hands and warm hearts, you can make your own shortcrust pastry but a shop-bought variety would also be fine. This is a fine meal on its own but also goes well with bacon and cabbage.

SERVES 6

25g butter

3 large onions, sliced

a dash of white wine

a sprig of fresh thyme

salt and freshly ground black pepper

150ml water

400g shortcrust pastry

300g young Brie or a full Camembert, sliced

milk to glaze the pastry

You will need a greased 20cm pie dish. Preheat the oven to 180°C.

Melt the butter in a large pan over a low heat. Add the onions and cook slowly until they are soft. Turn up the heat to medium and add the dash of wine, sprig of thyme, and season with salt and pepper.

Cook off the liquid entirely and then add about half the water. Cook until all the moisture is gone again and then leave the onion to cool while you roll out the pastry.

Take two thirds of the pastry and roll out to cover the base and sides of the pie dish.

Spread half the onions over the base and top with half of the cheese slices. Repeat with the remaining onions and cheese.

Roll out the remaining pastry to a size that will nicely fit over the top of the pie. Brush the edges with milk, then place the pie lid on top. Press the edges together with a fork to seal.

Place in the centre of the preheated oven and cook for about 40 minutes until the pastry is golden brown.

Serve warm with a tangy green salad or a good serving of bacon and cabbage.

SUMMER

Risotto with Saint-Marcellin and Asparagus

Risotto has to be in the running for one of the world's greatest ways to cook with cheese. You can use just about any cheese you wish and there are countless versions with vegetables. This is a nice basic recipe to start you off. Choose a Saint-Marcellin that is not too ripe. If you can't find one, use fresh goats' chese, feta, Parmesan or Robiola. You can make the dish without the asparagus or substitute it with any wilted greens. A few hints for a good risotto: never wash the rice, as the starch is vital; always try to use homemade stock and keep it warm at the back of the stove; use a heavy pan; and keep stirring to prevent the rice from sticking.

SERVES 4

> 1 onion
> 1 tablespoon olive oil
> 350g risotto rice
> 1 glass dry white wine
> 2 litres vegetable stock, seasoned
> 300g asparagus, chopped and blanched
> 150g Saint-Marcellin
> 50g butter

Using a large frying pan, soften the onion in the olive oil over a medium heat.

Add the rice and stir for a few minutes.

Pour in the wine and continue to stir until the rice has absorbed the liquid.

Now add two or three ladles of warm stock and, again, stir until the rice has absorbed the liquid. Keep adding stock for as long as needed to cook the rice – it should take about 20 minutes.

Taste the rice to see how well it is cooked. Some folk like the rice to have a little bite but many prefer a softer consistency. When it is cooked to your liking, add the blanched asparagus, cheese and butter and mix thoroughly. Serve immediately.

AUTUMN

Baked Camembert with Apple Crisps and Calvados Syrup

As the nights get chillier there's nothing better than bringing a whole baked Camembert in its box to the table, oozing creamy warmth. This recipe also celebrates the sweetness of the apple season to set us up for winter.

SERVES 4 AS A MEAL OR 6 AS AN AFTER-DINNER ALTERNATIVE TO A CHEESEBOARD

For the apple crisps
3 medium-sized apples, peeled and cored
2 tablespoons sunflower oil
2 tablespoons maple syrup
a pinch of salt flakes

For the cheese
1 whole Camembert in its box
2 cloves garlic, peeled and sliced into thin slivers
1 tablespoon fennel seeds
2 sprigs of fresh rosemary
olive oil, for drizzling
30ml maple syrup
2 tablespoons Calvados

Preheat the oven to 180°C.

Cut the apples into thin, round slices as finely as you can (a mandolin works brilliantly). Place some parchment paper on a baking sheet and lay the slices on top – be careful that they don't overlap (you may need several baking sheets).

Mix the sunflower oil, maple syrup and salt together in a bowl and drizzle this over the apple slices.

Bake in the oven for 10–15 minutes, until the edges are brown and crimped. Remove from the oven – they will crisp up as they cool.

While the crisps are baking, unwrap the Camembert and slice off the top rind. You can discard this or eat it on a cracker if you like, as a cook's perk. Place the cheese back in its box and press the garlic slivers, fennel seeds and rosemary sprigs into it. Finally, drizzle a little olive oil over the top.

While the apple crisps cool, bake the cheese in its box on a baking tray in the oven for up to 20 minutes.

Meanwhile, heat the maple syrup and Calvados together in a small saucepan over a medium heat and bring them to the boil. Boil gently for two minutes, stirring.

Arrange the apple crisps around the baked Camembert and drizzle the Calvados syrup over the hot cheese to serve.

WINTER

Cooleeney, Cranberry and Port Toasties

This is the perfect marriage of leftover seasonal treats. You can use cranberry sauce from a jar if you don't want to make it yourself.

MAKES 6

150g fresh cranberries
50g sugar
50ml Port
200g Cooleeney
1 loaf sourdough or brioche, cut into 12 slices
3 large eggs
50ml milk
olive oil, for frying

Put the cranberries, sugar and Port into a saucepan and cook over a medium heat, stirring occasionally, until the cranberries have begun to burst. Set aside to cool.

Cut the Cooleeney into bite-sized pieces leaving the rind on.

In a bowl, gently mix together the cheese and the cooled cranberry sauce.

Take a slice of bread or brioche and slather it generously with the cheese and cranberry mixture. Top with a second slice of bread and press them together well.

Beat the eggs and milk together. Dip the cranberry and Cooleeney sandwich into the egg wash – carefully pressing to keep it together. Make sure both sides are covered.

Depending on the size of your pan, fry one, two or three toasties at a time in a hot pan greased with olive oil. Repeat with the remaining cheese mixture and bread.

Keep the toasties warm in the oven as you cook the rest and slice each one into fingers to serve.

CHAPTER SIX

WASHED RINDS

FROM MILLEENS TO ÉPOISSES – PEOPLE, PLACES AND THE CHEESE THEY PRODUCE

Any fool can make cheese. It takes genius to ripen it. You are dealing with an innocent-looking blob of mainly protein and fat, which is the favourite food of almost every beast that roams the face of the earth. It must be protected from fliers and crawlers, drivers and walkers. It must be protected from the very small, like Listeria monocytogenes, to the very large, like the family dog, or an entire government.

Veronica Steele, Irish Cheesemaker

Washed rinds are the sticky and stinky cheeses. They've got pungent aromas and glorious earthy and meaty flavours. They ooze and run. Their name says it all – the rinds are washed as they ripen. They can also be called 'smear ripened' or sometimes 'semi-soft cheeses'.

Washing the rinds is not just a bit of housekeeping in the ageing room where cheeses mature. Most cheeses with a natural rind need their rinds rubbed or gently washed as they are aged to keep them clean. With propionic cheeses, though, it's a particular kind of washing that encourages a strong community of bacteria to make themselves at home on the rind. Like bloomy rinds, the rind of a washed-rind cheese has a big role to play in breaking down the cheese as it ripens to develop particular flavours and textures.

Washed rinds are a huge group of cheeses, probably the most prolific of traditional cheese types. They include the giants of French cheeses like Reblochon and Époisses, famous Irish cheeses like Gubbeen, Ardrahan, Milleens and Durrus, and Italian Taleggio. There are so many varieties and possibilities with this type of cheese and such a wide spectrum of flavour and texture. Many semi-hard and hard cheeses have a rind which is washed and have an ecology of bacteria and moulds; however, we define washed-rind cheeses as cheeses where the rind is the dominating influence in the structure and flavour of the cheese. With a washed-rind cheese, the rind sets the tone.

The first steps in making washed-rind cheeses are similar to the steps in making soft and bloomy rinds. The milk or a mix of milks is separated into curds and whey using starter cultures of acid-producing bacteria and the protein-munching enzyme in rennet. After that the steps vary depending on the type of cheese you are making. Some curds might be finely cut or left larger. Some are lightly pressed in moulds to drain the whey, others are left to sink under the weight of their own curd. Washed-rind cheeses can be dry-salted or brined by being soaked in salty water baths.

Most washed-rind cheeses are made round, with the exception of the odd heart-shape and some that are squares or blocks, such as Italian Taleggio. After salting by brining or dry-salting, the cheeses are typically stored on shelves in damp, cool curing rooms. The temperature is normally about 16°C, with the humidity above 95 per cent. The cheeses are then regularly washed with water or beer or wine. This can contain some of the bacteria which the cheesemaker is

encouraging to grow on the rind or it can have a little salt or alcohol, in the case of beer or wine. Salt and alcohol are used to inhibit the growth of unwanted moulds, giving salt-loving bacteria a better chance of domination.

You can tell a washed-rind cheese by the colour of its rind – they are pinkish to orange and the rind remains damp and slightly sticky. The colour comes from a bacteria called *Brevibacterium linens*, or *B. linens*. These bacteria can be introduced to the cheese as part of the starter culture, washed on to it in the washing solution or they can colonise the surface of the cheese from the environment of the maturing rooms and the skin of the cheesemakers themselves. These bacteria also give off a particular pungent smell. This varies in strength depending on the intensity of the *B. linens* and the mix of other moulds and yeasts. The aroma is reminiscent of human body odour because the *B. linens* found on cheese are very closely related to *B.*

linens found on human skin. The smell of feet comes from the fatty acids produced by our skin's microflora, just as the odorous cheese gets its stink from the action of the *B. linens* and other bacteria that produce fatty acids. If this all sounds a bit off-putting, the French describe the aroma more tenderly as *l'odeur des pieds de Dieu*, or the smell of God's feet. James Joyce brings it back down to a more earthy place in *Ulysses* when he describes a Gorgonzola sandwich: 'Mr Bloom ate his strips of sandwich, fresh clean bread, with relish of disgust, pungent mustard, the feety savour of green cheese.'

B. linens are the biggest characters in the washed-rind microbial world, but it would be a mistake to think of washed rinds as monocultural. They're a complex ecosystem of microorganisms. Each cheese type and each curing room has its own unique mix of microbes (yeasts, moulds and bacterias) and within each group there are almost infinite varieties and types all combining to make each cheese and each rind unique.

This process of colonisation begins with the yeasts. They grow on the moist rind, lowering the acidity of the cheese surface and making it more hospitable for the *B. linens* and other salt-tolerant bacteria. When the rinds of these cheeses are analysed at the end of ripening, many different strains of bacteria have been found, often with little or none of the originally introduced microorganisms remaining but a whole new landscape of unique bacteria.

It is not the rind itself which gives these cheeses their unique flavours but its action on the curds beneath. The cultures interact with the proteins and fat of the curd, producing flavours and breaking it down into a softer texture. Although the flavour and texture of washed-rind cheeses are heavily dependent on the microflora of the rind, other factors also have an influence. The strength of the rind and the thickness of the cheese affects how it will develop. A cheese made in a thin disk will have more of its interior broken down by the surface

bacteria, so it will develop a more pronounced flavour and softer texture. The effect of the surface bacteria on the curd diminishes the further from the rind it is, so the thicker the cheese, the less it is influenced by its rind. If the cheesemaker wants to make a more unctuous cheese, like Époisses or Milleens, they keep a larger amount of moisture in the curd. For firmer washed-rind cheeses, like Gubbeen and Taleggio, more moisture is taken out and small weights can be used to add a little bit of pressure to make a drier cheese. As with all cheeses, the origin of the milk and the starter cultures and type of rennet used all contribute to the shaping of the end cheese.

The monasteries of northern France are often pointed to as the origin of these cheeses. However, the relationship between *B. linens* and human skin would make it likely that as long as cheesemakers have been washing the rinds of their cheese to keep away unwanted mould, these bacteria have been colonising cheese, evolving and existing in a kind of symbiotic relationship between people and their cheeses.

RINDS – TO EAT OR NOT

THERE ARE NO set rules on this. Most rinds are made of moulds, yeasts and bacteria on a compacted layer of cheese – all of which are edible. There are of course some rinds that we don't believe anyone could recommend: the cloth on cheddar or the plastic coat used on some cheeses, although neither will do you any harm.

The rinds on most aged cheeses are practically inedible: they are just too hard to get your teeth through, as the outer paste dries with age. It is important, though, with these cheeses to make sure not to cut off too much of the cheese when you are discarding the rind. The most complex and interesting flavours are often found in the bit just beneath the rind. In any cheese the flavour and texture will change from the core of the cheese right out to the rind, so make sure to experience every bit.

This question really comes up when people are considering the rind of bloomy or washed-rind cheeses. Again, there are no set rules. Many would consider the rinds an integral part of the flavour of the cheese and are shocked to see anyone leave them behind on the plate. Others dislike the intense flavour or are put off by the idea of eating mould or bacteria. When tasting one of these rind-ripened cheeses, it is very important to first taste the paste without the rind: this way you can enjoy the more subtle flavours that are often masked by a strong rind.

MANY BREEDS

When we think of different milks making different cheeses, we generally mean cows', goats', sheep's, etc.; however, there are many breeds of these prolific animals, each with their distinct characteristics and variations in the milk they produce. Here is a little more detail about the main breeds used in cheesemaking.

Famous dairy cattle breeds

Brown Swiss: these large light-brown or grey-silver coated animals are the ultimate cow for cheesemaking. They originate in the Swiss Alps and so are hardy and sure-footed but also are very adaptable to different climates. They are still the main breed for cheesemaking in Switzerland but are used across the world. As well as their hardy nature, their high milk yield along with its high protein levels make them a great breed for cheesemaking.

Holstein-Friesian: bred from German and Dutch stock these are by far the most prolific dairy animal in the world. They have been bred to suit modern commercial dairying, producing huge volumes of milk with good fat and protein levels. They are instantly recognisable due to their black and white patch coat, though they can also have a red and white colouring.

Jersey: these are probably the most-loved cattle breed, with a light-brown, grey, cream or black coat and friendly face. They are a small animal with a curious and social nature. They originated on the British island of Jersey but are popular across the world. Their milk is famous for its high levels of cream. There are a few cheeses made from Jersey milk but in general they are kept as a part of mixed-breed herd.

Milking Shorthorn: a very versatile and hardy breed originating in England with a red or red and white coat. They are an all-purpose cattle, great for milk, beef and pulling power. Although still quite popular, they have been superseded by more specialist breeds.

Abondance: these hardy animals with chestnut-brown and white coats from the Haute-Savoie, France, are famous for their use in the classic Savoie cheeses. They are perfect for grazing at high altitudes and are able to thrive in extreme weather variations. They are good milk producers with balanced fat and protein levels.

Montbéliarde: most famous for their use in Comté cheese in Franche-Comté, France, these are large animals with red and white coats, suitable for varied climates and conditions. Their versatility along with good milk production is making them more popular with cheesemakers around the world.

Salers: large animals with a mahogany-red or black coat originating in Auvergne, France, they give their name to the Salers cheese of Auvergne and their milk is also used in other traditional cheeses of this area. They are more popular outside France as a beef animal rather than for milking.

Normande: a medium-sized animal with chestnut-brown and white or black and white coat, they are a very popular breed in France particularly, because of both their good milk and meat production. They are famous as the Normandy cow responsible for the region's great cheeses, milk and cream.

Kerry: Ireland's most famous native breed, the Kerry cow is present in quite a few of the herds producing Irish farmhouse cheese. It is a very hardy small animal which is particularly good for producing milk but also produces good beef. It has an entirely black coat with a little white on the udder.

Famous dairy sheep breeds

East Friesian: the East Friesian is the most popular sheep breed for commercial dairying. It has been bred for very high milk yields but at the expense of hardiness and can be quite delicate. They originate in northern Germany and have a distinctive long bare tail.

Lacaune: the Lacaune is a French breed that has become very popular around the world. They produce less volume of milk than the Friesians but the higher fat and protein levels make their milk great for cheesemaking and they are most famous as the sheep whose milk is used in Roquefort production.

Awassi: the Awassi sheep is a dairy sheep breed that was developed in what is now the Middle East. They tend to be hardier than the East Friesian or the Lacaune because they were developed in a much harsher environment. Their ability to survive in difficult climates and their efficiency at converting low levels of feed into relatively high milk yields make them the best choice of dairying sheep in what we would consider traditional sheep-farming regions.

Famous dairy goat breeds

Alpine: originating in the French Alps, these are great animals for milking and cheese production. Their milk has a very low fat content but good protein content. They are versatile, hardy and produce a lot of milk. They are large goats with erect ears, with varied markings and colours.

Toggenburg: these are the oldest registered breed of any animal and originate in the Swiss Alps. They have average milk production with good protein levels. They are of medium build and range in colour from light fawn to dark chocolate and have white ears and white on their lower legs.

Saanen and sables: these easy-going large goats also originate in Switzerland. They have a high milk yield and their milk has good protein and fat levels. Saanens are white or off-white in colour and are the largest of the standard dairy goats. Sables are Saanens that aren't white, due to a recessive gene.

Nubian: originating in Britain, having been bred from native stock crossed with Middle Eastern and North African breeds, they are a large breed with distinctive long floppy ears. This breed of goat produces less milk than other breeds but their milk tends to be higher in protein and butterfat content, giving a good return in cheese.

PEOPLE, PLACES AND THE CHEESE THEY PRODUCE

Travelling through the valleys and rugged coastline of the south-west of Ireland you can understand what has drawn artists and writers to this beautiful place for centuries. It's a wondrous painting, a masterpiece created over millions of years. But look closely and you can see a second layer painted over the canvas. It's the landscape of agriculture and existence. Between the mountains and rocky shores there is a patchwork of fields bounded by ancient stone walls. High pastures are populated by black-faced mountain sheep. Ancient potato drills on green slopes remind you that, just as this beautiful scenery attracted many, it also drove many away.

The drive down to Coomkeen on the Sheep's Head peninsula in the very tip of south-west Ireland feels like it takes for ever. A fast motorway will get you as far as Cork city, the capital of Munster, the province which covers the southern quarter of Ireland. If you've driven from Dublin or further north, you feel you should be almost there but, in fact, that's just the halfway point.

Durrus Farmhouse.

ABOVE: Janet Drew, Sheridans chutney maker.

RIGHT: Richard Graham-Leigh, Sheridans cracker baker.

Sheridans store, Co. Meath.

Gubbeen
Region: Schull, Co. Cork
Milk: Cow's
Rennet: Traditional
Maturity: 4–10 Weeks
Producer: Giana & Tom Ferguson

SHERIDANS
CHEESEMONGERS
chutney for cheese

Above: Aislin King, Meath warehouse.

Left: Mark Booker, Meath warehouse.

Below: Franck Le Moenner, Meath warehouse.

Durrus Farmhouse.

You travel away from the city heading south-west, continuing on a decent road until you reach the busy town of Bandon, the gateway to West Cork. From here the road gets a little narrower and more winding. The landscape becomes more hilly and the fields smaller as you continue west and pass through several small towns. At last you reach the south-west coast and the harbour town of Bantry, and you think, 'Surely we are nearly there.' But still you drive until you reach the village of Durrus, after which Jeffa Gill named her cheese. 'We've arrived.' Well, not quite.

Durrus is a lovely village servicing the local fishing and farming communities but also a fair amount of tourists who come for the landscape and the culture. There are plenty of places to eat and drink and, as with many West Cork towns, you may share the pub or restaurant with an artist, musician, farmer, fisherman or food producer. Now you drive through the village and take a sharp right turn at the old Protestant church. You head up through the steep hills trying to remember which turn to take. You're saved by the little sign pointing to Durrus Cheese. You continue up and over, travelling on what (even for Ireland) are tiny boreens, or narrow roads, walled by fuchsia and brambles. If you're lucky and it's not dark, or you're not driving through thick fog, halfway up the view of Dunmanus Bay, if you look back, will be spectacular.

After all that, you swing into the yard, get out and stretch your legs. And you see you're not in a typical concrete-paved farmyard but a small oasis nestled in hills at the end of the world. The garden blends into the landscape yet is obviously delicately cared for. The house is homely but perfectly kept. Almost attached but separate is a neat little building. A few small hints to the experienced eye give it away as the place where the cheesemaking happens. Just below this building a small stream runs down, pointing the way to the chicken run, poly-tunnels and reed beds, and coming around again to farm sheds converted into maturing rooms and a small shop. All of this Jeffa, with the help of her partner Pete, has managed to build into the landscape as if it were always there. Yet everything retains clean lines and a modern style.

The arriving is nothing to the experience of waking up on this farm on a clean, clear morning. A harmony and beauty makes you feel

Bantry Bay.

an odd mix of calmness and exhilaration. Unless you are up very early, you'll wake to quiet activity. There will be a delivery from one of the two neighbouring farms that supply the milk for Durrus, a semi-soft, washed-rind cheese. Jeffa might be in the kitchen having a coffee or in the office during one of the short breaks from cheesemaking, as she leaves the starter cultures or rennet to do their work.

This place might feel secluded now but imagine how remote it must have been in the early 1970s when Ireland's roadways were amongst the most basic in Europe, and post and the payphone in the village were the only ways of communicating with the wider world. This is the world that Jeffa chose to move to from the city when she left her life as a costume designer. It was 1973 when she arrived to an almost ruined farmhouse and rough land, and 1979 when she first started experimenting with cheese in her kitchen. Jeffa, like all cheese-makers we have met, is far from any cliché. She is in tune with her environment and her local farming community but she's also sophisticated and scientifically minded. Her cheese and cheesemaking operation reflect these characteristics.

When you enter the dairy, you are immediately struck by the traditional Swiss copper vat dominating the space on a raised platform. The height of the vat allows the curd to be fed through a large tube into the waiting moulds using only gravity. This is a much gentler method than using pumps and is more efficient than scooping by hand. The dairy is all stainless steel and clean white plastic. But when you are making cheese, a huge window allows you to look out across the fields and up into the hills. It also allows visitors to look in at the cheesemaking.

When Jeffa first began making cheese in her kitchen, it was with milk from her eight cows and she used a large, steel, jam-making pot. After a few years, she and Veronica Steele of nearby Milleens managed to persuade a local grant agency to help fund their expansions.

Jeffa Gill.

The grant helped Jeffa get a 60-gallon stainless steel vat made, convert half the kitchen into a dairy and turn a small outhouse into a ripening room. Increased production meant that her own cows weren't producing enough milk, so she began buying in milk from a neighbour. The quality of milk she was receiving combined with the increased workload led Jeffa to stop milking her own cows and focus on cheesemaking, as well as raising her young children.

The operation continued to grow slowly and a neighbour's daughter started to come up to the house after school to help wash the cheeses. When she left school, the young girl's mother Ann McGrath, who was already in the house every day for a cup of tea and a chat, began working with Jeffa. Ann was born and raised on the Sheep's Head peninsula and is now an intrinsic part of Durrus Farmhouse Cheese. She speaks with pride and deep understanding of the cheese, particularly the ripening and curing process. Other help has come and gone, including visiting cheesemaking students from France who travelled as part of their work experience every summer.

They brought with them some new ideas but returned to France having learned much about farmhouse cheesemaking.

Milk is still delivered from the same farmer about 15km away, along with a second farmer supplying summer milk from just 6km away. The milk arrives at about 6.30am and is pumped into the vat. As the milk warms, Jeffa mixes her starter cultures with a small amount of the milk to get them working. After about two hours, the mix is added to the vat and left to work for about an hour. She then adds traditional rennet, which takes about 30 minutes to set the milk into curd. Hand-held harps are used to cut the curd into uneven pearls. As the cutting action separates the curds from the whey, a sweet smell of milk and a yoghurty tang is released into the warm humid air.

Jeffa watches and feels the curd as it is swished around. Her hand dips into the whey, letting the curd pass through her fingers, giving it a squeeze. She takes a piece out and tastes it. The milk is never the same from day to day, season to season, year to year. Protein and fat content fluctuate in milk, depending on the lactation cycle, the type of food the cows are eating (grass, hay or silage) and the season. She has felt and tasted the curd countless times, consciously and subconsciously making calculations and decisions about when it is ready to stop cutting, stop stirring. She checks temperatures, textures and acidity with instruments and through taste, smell and feel. She understands what is happening to the milk and its constituents as well as any dairy technologist. But she also has a sense of it. It's that unarticulated understanding that cheesemakers have had for thousands of years before her.

When the timing is right, the curds are released down the large tube. They flow easily into the waiting white, circular, perforated plastic moulds. These are laid out ready on rows of stainless steel tables. Each tall mould is filled to the brim. Whey continues to drain from the curd, streaming off the tables and down the drains to the reed bed system that will purify the water, returning it to the hills.

The shiny curds stick to each other willingly, becoming one mass as they sink into their moulds. When they are all filled, each mould is turned. This is all done by hand and is quite a skill. The cheese is emptied out of its mould on to an open palm and then turned and flipped back into the mould downside up. With each turning, the pressure of its own weight begins to form the curd into something that looks like a round of cheese. The cheeses are turned several times until the surface of the curd is evenly compressed all over. Then they are left in the quiet. The stream of whey becomes a trickle and the cheeses slowly sink into themselves while Jeffa and her helpers get on with other jobs.

Over the remainder of the day, the cheeses are turned again

Making Durrus.

several times and then released from their moulds, still pure white but compacted under their own weight into a third of the height at which they started. The next day they are placed into large brine baths where they bob together gently, the salt in the brine binding to their skins, helping to form a protective layer and allowing the salt to penetrate the curd.

If after lunch at Jeffa's table the weather is fine, you can take a stroll up on to one of the tracks that walkers take along the Sheep's Head peninsula. These tracks will eventually lead you to a lighthouse cradled in rock and battered by the powerful waves of the Atlantic Ocean. But without going that far, just standing on the ridge of the hill above the farm, you can look down into Dunmanus Bay, north and west to the Beara Peninsula. There, almost within sight, is where Milleens Cheese is made. Turn and look south-west and beyond the hills and you're gazing at Mount Gabriel and the Mizen Peninsula, and hidden by the hills is the town of Schull where Gubbeen Cheese is made. They are both a decent drive away but if you were a flying crow you'd be there in no time. These three cheeses made on three close but separate peninsulas at the edge of western Europe are unique and exquisite. Although they are all technically of the same type of cheese and made in the same landscape, they offer such diverse experiences.

Each of the women behind these cheeses (Jeffa Gill, Veronica Steele who created Milleens and Giana Ferguson who makes Gubbeen) started to make their cheeses in the 1970s and very early 80s, when cheesemaking was not only unusual in this part of the world but it could have been (and probably was) described as lunacy. There didn't seem to be any market for farmhouse cheese. Dairy farmers sold their milk to the local creamery, and cheesemaking and cheese eating were a foreign idea to most people in Ireland.

For Jeffa and her small team, cheesemaking doesn't end when the curds have formed a solid mass. The rinds need to be minded and nurtured to form a stable covering that will work with the cultures and enzymes in the cheese. This rind doesn't just form a protective layer on the outside, it works its way through the curd inside its skin, breaking the curds down, transforming them into a smoothly textured cheese and developing the flavour and aroma. The rind takes the taste of the curd from yoghurty and tangy to a deeper, earthier set of flavours.

After they're removed from the brine, the cheeses are now in the shape that they will be when they are ready to eat. But the pure white gleam of the rinds, rather than the soft pink and beige colour that we expect, shows there is still a long way to go. The wheels are transferred into the curing rooms, where they sit on stainless steel racks. These racks are preferred to the traditional wooden boards as they allow the humid air to circulate around the cheese. Originally, Jeffa never added any cultures to the rind, rather she allowed the yeasts and cultures in the environment to find their way on to the cheese and she encouraged their growth by washing the rind with water and a tiny amount of salt. Later she began adding some *B. linens* to the washing water to make their growth stronger and counter some unwanted moulds that were invading the rind.

After just a couple of days in the ripening rooms, yeasts take hold and the surface of the cheese loses its white sheen and turns a blotchy yellow. With the surface now less acidic thanks to the yeasts, the *B. linens* in the water and in the environment begin to take hold. As they do, the typical pinkish blush of washed-rind cheese starts to cover the surface.

The cheeses do not have a defined period in the damp curing rooms but are judged to be ready when Jeffa and Ann feel they are right for the particular customer for whom they're destined. We like our cheeses a little more mature, so they tend to stay a little longer

than most. The cheeses remain there from roughly two weeks (for Jeffa's smallest 250g dotes – a pet word for something small and adorable) to eight or ten weeks for her larger 1.5kg wheels. The rind will tell them a lot about how the cheese has developed but they will also taste the batches to check that the flavour has developed enough. Even when the cheeses are packed and wrapped and the storage temperature is brought down, the cheeses continue to ripen. Jeffa sees her cheese more as a product of the rind than the milk. Just as the milk changes with weather, grazing and seasons, the rind is influenced by humidity and temperature in the maturing rooms and on the peninsula. These peninsulas jutting out into the Atlantic Ocean, sending salt-washed humidity up through the hills and valleys, provide an ideal environment for washed-rind cheeses and the microflora they depend upon. When dairy scientists analysed the bacteria on the surface of the finished cheese, they found no presence of the variety of *B. linens* introduced to the cheeses at the start of ripening; instead they found unique strains only found on these cheeses. These results were duplicated when the same study was carried out on neighbouring washed-rind cheeses Gubbeen and Milleens. These unique bacteria are native to this particular place.

The carefully packaged Durrus cheeses leave the peninsula to travel back over the winding roads and on to the motorway to shops and restaurants around Ireland and onwards, freighted as far away as San Francisco and the Middle East. Each cheese carries the imprint of the remote land it has come from and the farmers and cheesemakers who have translated an epic landscape into beautiful food.

THE FOOD WORLD'S FAVOURITE MICROBIOLOGIST

Rachel Dutton makes cheese. But it's not for eating. At least it's not for humans to eat. Her cheese eaters are microbes, single-cell organisms that love what she makes: an in vitro environment for their microbial communities. It's a place in which they thrive.

Rachel is a microbiologist who uses cheese rinds as a way to study how different bacteria and fungi assemble together like communities and work together. Along with her colleagues at Harvard University she replicates bloomy, washed and natural cheese rinds in the lab to study the interactions between these tiny single-cell organisms.

Thanks to new technology like powerful DNA sequencing, Rachel and her team are working in a frontier science. The study of microbes and the human microbiome (the millions of bacteria that coat our skin and line our gut) is an incredibly exciting area of investigation. An invisible patina of microbial life coats everything in most people's homes, schools, offices and food. The new wave of excitement around microbiology stems from the idea of an invisible universe that has been under our noses for millennia. The tools allowing us to begin to understand it are still being developed.

But why do Rachel Dutton and her colleagues love cheese? Because the cheesemaker's rind is the microbiologist's biofilm. Biofilms form when bacteria land and attach themselves to a surface and begin to produce a gooey covering, growing, multiplying and becoming a colony. Run your tongue over your teeth and you might be touching a biofilm. It's the plaque that forms on our teeth between brushing.

The Dutton Lab's study, published in *Cell* in 2014, used DNA sequencing to identify 14 bacteria and 10 fungi in cheese rinds from 137 cheeses made in different locations in the US and Europe. Two of the bacteria types had never been found in food microbial systems before. A full 60 per cent of the bacteria in the cheese rinds, along with one in four of the fungi, were uninvited guests. They were not added to the cheese during the cheesemaking process. They didn't come from any source that had been added deliberately by the cheese-maker to the milk. The study also identified three water-loving bacteria typically found in polar seawater. These cold-loving bacteria were found in cheeses that had been made nowhere near the Antarctic.

The Harvard team found that they could replicate these communities or families of bacteria and fungi in the lab. If they exposed milk curd to the same salt levels, temperatures, washing or not washing, and moisture conditions that happened in the cheesemaker's dairy and ripening room, similar colonies of bacteria and fungi colonised the curd and began to turn it into cheese.

So does this study trash the idea of *terroir*: the notion that beautiful cheeses come from beautiful places? If a team of scientists is able to replicate cheese-rind communities in lab conditions then where's the magic of landscape and mountain breezes and fields and salty air that we associate with ideas of artisan cheeses? Do we just need to perfect the conditions for a microbial workforce and let them get on with things, regardless of the view or whether the prevailing wind is blowing over an unspoilt land or seascape? If you build a cheese they like, they will come.

'We did find very similar types of microbes across all the countries that we sampled,' Rachel explains. 'We have a lot more work to do. I think we don't know the true potential microbial contribution.' So there could still be a link between place and cheese? 'It's still an open possibility that there is.'

And that's 'reassuring', Rachel says. Despite the similarity in the groups of microbes in the rinds, they didn't always have the same effects on the maturing of the cheese in the lab. Things often happened more quickly with the in vitro cheese than they did with the sampled cheeses, with obvious implications for how the cheese would taste in the end.

What you can read into the Harvard study is that much of the magic that makes cheese is in the milk. It's where Rachel Dutton thinks many of the mystery 60 per cent, those bacteria that were not deliberately introduced into the cheese by the cheesemaker, originate. 'Probably most of them are coming from the animals.'

The *Brevibacterium epidermidis*, or microbes that live on human skin in those warm crevices between our toes, also like to colonise animal skin. So the teats of the cow, sheep or goat are a likely source. The team saw no big difference in the cheese rinds of pasteurised milk cheeses as opposed to raw milk ones. Milk that started out with less bacterial content thanks to pasteurisation was still happily colonised by rind bacteria and fungi as the curds became cheese.

One of the many new ideas this fascinating study uncovered was that washed-rind cheeses might get some of their stinky qualities from the surprising water-loving polar seawater bacteria. The volatile sulphur compounds or gases released in the breakdown of the amino acids were always thought to have been the work of the *B. linens*, but a new flavour pathway was found in which the marine bacteria played a part in converting the fatty acids in the milk into the distinctive sulphurous stinky aroma we associate with washed-rind cheeses.

IS CHEESE FATTENING?

IF YOU EAT more calories, in whatever form, than you use, your body will store them as fat reserves. Cheese is a highly nutritious food that concentrates the proteins, calories, minerals and vitamins contained in milk. Relative to the amount of overall nutrition delivered to the body and flavour to the tongue, the amount of calories is balanced.

Interestingly, most people look at the oozing soft cheeses and think that these are the fattening ones, while they see the harder more austere cheeses as the 'sensible' choice. But the softer cheeses actually have less of everything including calories, and just more water, and the harder cheeses more nutrition, including calories.

HOW TO CHOOSE WASHED-RIND CHEESES

The biggest 'Don't' with washed-rind cheeses is never buy them vacuum packed. If a washed rind can't breathe, it can develop bad flavours. If you are buying pre-packed washed rinds, look for ones that are made in small rounds and wrapped by the manufacturer. When buying freshly cut washed-rind cheese, much comes down to the specific cheese and your own taste. A little bit of blue or black mould on the rind is generally fine, but be careful of cheeses where the cheese is browning under the rind.

HOW TO STORE WASHED-RIND CHEESES

The rinds of these cheeses are made up of a combination of bacteria, yeasts and moulds. Depending on the cheese and the stage of ripeness, some are more delicate than others. If the rind is damp and quite bright pink or orange, then it is a very active bacteria rind.

Cheeses with more muted colours and a drier rind are generally a little more stable. In every case a wrapping of breathable paper is best. Your fridge at home is fine but it is very dry and these cheeses like a humid atmosphere, so make sure to have plenty of wrapping. The biggest danger is smothering the rind with a plastic wrap, which can result in quite nasty flavours.

The best advice is to eat your washed-rind cheeses soon after buying them. Your cheesemonger will probably sell them at their optimum ripeness. If cheeses start to go brown under the rind, we would advise you to use them in cooking, as the flavours will be a little overpowering to eat raw.

FOOD WE LIKE WITH WASHED RINDS

○ The flavour and texture range within this category is quite large and so a lot will depend on the particular cheese. As with all cheese, it is hard to go wrong with fresh apples and pears but these cheeses can also take some more robust accompaniments.

○ One of our favourite flavour partnerships is Sheridans Onion Marmalade and Durrus. The syrupy marmalade doesn't overpower the rich earthiness of the cheese but echoes its sweetness and the textures work really well.

○ A runny, stewed rhubarb and ginger compote that is not too sweet works well drizzled on to a slice of washed-rind cheese on a crisply toasted slice of good bread or a Sheridans brown bread cracker.

○ We would avoid very sweet fruit jellies or honey – look for sweetness but also some acidity to cut through the meaty flavour of a washed-rind cheese. Go for chutney or fruit-rich preserve, like a good quince paste.

○ If you are hoping for a vegetable match, look to the sweeter end of the spectrum, as sulphurous brassicas can have too much of a base note with a washed-rind cheese. Small summer courgettes briefly fried in a little butter with some sweet fried shallots are great topped with slices of Milleens and flashed under a grill. If you're lucky enough to get fresh courgette flowers, fry some diced spring onions, stir through small chunks of Gubbeen and spoon the mixture into the flowers. Roast in the oven briefly until the cheese starts to ooze and serve with a vinaigrette for dipping. Try not to dribble.

DRINKS WE LIKE WITH WASHED RINDS

○ These can be one of the more difficult styles of cheese to pair up. Often more fragrant styles of wine can provide a counterbalance to the earthy and often pungent flavours associated with washed-rind cheeses. Try an Alsace or Austrian Gewurztraminer, Pinot Blanc or Pinot Gris. An earthy but not tannic Pinot Noir or a mellow Cabernet Franc can be a success too.

○ As with bloomy-rind cheeses, we find that beers generally bring out the bitter flavours of washed rinds and so we much prefer a glass of dry cider with them, which cuts the pungency but also brings out the sweetness.

○ You can go for quite blousey flavours with a powerful washed-rind cheese, so for a non-alcoholic drink try some passion fruit juice, diluted with soda and finished with a slice of lemon.

SOME OF OUR FAVOURITE WASHED-RIND CHEESES

ARDRAHAN

PRODUCER: Burns family
MADE: Cork, Ireland
PRODUCTION: farmhouse, using milk from their own farm
MILK: cows'
RENNET: vegetarian
TYPE: washed-rind, semi-soft

RIND: thick *B. linens* with some moulds
RIPENING: 6 to 10 weeks
APPEARANCE: 1.4kg and 300g wheels
TEXTURE: thick, creamy paste
TASTE: pungent and nutty

MARY BURNS and her late husband, Eugene, began making Ardrahan in 1983. Mary continues at the helm with the help of her children, several of whom are involved on the farm and the dairy. This cheese is often sold quite young when the paste is still chalky and the flavours and aroma subdued. It is very pleasant in this condition and very popular. However, since Eugene first drove up to our little kiosk in the Galway shopping centre with a boot full of stinking, very ripe cheeses that no one else would buy, we have had a particular affection for the quite ripe, often misshapen and broken-rinded Ardrahan. When the slightly gritty beige rind has softened the paste right to the centre, the aroma becomes quite powerful. At this stage the flavour is rich vegetal, nutty and a little salty.

DURRUS FARMHOUSE CHEESE

PRODUCER: Jeffa Gill
MADE: Coomkeen, West Cork, Ireland
PRODUCTION: farmhouse, using milk from two neighbouring farms
MILK: cows' and seasonally raw cows'
RENNET: traditional
TYPE: washed-rind, semi-soft

RIND: *B. linens* with natural moulds and yeast
RIPENING: 6 to 10 weeks
APPEARANCE: 1.4kg, 360g and 225g wheels
TEXTURE: slightly elastic, soft through
TASTE: earthy, sweet milk with a soil and hay aroma

JEFFA GILL has been making Durrus at her hillside farmhouse in West Cork since 1979. The Durrus rind varies from smooth and pale with a pinkish bloom to slightly gnarled with mottled pinks, ochres, browns and blacks. The variations depend on the season and age of the cheese but always the rind is complex and beautiful of itself. Under the rind, the paste is moist, elastic and slightly bulging. The aroma varies in intensity but is consistently of earthy wet soil, fresh hay and yoghurt. The flavour varies with age, the development of the rind and the size of cheese being tasted – there are earthy, rich, savoury flavours alongside a sweet milk. With age and particularly with the raw milk cheeses, the flavour and aroma grow more complex, deepening and developing more meaty elements. Jeffa has recently teamed up with the great Irish fish smoker Sally Barnes to produce a smoked Durrus Óg that works surprisingly well.

GUBBEEN CHEESE

PRODUCER: Ferguson family
MADE: Cork, Ireland
PRODUCTION: farmhouse, using milk from their own farm
MILK: cows'
RENNET: vegetarian
TYPE: washed-rind, semi-soft

RIND: *B. linens* with light, yeasty bloom
RIPENING: 6 to 10 weeks in warm, humid maturing room
APPEARANCE: 1.4kg and 450g wheels
TEXTURE: moist with a bounce
TASTE: forest mushroom aroma with a milky, nutty flavour

GIANA FERGUSON first encountered cheese during her childhood in Spain. She and her husband, Tom, have been making Gubbeen on the Ferguson family farm since 1980. Since that time, Gubbeen has become one of the best known of all the Irish farmhouse cheeses. All the milk used comes from their own mixed herd of Jersey, Friesian, Simmental and Kerry cows. We have always liked Gubbeen before it becomes too mature at about five weeks. This is before it develops deeper, oakier flavours as the rind turns from dusty pink to beige. At this younger stage the cheese retains a milky, yoghurty flavour that has a little pungency and light nuttiness. The texture has a real bounce. The Fergusons also produce a version smoked by their son Fingal. Fingal built the smokehouse rather than shipping the cheeses to a local smoker and has since developed the leading Irish charcuterie and smokehouse in the country. The young smoked cheese is very mild but when produced in large wheels and aged for six months it has a real depth of flavour.

SAINT-NECTAIRE FERMIER, MORIN

PRODUCER: Affinage Fromageries Morin
MADE: Auvergne, France
PRODUCTION: farm, using milk from their own herd
MILK: raw cows'
NAME PROTECTION: AOC, PDO
RENNET: traditional
TYPE: washed-rind, pressed

RIND: B. *linen* cultures and later growth of dark moulds
RIPENING: 5 to 10 weeks
APPEARANCE: 1.5kg wheel
TEXTURE: soft but compact
TASTE: sweet cabbage and raw cauliflower with a strong cellar and mushroom aroma

AS WITH MOST French AOC cheeses, Saint-Nectaire may be made from raw, thermalised or pasteurised cows' milk on farms (*fermier*), by co-*opératives* or in larger factories. We sell Saint-Nectaire Fermier aged in Aurillac by *affineur* Xavier Morin. An *affineur* (from the French verb *affiner* to fine-tune or mature) is a professional who takes cheese from the producer before it is ripe, ripens the cheese and markets it. The surface of Saint-Nectaire is characterised by a furry grey mould, which grows on the beige, natural rind beneath. The cheeses first develop their pinkish rind of B. *linens* but then the *affineur* allows and encourages moulds to grow over this layer of cultures. Each *affineur* has a different style and develops a different balance of mould and cultures on their cheese. The paste is quite dense without any holes and is smooth and elastic. The aroma of Saint-Nectaire Fermier is quite distinct and one of the most pleasing of any cheese. Although there is a dominant smell of damp mould, there is simultaneous freshness. The best way to describe it is the aroma of moss-covered stones at the edge of a mountain stream. The flavour has a gentle pungency and sweetness, along with hints of cooked vegetables and nuts.

MONT D'OR/VACHERIN DU HAUTS-DOUBS

PRODUCER: various dairies
MADE: Franche-Comté, France
PRODUCTION: small farmers
co-opératives and large dairies
MILK: raw cows'
NAME PROTECTION: AOC, PDO
RENNET: traditional
TYPE: washed-rind

RIND: B. linen cultures with a
yeasty bloom
RIPENING: 3 to 12 weeks
APPEARANCE: 500g, 800g and
3kg disk
TEXTURE: soft, oozing
TASTE: sweet and milky with a
very light pungency

MONT D'OR IS a truly great cheese and one of our most loved – partly because its thick, oozing paste is so appealing and partly because it's appeal is enhanced by its seasonal availability. The rules of production, as laid out in the AOC, stipulate that it must be made between 15 August and 15 March and that the cheese may only be sold from 10 September to 10 May – we tend not to sell it until October. During the summer months, the milk from the same herds of Montbéliarde and Simmental cows would be used in the production of the region's other great cheese, Comté. Traditional farming methods would have meant that there was less milk available in winter time, and you need a lot of milk to produce the large 35kg wheels of Comté. In addition, the cattle are in sheds in winter, feeding on hay rather than out on the communal summer grazing. The harsh winters in this region would have made it difficult for the eight or ten farmers, who would normally pool their milk for Comté, to transport it to a central cheesemaking facility. Instead, smaller Mont d'Or cheese was made at each farm. All of these elements combined to create a winter-only cheese and this tradition has thankfully been preserved by the AOC regulations. Another unique characteristic of Mont d'Or is that it is bound by a strip of spruce bark around the circumference and ripened on a wooden board. The spruce band and the board stay with the cheese all the way to shop counter or, for the smaller cheeses, on to the kitchen table. Although the paste is oozing and the pinkish hue and often fuzzy grey moulds on the rind give the appearance of a powerfully tasting cheese, the flavour and aroma are actually quite gentle. They are a lovely mix of hay, cream, forest mushroom and spruce forest.

MILLEENS

PRODUCER: Steele family
MADE: Beara, West Cork
PRODUCTION: single farm
MILK: cows'
RENNET: vegetarian
TYPE: washed-rind, semi-soft
RIND: *B. linen* cultures with
  speckled moulds

RIPENING: 4 to 10 weeks
APPEARANCE: 200g (dotes), 1.2kg
  disc and 1kg '0'
TEXTURE: semi-soft
TASTE: from light, fermented hay
  to deep pungency with aromas of
  cooked vegetables and yoghurt

VERONICA AND Norman Steele began making cheese on their farm at Milleens on the Beara Peninsula, Co. Cork, in 1976. It is generally seen as the first of the modern Irish farmhouse cheeses. Their son, Quinlan, has taken over cheese-making and milk is bought in from a neighbour, as the Steeles no longer keep their own herd. Depending on the season, the weather, which of the three variations of Milleens you are eating and, perhaps, the humour of the cheesemaker, this cheese can vary quite a bit. This should not be seen as a fault but a great advantage, as each variation is wonderful and full of unique flavours. The paste, particularly of the small dotes, can be bulging, almost spilling, or it can be a little chalky yet moist. The flavour of the less attractive chalky cheeses can be surprisingly complex and satisfying, while the softer cheeses tend to be sweet and pungent.

DILISKUS

PRODUCER: Maja Binder
MADE: Co. Kerry, Ireland
PRODUCTION: seasonal, single
  herd
MILK: raw cows'
RENNET: vegetarian
TYPE: washed-rind, pressed

RIND: *B. linen* cultures with
  speckled moulds
RIPENING: 6 to 20 weeks
APPEARANCE: 1 to 2kg wheels
TEXTURE: semi-firm
TASTE: earthy, pungent, a little
  salty

Mixing herbs or spices into a cheese can often be a sign of a mediocre cheese being disguised by strong added flavours. This is certainly not the case with Diliskus. Maja uses the native Irish sea vegetable dilisk to add another dimension to her cheese. Maja makes and matures her cheese metres from the edge of the Atlantic Ocean. The cattle that produce the milk graze on hills enveloped by the salty humidity of the sea. This combination of land and sea carry through in the flavour of the cheese. When fully developed, the rind resembles an algae-speckled stone on the seashore. It is washed with whey and ripened in humid stone sheds. The washed rind imparts a little pungency and this is combined with a salty earthiness and a slight sharpness that develops with age.

REBLOCHON FERMIER, MISSILLIER

PRODUCER: Jean-Pierre Missillier
MADE: Savoie, France
PRODUCTION: farm, using milk from a single herd
MILK: raw cows'
NAME PROTECTION: AOC, PDO
RENNET: traditional
TYPE: washed-rind, soft

RIND: *B. linen* cultures and light *candidum* bloom
RIPENING: 4 to 10 weeks
APPEARANCE: 500g wheel
TEXTURE: soft, almost liquid
TASTE: delicate pungency, sweet milk

REBLOCHON PRODUCTION may be *fermier, co-opérative* or industrial. By far the best cheeses are raw milk and *fermier* like this one made by Jean-Pierre Missillier, which we have sold for many years. This wonderful cheese has its origins in a form of tax evasion. Knowing that village-dwelling tax collectors were unlikely to be fully acquainted with agricultural practice, canny mountain farmers, who had to pay tax on all milk produced, would only partially milk their cows, leaving the rest of the milk in the beast. Satisfied that he had seen the animals milked before his very eyes, the taxman would move on to the next farm, where the trick would be repeated again. Once the coast was clear, a second milking would take place. This second milking produced a thicker, richer milk that would then be used to make the small soft cheese eventually known as Reblochon – taking its name from the French verb *reblocher*, to pinch a cow's udder again. The rind of this little disc-shaped cheese is velvety pink. The *B. linens* are veiled in a gentle bloom of *candidum* moulds. The paste is soft and almost liquid when ripe. The aroma is really special. If you have ever milked a happy, clean cow in a stone shed, your nose close to her warm body, then the smell of this cheese will bring you straight back to that place. The flavour is quite delicate with a sweet, rich creaminess and light nuttiness.

TALEGGIO

PRODUCER: various large and small dairies
MADE: Bergamo, Lombardy, Veneto and Piedmont, Italy
PRODUCTION: large and small dairies
MILK: cows' and a few raw cows'
NAME PROTECTION: DOC, PDO

RENNET: traditional
TYPE: washed-rind, semi-soft
RIND: thick *B. linens* with spots of mould
RIPENING: 5 to 10 weeks
APPEARANCE: 2.2kg squares
TEXTURE: semi-soft to soft
TASTE: gentle pungency, fruity

ALTHOUGH IT only acquired the name Taleggio in the early twentieth century, this style of cheese has been made in the Val Taleggio, in Upper Bergamo, since at least the tenth century and it is from here that the cheese takes its name. Taleggio is characterised by a slightly pungent, pinkish-orange rind and a semi-soft white paste, along with its distinctive square shape. There are many producers and many styles of *affinage*, which all produce a myriad different styles of this cheese. Some can have quite a chalky paste and lactic, light flavours, others can be long matured with thick, creamy pastes and rich, deep, pungent flavours. We like our Taleggio to have an active, bright-pink-orange rind and a soft, bulging paste, giving a pungent but still sweet and slightly fruity tang.

ÉPOISSES DE BOURGOGNE, BERTHAUT

PRODUCER: Berthaut
MADE: Burgundy, France
PRODUCTION: dairy with milk
from surrounding farms
MILK: cows'
NAME PROTECTION: AOC, PDO
RENNET: traditional
TYPE: washed-rind, soft

RIND: *B. linens*, washed with Marc
de Bourgogne
RIPENING: 5 to 8 weeks
APPEARANCE: 250g and 1kg
wheels
TEXTURE: soft to runny
TASTE: gentle pungency, floral

THE ORIGINS of this cheese have, as with so many great washed-rind cheeses, been traced back to monastic settlements, in this case to the Cistercians. In 1956, sensing an opportunity, two young farmers from the village of Époisses harnessed the cheesemaking expertise still available in their community and reintroduced the cheese to France. The award of the AOC to Époisses in 1991 is testament to the success of their endeavours. One of those farmers was a M. Berthaut, whose family continue to make Époisses today. The *B. linens* rind of this cheese is bright orange and grows thickly over the moist paste beneath, encouraged by regular washing with water and Marc de Bourgogne, a kind of brandy made from the pomace left over when grapes are pressed. The high-moisture paste and the thick, active rind mean that the paste quickly turns from chalky to spilling semi-liquid. We have quite often served it to very happy customers in a paper cup! The flavour is less pungent than the rind would suggest and has a very pleasant sweetness. Berthaut also makes similar cheeses ripened with Chablis wine instead, which are slightly milder.

SERRA DA ESTRELA

PRODUCER: various small dairies
MADE: Serra da Estrela, Portugal
PRODUCTION: farm, using their
own milk
MILK: raw sheep's
NAME PROTECTION: DOC,
PDO
RENNET: vegetarian, cardoon
thistle

TYPE: washed-rind, semi-soft
RIND: *B. linens* with muslin band
tied around the circumference
RIPENING: 1 to 6 months
APPEARANCE: 1.5kg cylinders
TEXTURE: semi-liquid to firm,
creamy depending on ripening
TASTE: strong herbal and floral
aromas and sour notes

THE TERM handmade was never so deserved as with this wonderful cheese. It has been produced in the same way for centuries by the shepherds of the Serra da Estrela, 'Star Mountains', the highest mountain range in Portugal. Serra is made from native Bordaleira and Churra Mondegueira sheep's milk between November and March when the ewes produce milk naturally. Production is simple but unique. The strained petals of the cardoon thistle are added to the warm milk. After about half an hour, the milk has curdled and separated. The curds are then scooped up into a muslin cloth and whey is pressed out through the cloth by hand. The curd is then emptied out on to a table where it is broken up and massaged by the cheesemakers' hands. The curd is then put into a cloth-lined mould and pressed to push out more moisture. The resulting cheese is rubbed with dry salt and wrapped in a band of muslin. The cheeses are stored on wooden boards in humid cellars or cupboards, where they are turned and washed with water. For the younger cheeses, called *amanteigado*, the maturation period is between 30 and 45 days. The bulging cheeses develop a natural, sticky *B. linen* rind. At this point the paste is unctuous and almost runny; it can be eaten by slicing the top rind off like a lid and spooning out the flesh. The more mature versions, called *vehlo*, are allowed to mature for up to six months. The paste then becomes firmer but still creamy. The older cheeses have a more intense flavour with a stronger bitterness and nuttiness.

LANGRES

PRODUCER: single farm and various dairies
MADE: Champagne-Ardenne, France
PRODUCTION: farm, using milk from a single herd
MILK: raw cows' and cows'
NAME PROTECTION: AOC, PDO
RENNET: traditional
TYPE: washed-rind with addition of colourant
RIND: *B. linen* cultures and later growth of *Penicillium candidum*
RIPENING: minimum 15 days
APPEARANCE: 180g, 300g and 1kg concave wheel
TEXTURE: soft but compact
TASTE: mildly pungent and sweet, getting saltier with age

THIS IS A really delicious, very lightly pungent cheese. Unfortunately, only one farmhouse or *fermier* producer is still making the cheese, though there are quite a few very good larger-scale producers. Although the rind is washed to encourage the growth of a light covering of *B. linens*, the colourant annatto is also added to give the impression of a stronger rind. A gentle *candidum* bloom grows over the washed rind later in maturation. Most cheeses are turned frequently during maturation to avoid the danger of the cheese collapsing in on itself. By contrast, Langres is purposely left unturned during its *affinage*, which takes place on oat straw. This allows the formation of the 'fountain' or dip on the topside of the cheese. Some people like to pour a drop of Champagne or Marc de Bourgogne into this natural indentation before sampling the cheese. The aroma can be quite pungent but the flavour is very gentle. The paste remains quite firm, though creamy and moist.

And here are some favourites from our friends around the world.

CARDO

PRODUCER: Mary Holbrook
MADE: Timsbury, Somerset
PRODUCTION: single farm, using their own milk
MILK: raw goats'
RENNET: vegetarian, cardoon thistle
TYPE: soft, washed-rind

RIND: *B. linens* with natural moulds
RIPENING: 4 to 6 weeks
APPEARANCE: 600g wheel
TEXTURE: dense heart with breakdown around the edges
TASTE: rich cooked cream notes with a herbaceous finish

THIS CHEESE has a lovely mouth feel. It's creamy soft without being elastic or gooey. Flavours are always present, distinctive and thought-provoking, and yet always slightly different from batch to batch. Made by Mary Holbrook, the 'grande dame' of the British farm cheese world. I watch them all growing up, since Mary brings the cheeses to London every week and spends a couple of days in the maturing rooms with us washing and nurturing the cheeses. *Jason Hinds, Neal's Yard Dairy, London*

GRAYSON

PRODUCER: Meadow Creek Dairy
MADE: Virginia, USA
PRODUCTION: single farm, using
  their own milk
MILK: raw cows'
RENNET: vegetarian
TYPE: washed-rind, semi-soft

RIND: *B. linens*
RIPENING: minimum 60 days
APPEARANCE: 3kg square
TEXTURE: supple, silky
TASTE: slightly sweet, nutty notes
  and a solid earthy undertone

THIS WASHED-RIND cheese made in Meadow Creek Dairy is truly unique. The pasture-fed cows produce fine milk that is masterfully turned into cheese. The texture is gooey and the aromas are assertive, almost savoury. A great cheese to eat melted on top of new potatoes. It also pairs with IPAs or other hoppy beers. *Carlos Yescas, Lactography, USA (ex-Sheridans Cheesemonger)*

RECIPES

SPRING

Durrus and Potato Pizza

This lets the rind sing! Potatoes on pizza might sound a bit much but they're surprisingly good. The trick is to slice them very thinly and only use a single layer so they don't make everything too claggy and thick.

SERVES 6

375ml warm water

1 teaspoon dried yeast

110ml olive oil

salt and freshly ground black pepper

600g 00 flour

3 sprigs of fresh rosemary

6 cloves garlic

2 medium Rooster potatoes, peeled

1 large sweet potato, peeled

250g crème fraîche

360g Durrus, sliced

To make the dough, pour the water into a jug and mix in the yeast, smoothing it against the sides to ensure it's dissolved. Add 50ml of the olive oil and 1 teaspoon of salt to the liquid.

Pour into a bowl with the flour and mix to form a dough. Leave for 10 minutes.

Turn the dough on to an oiled surface and knead lightly until it comes together. Put it back in the bowl, cover and leave for 90 minutes to prove.

Meanwhile, remove the leaves from the rosemary sprigs and combine in a mortar and pestle with the garlic and a pinch of salt. Bash this into a paste and then add the remaining olive oil. Transfer the entire mixture to a saucepan and heat the oil gently for about 10 minutes. Turn the heat off and leave the oil to infuse with the garlic and rosemary flavours.

Roll out the dough and dimple it with your fingers. Fold it over like a sheet on itself and dimple again before rolling and repeating this a second and third time.

Return the dough to the bowl to rest for a further 30 minutes.

Divide the dough into three and roll into rounds or rectangles, whichever you prefer.

Preheat the oven to 220°C – or as high as it will go!

Finely slice the potatoes and sweet potato into paper thin rounds and arrange them on the pizza bases in a single layer.

Dot the potatoes and sweet potato with blobs of crème fraîche and place the slices of Durrus in between the blobs.

Finally, drizzle the pizzas with the garlic and rosemary oil and give them a good sprinkling of freshly ground black pepper. You can strain out the rosemary shards or leave them in, whichever you prefer.

Bake the pizzas for 10 minutes and serve immediately.

SUMMER

Pickled Vegetables

Giving a tangy crunch to things, these vegetables make a nice partner to washed-rind cheeses and can be served as part of a cheeseboard or with cheese on a cracker. They will keep in the fridge for up to a week and benefit from spending some time in the pickling liquid before you serve them.

SERVES 4 AS A SIDE DISH

100ml rice vinegar

2 tablespoons sugar

1 teaspoon coriander seeds

a pinch of salt

a pinch of whole peppercorns

2 medium carrots, peeled

½ head cauliflower, or 1 small head

Scald a Kilner jar or large jam jar with boiling water and leave to one side.

Heat the vinegar, sugar, coriander seeds, salt and peppercorns gently in a saucepan until they start to bubble and the sugar has dissolved. Meanwhile, slice the vegetables as thinly as you can. A mandolin is really useful here but make sure to use the finger guard.

Tip the vegetables into the warm pickling liquid and stir them well together. Transfer to the Kilner jar and ensure all the vegetables are covered in liquid.

Let the mixture cool and then store in the fridge.

AUTUMN

Taleggio Tartiflette

*It's no coincidence that tartiflette is a classic après-ski dish.
It's a rib-sticking, cockle-warming lump of a meal, best used
as a reward after strenuous activity. But it's so delicious you
can simply take a smaller helping if your step count doesn't
warrant a heftier one.*

SERVES 4

1kg potatoes, peeled and cut into 1cm dice

rapeseed oil

2 thick rashers smoked streaky bacon, cut into
4cm dice

1 large onion, peeled and diced

½ glass Eight Degrees Brewing Barefoot
Bohemian Pilsner Lager

350g Taleggio, diced

1 garlic clove, peeled and cut in half

sea salt and freshly ground black pepper

Preheat the oven to 200°C.

Boil the potatoes for 3–5 minutes until just tender and then
drain them and season with salt and pepper.

Heat a good splash of rapeseed oil in a large, heavy pan over a
gentle heat. Fry the potatoes for a minute or two and then add
the diced bacon and onion. Cook until the bacon has begun to
crisp.

Pour in the Pilsner, stir and then add the cubed cheese. (You could also add some spinach, chard or kale at this stage.) Remove the pan from the heat.

Prepare an ovenproof earthenware dish by rubbing it well with the halves of garlic and greasing with rapeseed oil.

Empty the contents of the pan into the dish and bake for 20–30 minutes, until the cheese has melted and begun to crisp.

WINTER

Baked Mont d'Or

The seasonality of this cheese, together with the convivial nature of how the dish is shared, makes it one of our favourites for a cold winter evening. It can be served at the end of a meal to replace the cheese board or as a main course, if accompanied by plenty of winter salads and cold meats.

You can use Swiss or French Mont d'Or and you can also adjust this recipe to suit other washed-rind cheeses. Our favourites are Durrus 360g or Gubbeen 450g. Because they don't come in boxes, you need to make the following adjustments – rather than score the rind, cut a thin lid off the top and put your garlic and thyme into the paste, replacing the rind lid. Place the cheese in the centre of a sheet of foil, bring up the corners of the foil, covering the cheese, but leave a 'chimney' in the centre, formed with the foil. Pour the wine in through the chimney and leave it open during baking.

SERVES 6 AFTER DINNER, 4 AS MAIN COURSE

500g Mont d'Or in its box, with lid on

1 clove garlic, peeled

2 sprigs of thyme

½ glass of whatever white wine you are drinking

crusty bread to serve

Preheat the oven to 180°C.

Cut an 'X' through the rind of the cheese from edge to edge. Using your thumb, press the sprigs of thyme and the clove of garlic through the centre of the x and into the paste of the cheese.

Pour the wine over the cheese.

Fit the wooden lid back on to the cheese and place it on an ovenproof dish or baking tray to catch any leaks.

Bake in the preheated oven for ten minutes.

Remove from the oven, take off the lid and peel back the scored rind to reveal the warm gooey paste.

Place in the centre of the table so that you and your guests can scoop out the melted cheese with chunks of crusty bread.

CHAPTER SEVEN

PRESSED UNCOOKED CHEESES

FROM CHEDDAR TO GOUDA – THE FARM BEHIND THE CHEESE AND NEW TRADITIONS

'The butter your sister is sending us is very good,' I said to my neighbour one day. 'Yes,' he said, 'that field always made good butter.'

Myrtle Allen, Ballymaloe House

The cheeses in this category are a bewildering array of types, shapes, sizes, tastes and traditions. The category covers all cheeses that are not defined within the other chapters. Pressed uncooked cheeses include English territorials such as Cheddar and Cheshire, Dutch Goudas, the mountain Tommes of France, and the great sheep's milk cheeses of the Pyrenees, Spain and Italy.

This array of cheeses all share two common features: they are firm and longer aged than the fresh or rind cheeses we've dealt with so far. And they are made without heating the curd above 40°C. This is what we mean when we describe them as 'uncooked'. This doesn't mean the curd isn't heated – Cheddars are made with warmed curd and the Gouda curd is scalded in hot water – but cooking the curd for longer at higher temperatures is something we'll get on to in the next chapter.

Although many of these cheeses have rinds covered in moulds and cultures, the rinds don't play as significant a role in developing flavour and texture as they do in bloomy- and washed-rind cheeses. Traditional English cheeses like Cheddar and Cheshire have a protective layer of cloth and lard, but they still develop a significant rind of moulds and yeasts, like a skin underneath their clothing that influences their flavour. The maturing process in these firmer cheeses is slower moving than in rind-ripened cheeses and is down to agents that work within the body of the cheese rather than a rind working from the outside in.

The enzymes and bacteria present in the cheese when it is first produced continue to work slowly as the cheese matures. Ageing or ripening will take at least two months and some will be matured for more than a year. Each type of pressed uncooked cheese was primarily created as a way of preserving the nutrients in milk over a long period. As much, if not more, of their success has been down to their practical use as tradable commodities that could be shipped and stored, with great nutritional value, than as foods with an ability to please the palate. The development of the wonderful flavours and aromas we have come to love in these cheeses are a happy by-product of the ingenious ways people have invented to preserve milk.

Most of the rinds are made up of salted, hardened curd. These rinds then attract moulds and cultures from the environment. Although the fungi which populate the rinds contribute to the flavour of the cheese, their influence is mild compared to the surface-ripened bloomies and washed-rind cheeses. Their function is principally to protect the precious food within, allowing moisture to escape very slowly, protecting the cheese from unwanted moulds and other microorganisms.

These cheeses tend to be larger than the ones we've met so far because they're not as dependent on their rinds to develop their flavours and don't, therefore, need to be thin enough to let the rind work its way quickly to the middle before the outer layer spoils. The lack of moisture in the curd and their large size means that their flavour develops at a slower pace. The enzymes and bacteria already present in the cheese when it is first produced work slowly as the cheese ages. More recently technology has allowed the development of new materials to protect the cheese from unwanted microorganisms and to slow down or prevent moisture loss during maturation. Plastic used in vacuum packing or thick wax coatings are mostly used in the pro-

duction of industrial cheeses. The use of these impenetrable rinds means that there is virtually no loss of moisture in the cheese, resulting in little weight loss. These coverings produce a cheese with no rind, perfect for cutting and pre-packing. The disadvantages are a sometimes less appealing rubbery texture, flavour development is slower and the end result lacks the extra dimension given by the natural rind.

The flavour and texture that each cheese develops is determined by many factors. First, how the curd is treated from when it is separated from the whey to when it is packed into moulds has a great influence. In these types of cheeses, the curd can be subject to many different treatments during production. How fine the curd is cut is a major factor in how much moisture the cheese will have; the finer the curd, the drier the cheese. The curd can be 'washed' in hot water, causing it to lose moisture but also reducing its acidity. The curds and whey can be heated up to 40°C, causing them to lose more moisture. The longer the curd is left in the whey, the more acidic the cheese becomes. Also, salt can be added into the curd rather than waiting to introduce it through the rind of the cheese.

These and many more small differences change the moisture content and the structure of the curd as well as the acidity. The different methods affect the resulting formation of the cheese but also encourage and discourage different bacteria and how they react with the curd as the cheese matures. In the early stages of production, some of the bacteria work to transform the lactose to lactic acid but others work later, continuing the transformation of the curd many months after it was first pressed into a cheese.

The flavour and aromas can go from light to stronger sweetness, ranging from the sweet hay smell and taste of a mature Brebis, to the deeper cooked caramel taste of an old Gouda. Meanwhile, the English traditional cheeses give the most beautiful sour and tangy flavours wrapped in the delicious smell and taste of leaf mould and wet stone cellars. The sheep's milk cheeses of Spain and Italy, Manchego, Idiazabal and pecorino, can have rich, brothy, almost fatty flavours and aromas. These tastes get heightened by a sharpness as they age and are often salty. When these cheeses are made with raw milk and their rinds are allowed to develop naturally, their cultures provide the most complex flavours in cheese. It's a more sophisticated set of flavour combinations than those dominated by the action of their rinds.

TOMME, TOME, TOMA

The French word *tomme*, sometimes spelt *tome*, and the Italian word *toma* are very general terms describing small- or medium-sized cheeses normally made in mountainous areas. They have natural rinds similar to those of washed-rind cheeses but these cheeses are generally matured for longer and have developed a natural diversity of moulds and cultures. The curds are never cooked but moisture is usually extracted by gentle pressing of the fresh cheeses, allowing them to last for several months. They can be made from cows', goats' or sheep's milk.

There are many varieties of Tomme, usually identified by their place of origin together with the word *tomme*. They are mainly produced across the Alps from Savoie through Switzerland and down to Piedmont, though the term is often used to describe cheeses of the Pyrenees.

The best known of these cheeses is Tomme de Savoie: a cheese that itself has many variations made across Savoie. The flavour of these cheeses varies from type to type and region to region but in general they tend to have rich but subtle flavours, including nuttiness, floral, hay and grass, and mild pungency. They do all tend to have a rich, earthy, loamy aroma, coming from their natural and often complex rinds.

CHEESE MITES

THESE ARE TINY little spider-like fellows who just love cheese. They live on the dry rinds of aged cheeses. They are generally seen as a nuisance by cheesemakers and *affineurs*, as they consume valuable cheese, literally leaving dust in their wake. For some cheeses, however, they are seen as bringing an extra level of flavour and are even encouraged. The most famous cheese where these small beasts are integral to the maturing process is Mimolette. This Edam-style cheese is produced on either side of the border between France and the Netherlands. Both Dutch and French versions exist, although the majority of *affinage* is carried out on the French side. It derives its name from the French *mi-mou mi-mol*, meaning half

soft, half hard. Mimolette is also known as Boule de Lille, after the town of Lille in northern France where many of the *affineurs* of this cheese, including the celebrated firm of Cesar Losfeld, are based. Here in their dark cavernous cellars Losfeld allow the mites to slowly eat into the rind of the cheese; over a year the rind becomes poked as the mites bore down into the hard paste. The resulting cheese resembles an ancient cannonball recovered from the floor of the ocean. The action of the mites is said to be responsible for an additional fruitiness in the flavour. You will find a small amount of mites on almost all hard cheeses, including Comté, farm Cheddars and even Stilton. They are still seen by many as a sign of a well-matured cheese.

CHEESE IN CLOTH AND LARD

Cheddar is one of many British territorial cloth-bound cheeses. All of these cheeses have a similar production method – draining the whey in a vat and pressing finely milled curds into moulds. The result is a particularly crumbly texture and a distinctive acid flavour, along with an extra dimension under the rind brought by the moulds which flourish on the cloth and lard covering.

Another unusual aspect of these cheeses is that salt is added directly into the curd. Because salt is added throughout the curd rather than on the surface, the cheese has no natural skin. The salted curd is pressed into moulds to give them their form and various types of presses are used to expel moisture and to compact the cheese. The cheeses are finally bandaged in muslin cloth that has been soaked in lard. It's how you might imagine bandaging a mummy. The lard and

cloth act to protect the cheese from drying out too fast and cracking, and it is this last stage that gives these cheeses their distinctive look but allows moisture to continue to leave the cheese during maturation.

In cloth-bound Cheddars, the odd small blue vein running a few inches into one of these cheeses, particularly the more mature ones, is a lovely indicator of a cheese with a natural rind. However, if that small vein grows into a web of blue by linking with tiny cracks and fissures throughout the body of the cheese, it can be a problem. Some customers enjoy the resulting flavour but most prefer their Cheddars white (or red) and their blues blue. These blue veins are a result of small cracks that occur when the cheese dries out too quickly. This veining can be made much worse if the cheeses are not treated gently in the maturing rooms. When turning the cheeses, it is very easy to bang the heavy rounds back on to the boards. This sends little shock-waves through the cheese and any small blue veins will expand through the newly created highways. To reduce drying out and the resulting cracks, cheesemakers can increase the amount of lard applied. But if too much is applied, the cheese seals almost completely and the result can be worse. Without the ability to breathe out moisture, the cheeses become rubbery and the flavour does not develop properly. It's a delicate balance.

RED LEICESTER, RED CHESHIRE, RED CHEDDAR. WHAT MAKES THE CHEESE RED?

LIKE RED LEMONADE, red Cheddar is a favourite with Irish consumers. We'll fairly frequently hear a new customer looking for red Cheddar: 'I much prefer red Cheddar,' they'll say.

The red dye in Cheddar and other cheeses does not affect the flavour. It is a tasteless food colouring, typically annatto, which comes from the skin of the deeply coloured seeds of the tropical achiote tree. On Irish supermarket shelves there are always two Cheddars, red and white. The colour is the only difference. In a blind test both cheeses taste exactly the same. We eat with our eyes first and so it makes sense that the colour of a cheese makes a difference to us, though.

Colouring cheese goes back a long way. It's believed that Cheshire cheesemakers coloured their cheaper, lower fat cheeses with carrot juice in the seventeenth century to make them look more alluring (traditionally a richer, more yellow cheese is generally higher in fat content and has more carotene, which comes from fresh grass rather than other feeds). When they sent these inferior cheeses to market, they found the coloured cheeses sold even better than the higher quality, full-fat cheeses and so more and more cheesemakers began to dye cheese a richer colour.

We never received instruction in the art of opening a cloth-bound Somerset Cheddar. We had to work it out for ourselves using simple logic. When you have done it countless times, it takes on a sense of ritual. It's one of the jobs that reinforces the feeling that you are a cheesemonger and not just a cheese retailer. We once witnessed the horror on Jamie Montgomery's face when a very well-meaning Italian opened a wheel of his Cheddar using a method more commonly used to crack a wheel of Parmesan. Jamie is the man behind the renowned Montgomery Cheddar. He's the third generation in this cheesemaking family. His face fell during the biennial Slow Food Cheese Festival in Bra that year. In a flamboyant experiment, the organisers decided to age some of the best Slow Food Presidia cheeses in the Piedmontese caves of Beppino Occelli. Montgomery Cheddar was one of the cheeses that had been chosen and with great ceremony each one was being opened for tasting after its year in the Italian cave. In the end, the experiment didn't seem to have any lasting effect on the flavour of the Cheddar. It was just a year older, having already stabilised its flavours before it went into the cave.

The wheel of Montgomery was placed on a table, the cloth rind left in place like it was part of the cheese, and the Cheddar was scored and prised open with a set of Parmesan knives. The result was quite beautiful, with the natural texture of the well-aged cheese emphasised in the rough surface of each quarter. Jamie would have preferred the more traditional approach, though. The wheel of cheese should be rested on its side and the tight cloth scored, top to bottom. With a little help from a small knife, you can get a grip on the cloth and pull. The cheese rolls on the spot and the cloth pulls off in a little cloud of dust. The edges of the cloth covering the top and bottom of the cheese can then be gripped and similarly pulled off. The cheese is now much paler, mottled beige and ochre, sometimes with rusty orange spots.

One more layer of cloth remains and again this is scored, pulled and released from the surface. The cheese rolls out of its inner skin and is naked. There is the thinnest layer of lard remaining with the imprint of the cloth and this merges with the cheese. We always cut our Cheddars horizontally in thirds. A little score with a knife so that a wire can get a grip, then the tight steel wire is pulled through the cheese in a cut so fine that it leaves it looking intact. The top third is lifted off like the silver-plated cloche from a grand last course at a posh restaurant. Immediately you bring your nose to the open surface and

Franck Le Moenner opening Cheddar.

breathe in, the aroma of hay, wet stone and a hint of ripe butter and a hundred other indefinable aromas meet you and fill your nose and mouth.

Drag a taster tool (like a cheese slice or a large vegetable peeler) across the newly revealed surface, the cheese comes up in a long sliver and you'll notice the broken edges and the brittle look, which reveals the distinctive, cloth-bound Cheddar's texture. The flavour varies from cheese to cheese, from year to year, from batch to batch. You hope for and often get jaw-filling flavour with only the tiniest sharpness. The aroma, which was revealed a minute ago, is intensified through your mouth and there is the addition of a flavour, only present when the cheese has had a natural rind. We can best describe it as delicious, wet mould.

Farm Cheddar seems to be the most difficult cheese to make well. We say this because we have tasted so many disappointing wheels, not only from new producers but even the most experienced and celebrated Cheddar makers when they have their bad patches. Production is a complex process, balancing moisture content and acidity. Even after the cheeses are pressed and wrapped, there are plenty of opportunities for problems in the maturing rooms.

As with all long-aged cheese, solving flavour faults is extremely difficult. They are often not apparent until after six months or more of ageing and so the time lag between trying out a solution and seeing a result slows down progress. We once had the pleasure of listening to Jamie Montgomery and Randolph Hodgson of Neal's Yard speak about their approach to tasting, selecting and improving Montgomery Cheddar. What was striking was their relentless attention to detail and emphatic note-taking at every stage of production and maturation. Every small change in the day's milk and even weather is recorded. Every detail of the cheesemaking process, particularly times, temperatures and acidity of the curd, is logged. At regular intervals during maturation the cheeses are tasted and their development noted.

Greatness in a cheese, and especially Cheddar, doesn't appear from the sky but comes from much hard work and dedication. There were once more than 400 farm Cheddar makers in Somerset; there are now only three remaining who use raw milk and traditional methods. At different times we have worked with all of them – they are Keen's, Montgomery's and Westcombe. Each have their own characteristics and each have evolved and developed over the years. It's impossible to pick any one as being better than the others. We select the ones we believe our customers will like the most. We pick cheeses with a strong flavour but a balance to how the flavour is experienced. Flavours should be knitted together and arrive smoothly connected to each other without any jarring notes interrupting that experience.

THE POWER OF MARKETING OVER THE POWER OF MARKETS – THE RISE AND RISE OF THE CHEESTRING

Around 85 per cent of the milk produced in Ireland is processed by eight companies. It's a common story of modern food. Fewer larger players control the bulk of our modern food supply chains. The holy grail in the dairy world is a new product or new market in which Irish milk can be used. With the lifting of the dairy quota system, Irish farmers are now free to produce as much milk as they like. But the more milk that is produced across Europe, the cheaper milk becomes.

So how do you persuade people to eat something they've never encountered before? The answer seems to be to spend a lot of money on marketing. Almost twenty years ago, Kerry Foods put a new cheese-based food product on supermarket shelves with a marketing budget of €4 million. Now it's a multimillion-euro seller and it's made in Charleville, Co. Cork.

Inside the Kerry factory in Charleville, a thin wall of stainless steel screens is all that separates you from one of the biggest industrial secrets in the Irish food business. The air smells of baked milk. Everyone is dressed in hairnets, bright orange jackets and disinfected white shoes.

A swift dive to the floor and you might get a glimpse underneath the screens. Roald Dahl would have a thousand squirrels behind here playing cat's cradle with lengths of molten cheese. But only people who have signed a confidentiality agreement are allowed to see what really happens.

Welcome to the home of the Cheestring, an annual €80 million success story and one of Ireland's most successful food exports. It's a windowless building in the middle of the Kerry Foods complex in Charleville. At one end of the production line, sofa-cushion size blocks of cheddar curd are being warmed into a molten rubbery mass that falls steadily from a large funnel into a stainless steel vat.

Then comes the secret part in an area roughly the size of a tennis court. Here the warm bubble-gummy cheese is somehow being turned into sticks of cheese that will peel into strings when cold. This is where the straw that is raw curd is spun into gold.

In the final section, a machine is spitting Cheestrings into a brine river where they float around stainless steel bends to cool before they're packed and shipped. In days, they will be in millions of lunchboxes in Ireland and Britain, and fridge doors of families in Holland and France. In this small factory, roughly a million Cheestrings are made and packaged on a relentless 24-hour production line, day and night, stick of cheese after stick of cheese.

Cheestrings are a brand marketed at children with a nod to their time-pressed parents. As an adult you might eat chocolate or crisps but you are almost as unlikely to eat a Cheestring as you are to down a glass of baby formula. Cheestrings are a fascinating story of adding value to milk. They are adored by children and vaguely distrusted by adults. In nearly twenty years of existence, they have changed their message and their ingredients to chime with the zeitgest and grow the brand. And they are marching ever forward.

The key man behind the phenomenon is the affable Kerry Foods cheese marketing director Denis O'Riordan. He sat in an office in Canada twenty years ago and heard about a string cheese product. He was an executive with Golden Vale (since swallowed by Kerry Foods), searching for a brand that they could use as a battering ram into the lucrative world of the British lunchbox.

Ault Foods in Canada (since swallowed by Parmalat, itself swallowed by French dairy giant Lactalis in 2011) had an innovative chief executive and two new ideas: a filtered milk and the Cheestring. O'Riordan and his board went for the cheese. The manufacturing process was tricky enough to prevent copies hitting supermarket shelves for at least six months. They invested €2 million in plant and the same again in marketing before a single Cheestring was sold.

O'Riordan was wondering if he had just gambled €4 million when he heard the magic words in a supermarket in Glasgow. Small twin girls being wheeled in a trolley down the cheese aisle: 'Mum, Mum. There are the Cheestrings,' they said. And he knew it was going to work.

Cheestrings launched in Britain in 1996 with a TV ad showing a dancing child playing with the product and the tagline 'Real A-peelable Cheese'. And Cheestrings went viral with sales of €16 million in the first year. The Golden Vale team soon learned to ask supermarkets to reposition them from the coveted top left-hand corner of the aisle to the child-reach position of the middle shelf. 'The basic concept got traction from day one,' O'Riordan explains.

By 2001, Cheestring sales had reached €25 million in Ireland and Britain but things were levelling off. The marketing team realised the window was too narrow. Children were starting to eat them at the age of four or five and stopping at seven. A new ad ran showing an older child faking a calcium deficiency to hoodwink his gullible adland mother into rushing out to buy Cheestrings.

They also discovered through focus groups that kids were playing with the packaging. A numbering system printed on each Cheestring for traceback was being used as a game to compete with each other over who got the highest number in the pack.

'The kids had invented a game that we never thought existed,' O'Riordan explains. So they started putting games and trivia on the packaging,'adding another layer of entertainment.'

By 2002, one in every two households with children in Britain was a Cheestring consumer, according to O'Riordan. In 2004, they crossed the Channel to France. There were some cultural teething problems. 'French children were finding it difficult to pronounce. And it was embarrassing because it was reminding them of a word for female underwear,' O'Riordan explains.

After 18 months, Cheestrings were rebranded as Ficello (after *ficelle*, the French for string). The other cultural barrier was the French palate. The red cheddar was 'positively disliked' by French children and they wanted a softer string. A Gouda–Emmental cheese mix was tested instead and it went down a treat. In Holland, the plain Gouda cheese also went down better than the British and Irish Cheddar version.

'In France, the lunchbox doesn't exist,' O'Riordan explains. 'So the "home-from-school-and-starving" moment was the one which we were playing for.' Today, Ficello is in 7.5 per cent of French households, according to Kerry Foods estimates.

Between 2001 and 2005, the fight back against fast food stepped up several notches with Eric Schlosser's *Fast Food Nation* and Morgan Spurlock's television documentary *Supersize Me*. Finally, in 2005, Jamie Oliver waved a Turkey Twizzler at millions of television viewers during his campaign to improve school dinners. The snack-food industry was in the spotlight.

As a result, the world got the McDonald's salad, crisps that were baked instead of fried and in 2007 Cheestrings quietly dropped the smokey bacon and pizza flavours. 'It was part of a genuine effort to make the brand a cheese-only.'

The head of technical development at Charleville, Joan Tobin, has been working on Cheestrings for more than ten years and is the expert on the kind of milk needed to produce them, 24 hours a day, five days a week. 'They are two thirds of the fat of normal Cheddar,' she says. They contain salt, but that has been reduced by 10 per cent. And she says they will do what they can to reduce it further as food scientists research new production methods. 'But then if you don't have salt, you don't have cheese.'

But why are they so expensive? Despite being a mass-produced processed food, Cheestrings are equivalent in price to most artisan cheeses produced in Ireland. A Cheestring costs between €18 and almost €30 a kilo depending on the quantity you buy, the most expensive option being the Minis, which at €1.79 for 60g take it into the gourmet cheese price bracket of €29.80 per kilo. One of the reasons for the high cost, Tobin says, is the high-protein curd needed to make them. Most people don't think of milk as a seasonal product but in the winter months when many cows are taken off grass and housed, the protein content of their milk falls. The result is a less frothy cappuccino and a less stringy Cheestring. 'We have a bespoke blend made for us and it has to be used in 48 hours. What's milk on a Monday will be a Cheestring by Thursday,' Tobin explains. In 2011, the high-protein milk curd was coming from Welsh, Northern Irish and West Cork cows. So while the product is made in the Republic, much of the raw material comes from farms outside the border.

Back on the production line, the Cheestrings fresh out of the brine river are even more fibrous than they will be by the time they are on supermarket shelves. The cheese is tearing into hair-sized filaments and tastes salty. They will taste less salty and be less stringy after a few days, Tobin explains. The cheeses are shuttled along a production line, lifted by robotic arms adapted from a German car manufacturer and finally packed onto pallets for shipping.

Outside the plant, Charleville is a town built on cheese. The milk plant is its largest employer and supports several other industries, including stainless steel fabricators. A new sculpture of a cow made from galvanised steel has been put on a patch of grass near the plant, with 'Charleville Says Cheese' painted on its ribcage.

A few miles outside Charleville, Tom Biggane farms goats and a dairy herd. The Cork farmer and his wife Lena have been making Clonmore goats' cheese for more than ten years. More recently they started making a cows' milk cheese called Shandrum. Both cheeses are Gouda style and Clonmore is one of our favourite cheeses at Sheridans. At about four to six months it retains a creamy texture and has the most delicious vanilla and almond aroma.

Biggane was supplying goats' milk to other cheesemakers when he decided to try it himself in the late 1990s. It wasn't long before we came across his cheese and fell in love with it.

When we visit, it is the end of the summer, he has just made one of his last batches of Clonmore for the year in the small extension at the end of his bungalow outside Charleville. The equipment is simple: a paddling-pool-sized stainless steel vat with a lid where the milk is stirred and heated, a press where the large rounds of pale curd are compressed in a brine bath before being transferred to a small long room where they sit on wooden shelves and quietly mature, their skin going from a pale yellow to beige as they age.

'We'll be stopping the cheese in a week or two,' he explains, 'and then we start again around St Patrick's Day.' Across the road, some of his herd of nearly a hundred goats bleat over the fence at us. Their milk, up to 500 litres of it a day, is heated in the vat to pasteurise it. Then it is cooled and has a starter and rennet added to separate the curd from the whey.

When they were learning to make cheese, the couple wrote down everything they did and compared the end result. 'You'd get a slightly different cheese depending on what you did.' Does he like making cheese? 'It's very satisfying. It's nice to be doing something that hopefully someone else can enjoy.'

The subtleties of handmade cheese are like bread-making, he believes. 'You won't find any two alike.' He likes the differences in texture and flavour that happen with the changing of the milk. 'My favourite would be a cheese made from milk in May. You can taste the growth of the grass.'

He likes to eat his cheese as it is or grilled with tomatoes on top. The Shandrum is particularly good with mushrooms and bacon or ham, he says. At the market in Limerick, he recently got some feedback from the Cheestring generation. 'A lady had two small boys and I gave them a taste of the cows' cheese and the goats' cheese.' The boys liked the cows' cheese and their mother loved the goats' cheese. When the children tasted the goats' cheese, their hands went to their mouths to spit the cheese into their cupped palms. 'Three-year-olds are not my market,' Tom says, grinning. His cow's cheese, Shandrum, sells for a little less than Cheesestrings.

The difference is that a time-pressed parent can't lob a chunk of Shandrum and a knife into the back of the car when plaintive cries of 'I'm hungry' begin. Of course there are ways around that but we have grown used to the convenience of an individually portioned piece of cheese that can be fished out of a fridge or a handbag and opened by a moderately dextrous two-year-old. By positioning itself as the least of the evils in the array of children's snacks, the Cheestring has triumphed. Blessed are the cheese-makers, it seems, especially those with focus groups, a large lump of capital and enormous marketing budgets.

Eamonn and Patricia Lonergan.

THE FARM BEHIND THE CHEESE

In Ireland we have a strong tradition of Cheddar-making. This has almost entirely been concentrated in industrial production, where volume and price have taken precedence over flavour. There are, however, a few farm Cheddar makers. Eamonn Lonergan is one of them. Eamonn is first and foremost a dairy farmer. He is rightly proud of his farm, his herd of pedigree Friesians and the wonderful milk they produce. If you visit his farm he will show off his cows before he shows off his cheese.

It was Eamonn's pride in this milk, along with his entrepreneurial spirit, that led him to cheesemaking in the late 1980s. He doesn't fit into the popular perception of a raw milk artisan cheesemaker as Bohemian. He dresses casually but carefully and has a thatch of pepper-and-salt grey hair and a neatly trimmed moustache. He looks like the solid family and dairy man that he is. He and his wife, Patricia, a schoolteacher, are very much a part of the rural community where they live and farm. Their farmhouse and yard in the townland of Knockanore in Co. Waterford are typical of many in Ireland. The house feels and looks like so many other well-kept Irish farmhouses, with proudly hung photographs showing the family's links to Waterford hurling.

There is nothing you can see from outside its walls that gives a hint of the extraordinary work that takes place inside the simple grey shed at the back of the Lonergans' house. Eamonn has been producing a Cheddar-style cheese called Knockanore from the raw milk of his herd on his farm for almost 30 years. Along with his plain Cheddar he also makes a naturally smoked version as well as cheeses with different combinations of herbs and spices. We have been stocking Knockanore since our first stall in Galway, although it wasn't until a few years later that it became one of our big sellers.

To our shame, we used to sell an awful lot of a particular English 'smoked' cheese. This cheese was, in fact, flavoured with an artificial smoke and dusted with pimento to give it a smoked colour. We got it in before we knew better, and our customers became addicted. The awful outbreak of foot-and-mouth in 2001 meant we weren't able to bring in any British cheeses, so our supply of the fake smoked cheese was cut off. It gave us the opportunity to introduce customers to Eamonn's Smoked Knockanore. We weaned them off the impostor and everyone became very happy with Knockanore. Needless to say, we never went back to the fake smoked cheese.

The thing that makes Eamonn's smoked cheese so good is that, first, it is a really good cheese. He ages it for six months before smoking it with smouldering oak and beech chippings. Then he vacuum packs the cheese and ages it for a further few months. The smokey flavour is powerful but there is enough strength and depth in the aged cheese to give it a rich, savoury base, so it's far from the sometimes one-dimensional flavour you get from some smoked cheeses. There are more things going on in the cheese than just smoke.

We always felt it was a pity that Eamonn vacuum packs all of his cheeses just after they are made. It means his cheese misses the influence of a rind and the slow, subtle development of flavour and texture that a rind can bring. Eamonn's decision to seal and mature his cheeses in this way has probably been the right one, though, as a cleaner appearance and a less expensive maturing process has allowed him to reach a broader market. So a wonderful authentic farmhouse raw milk cheese is available for many people to enjoy.

But we haven't been able to let go of a hankering to taste a slower more gently matured Knockanore. We've been talking to Eamonn for the best part of ten years about working together on a cheese that might fully show off the quality of his milk and cheesemaking skills. A few years ago Eamonn began collaborating with a superb group of organic dairy farmers to make a cloth-bound Cheddar using their

Lonergan Farm.

milk. The result is wonderful but still not what we were looking for. This may be because the milk used is not his own.

Eamonn makes cheese every year when his cows start to go out to grass. This begins to happen in late January or February as the temperatures rise and the grass begins to grow again. They have been inside sheltering and being fed on silage and some supplements since the previous November. They are only out during the day at first, returning for shelter and extra feed after the evening milking. As the ground becomes firmer and the grass growth improves, they stay out in the fields day and night. During these eight or nine months when his cows are on pasture, he makes cheese more or less every other day.

The cheesemaking day starts at 6am, when the milk kept chilled from the previous two days is pumped into the cheesemaking vat, a large rectangular stainless steel bath about a metre deep. The vat holds 6,000 litres of milk, perfect to hold two days' milk from Eamonn's more than 100 milking cows. As soon as the milk is in, he adds his first cultures and then hot water is pumped through the lining of the vat to slowly raise the temperature. As the milk warms, he adds another set of cultures. By 9.30am the milk should have reached the target temperature of 32°C and the cultures will have begun to convert much of the sugars in the milk to lactic acid. Rennet is then added to the milk. Graham Lee, who has been working for Eamonn for 23 years, keeps a close eye on the milk for the next 20 to 30 minutes. Eamonn describes the transformation as a magical moment.

'You are staring at the milk wondering, "Will it not happen today?", then you look away for a minute and when you look back it has turned from liquid to solid, a miracle every time.'

To judge when the curd is ready to be cut, they do 'the knife test'. A knife is drawn across the curd, making a clean incision. The knife is then placed back into this incision and dragged along with its flat side forward. If the curd continues to break cleanly ahead of the knife past the original incision, the curd is ready. The mass is cut and stirred, separating small white curds from the yellowish whey. The temperature of the vat is increased again, taking about 40 minutes to reach 39°C, and held there for about another ten minutes. This gentle heat tightens the curd, helping it to become drier. All the time the curd is continuously but gently stirred in its warm bath, preventing it from sinking to the bottom and clumping together.

Using a special pump, which pushes rather than sucks, the wet curds are transferred to what Eamonn calls the draining table, though it is more like a shallow rectangular vat about 30cm deep. Here the curds are raked to each side, allowing the whey to flow off. The curds begin to clump together and form a big spongy mass on each side of the table. This mass, now pretty solid, is cut into square blocks and stacked, releasing more moisture as its own weight bears down on the curd. All the time the busy bacteria continue to raise the acidity of the curd. Eamonn calls this the 'chicken breast stage', describing how firm the curd should feel when it is ready to mill.

At every stage in production, acidity, temperature and timing are checked and recorded but it is more the experienced eyes of Graham and his helpers, rather than thermometers or pH-meters, that determine when to stop and start each stage. The process is exact and consistent but the cheesemakers need to respond to daily differences in the curd. Eamonn ascribes these differences to weather and season, and also to which field the cows have been grazing in. Each of the farm's 15 fields is different. This is not a romantic notion but comes down to elements such as the protein content of the grass, which is different in each field. Some fields have more mature grass while others are more recently sown. He says that he and Graham could probably tell you which field the cows have been in just by looking at the curd.

The blocks of curd are fed into the mill and salted as they go in. In

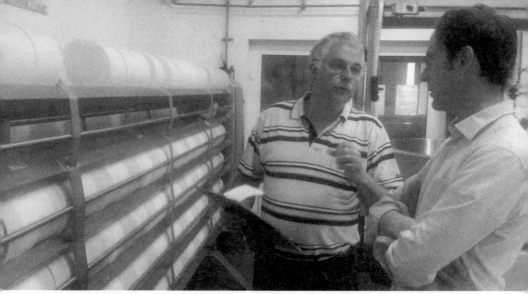

Eamonn and Kevin.

the mill they are cut down to smaller 3cm cubes and the action of the mill pushes even more moisture from the now tight curds. The remainder of the salt, about 3 per cent of the weight of the curd, is added. Cylindrical steel moulds are filled by hand, pushed tight and pressed in. It's 4pm by the time the moulds are put into the horizontal presses, each pushed tight against the next, slowly squeezing out more moisture and packing the curds firmly together. It is 4.30pm by the time the doors are closed, the dairy is silent and the new cheeses wait in peace for the time when they will be prised free from their moulds the next day.

In 2013 we finally began to work with Eamonn on the cheese we felt was attainable from his farm and which we felt was missing from our range of Irish cheeses. By using Eamonn's milk we had the most important element – great raw milk from summer grazing on a single farm. With Eamonn's and Graham's cheesemaking skills, we knew this could be translated into a great cheese. We tweaked his original recipe slightly in different directions to produce a few options. We matured these different batches in our warehouse in Co. Meath, trying slightly different techniques. We tasted the cheeses at different stages, from about three months to 12 months, which allowed us to settle on a single recipe. In the summer of 2014 Eamonn made us two full batches of about 250 wheels each.

Within a couple of days of each batch being made, we had them shipped up to our warehouse in Co. Meath. Here we have a nice maturing room with wooden shelves brought in from France. We originally got them to mature the cheeses that came from a great but sadly deceased cheesemaker, David Tiernan. With a decent dollop of romanticism we feel the yeasts and moulds embedded in the wooden boards and maturing room from his wonderful Comté-style cheese are now passed on to this new creation. After receiving the new cheeses, we gave them a light covering of a modern plastic coat, one without any antibacterial or antifungal properties. This coating allows moisture to be released slowly over the maturation of the cheese but also allows the development of natural microorganisms on the rind. We are big fans of cloth and lard for the rind of Cheddars but we have found that this more modern version suits this cheese and gives us the result we wanted. We have named the cheese 15 Fields, referring to the 15 fields in Eamonn's farm. We are still very early in the development of the cheese but we are really happy with how it is going. No doubt we will make some changes and always work to improve it. We have found the cheese is ready at about eight months but, depending on the batch, can continue to improve up to about 18 months. The texture is firm and has a lovely Cheddar structure, not quite crumbly but with enough moisture so it doesn't feel dry in the mouth. The flavour has a light acidity with a gentle, nutty sweetness and, delightfully, it has a yeasty, earthy background flavour that comes from the rind.

This page: The cheese counter.

Overleaf: A selection of cheese pastes and rinds.

DUNMANUS

A fruity flavoured mature cheese from
Durrus Farmhouse Cheese, West Cork.

€25/KG

KILMORA
MAASDAM-STYLE
FROM KILLEEN
€21·50/KG

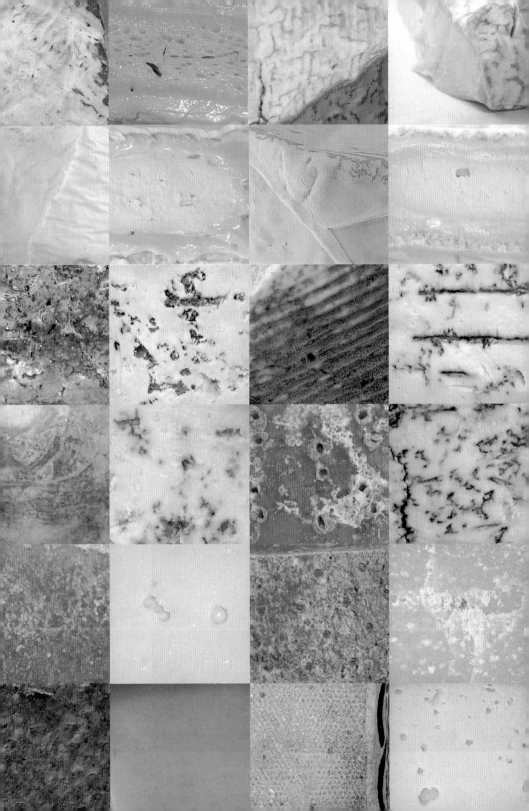

Cheesemaking at Coolea Farmhouse.

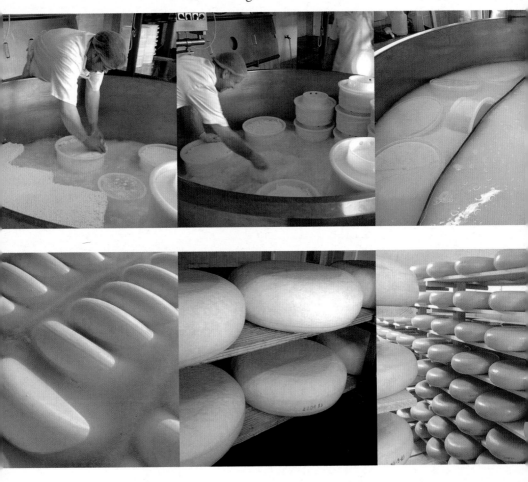

A NEW TRADITION

It is funny that it has taken us 20 years to become *affineurs* with 15 Fields. When we first became cheesemongers, we felt a pressure to be *affineurs*. We didn't understand what it really meant but we were inspired by the great work of Neal's Yard and had ideas about traditional French *affinage*. An *affineur* will typically work with more than one producer of a particular cheese from a specific region, maturing cheeses from different producers together. In many cheese cultures the *affineur* is a lynchpin to the whole system. They buy the cheese from the farms when it is young, which provides cash for the farmer. They use the economies of scale provided by working with many small farms to mature and market the cheese properly, where the farmer perhaps could not. An *affineur* has a very close relationship with their cheesemakers, advising and collaborating on production.

When we opened our shop in Kirwan's Lane in Galway, we simply turned the whole space into a cold, damp maturing room. It was a space where we could care for the cheeses reasonably well. We repeated this system when we opened our larger shop in Galway and our shop in Dublin. We made sure the cheeses were not too dry and tried to ensure we sold them neither too young nor too old. When we got our first warehouse, we began to play with the idea of turning part of it into a cheese cave to do our own *affinage*. We learned the hard way that, at that stage of our careers, we were not *affineurs*. In our experiments with maturing cheeses we found we were adding little to the quality. In some cases our efforts were damaging the cheeses. We were chasing the idea of being *affineurs* because we thought that was what we needed to be, rather than just working out what was the best system for each cheese. Eventually, we established that, for example, working with the makers of West Cork washed-rind cheeses to keep the cheeses in their native environment until they are at their best results in much better cheeses than taking them early and maturing them a couple of hundred miles away in Co. Meath. By no longer chasing the idea of being *affineurs* we became better cheesemongers. Timing is everything. We try to take cheese directly from the farms or from *affineurs* at the right point, allowing the cheeses the time to develop properly in their natural environment. We then use our experience and knowledge of each cheese and how the cheese develops after it leaves the farm to give our customers the cheese at its best.

After that our main job is damage limitation. We try to ensure that transport and storage and packaging do not decrease the quality of the cheese before we manage to get it to our customers. Of course we time the release of our cheese to ensure the optimum ripeness, but it is our relationship with our producers which more than anything allows us to sell the best cheeses. In many ways this relationship is about trusting and allowing our producers to make the best cheeses and not forcing them to focus on unnecessary commercial and operational demands that impede great cheesemaking.

So while we had figured out we were not *affineurs* and we wanted to work as much as possible directly with producers, we also knew the importance of *affinage*. There is a place for genuine *affineurs*, particularly within very traditional cheesemaking cultures. Many of the farmers producing cheese don't have the skill or commercial weight to select, grade and ripen their cheeses. Within these cultures there has always, and still is, a great need for *affineurs*. We work with several across Europe and these skilled people work with small producers, gathering their cheeses, selecting the best ones to be matured on and then looking after the packing and shipping of the cheeses. Very often these *affineurs* also give help and advice to their cheesemakers, guiding them towards producing the best possible cheeses and often providing financial help when things may be difficult. The *affineurs* we work with know the types of cheeses our customers want and are able to select the right ones at the right maturity.

Although these firm, aged cheeses are less delicate than softer ones, they still require careful handling to bring out their best characteristics. All of the wonderful varieties of cheese that have been developed by dairying cultures to preserve milk give us a vast range of flavours and textures. Our job is to seek out the ones that translate their tradition and landscape into something extraordinary and get them to our customers.

NOT-SO-MICROORGANISMS

DURING A TRIP to Italy, we visited a small farm that produced a ewe's milk cheese they matured in a tradition more famous in Sardinia but also practised in Campania. Part of the maturing process involves introducing the larvae of a particular fly to the cheese. Much like the more invisible microbial communities of yeasts and bacteria, these larvae help to break down the cheese, softening the texture and increasing the pungency.

None of our hosts spoke English and we literally had a few words of Italian, so we were introduced to this cheese with a lot of hand waving and a few words like 'special' and Italian words we could understand like 'pecorino', to indicate it was a sheep's cheese. It was presented on a heavy ceramic plate – a small piece of very white cheese with some honey drizzled over it. Maggots were hopping around on it. There was an internal gasp but we were not going to miss this opportunity to try something new. The flavour was typical of the farm pecorinos from southern Italy, particularly ones matured in natural stone buildings where the temperatures can sometimes be quite high. It was more pungent and had a little rancidity. The honey countered this well. The maggots didn't seem to add anything to the flavour but it was surprising how far they could hop. One landed in the wine glass. A swirl and a gulp and it was gone.

GOUDA

Gouda is, in many ways, the perfect cheese. It can be eaten quite young at a couple of months old when it is milky and sweet and smelling floral. It can be aged for many months or even for two or three years. As it ages the flavour intensifies as if cooked down, like caramel or fudge. The sweetness comes from the particular bacteria introduced at the start of cheesemaking and also the production method where the curd is 'washed' or scalded before pressing, reducing the production of tangy lactic acid.

The sweet flavour is instantly appealing and, although aged Gouda can carry powerful flavours, it is rare to find one with the nuances and complexities of other aged cheeses. The name Gouda is not protected and so any factory or farm can use the recipe and label their cheese Gouda. Not only is Gouda one of the most popular industrial cheeses, available in every supermarket around the world in wedges and slices, but it is the most common recipe used by farm-house cheesemakers in areas where there is not a dominant traditional recipe. And it can be made successfully with cows', sheep's and goats' milks.

It is, of course, a traditional cheese of the Netherlands. The Dutch have always been great international traders and this cheese is built to travel. The sturdy wheels can be piled high, their tough rind can take the odd knock, and this, together with their appealing flavour, made them a very successful Dutch export.

The Dutch eat one cheese: Gouda. But that is just a starting point. They take Gouda and flavour it in more ways than you could imagine. They use everything to flavour cheese, from herbs and garlic to cumin, all the way to 10-year-old clove cheese. You can see how many varieties of one cheese one nation of cheese lovers can produce.

MIXED-MILK CHEESES

CHEESES DON'T NEED to be made with either cows' milk or goats' milk, etc.; they can and quite often are made with a mix of milks. These mixed-milk cheeses tend to originate where farming communities herd two milking species together. The most famous of these is Greek feta cheese, where herds of sheep are farmed together with smaller numbers of goats and the milk is mixed for cheese-making. A more modern example is Rogue Creamery's Echo Mountain blue cheese, which uses a combination of cows' and goats' milk to achieve a particular quality rather than for practical purposes.

HOW TO CHOOSE PRESSED
UNCOOKED CHEESE

In general these are reasonably stable cheeses as the rinds are mostly inactive, which means they can take more abuse than the cheeses in the previous chapters and still retain their good flavour and texture. Goudas, in particular, are very hardy and even do quite well in pre-pack sections. The rind of the cheese, or the lack of it, will tell you a lot about the quality of the cheese. Look out for mottled colours and signs of mould and yeast growth, rather than uniform colours and a polished look. Interesting-looking rinds mean that the cheeses have been matured in a way that has allowed the cheese to breathe and develop. The presence of cloth on a Cheddar or other English territorial cheese is a sign of authenticity and will generally mean a decent farmhouse cheese. It is unlikely that any cheese packed in a rindless rectangular block will offer much more than a simple, if not bland, flavour.

Pressed uncooked cheeses are made to age and so should show

some sign of the ageing process – a natural speckled rind and a paste that is a little drier and has a deeper colour under the rind. As always, the best way to choose is by tasting first.

HOW TO STORE PRESSED UNCOOKED CHEESE

Uncooked cheeses are generally well matured and stable. There are, however, cheeses in this category that, although pressed and aged, still have an active rind – such as Tomme. These don't like to be smothered, so stick with a wax paper that will give them some opportunity to breathe. The more sturdy nature of these cheeses allows you not to have to be particular about refrigeration and, if you are blessed with a cool room or an airy cool cupboard in the house, they will generally do better in this environment than in your fridge. A traditional ceramic cheese bell is great. Or an overturned flowerpot on a plate is just as good.

FOOD WE LIKE WITH PRESSED UNCOOKED CHEESE

○ The flavour profiles of these cheeses are quite broad. They range from the tart English territorials to sweet fudgy Gouda. We like sweet acidic chutneys and pickles with the full spectrum of flavours in these cheeses. The ploughman's lunch of cheese, pickle and bread was only given its name in the 1960s as part of a marketing campaign by the British Milk Marketing Board, when ploughmen had long since been replaced by farm machinery. However, ploughmen, builders, roofers and every other type of worker have been eating cheese with homemade pickled vegetables and beer for hundreds of years.

○ There's something about pressed uncooked cheeses that calls for piquancy, a spiky tang rather than a subtle partner. But you don't want anything too vinegary. Naturally fermented sauerkraut, where salted cabbage is pickled in its own acid, is a great partner to Cheddar.

○ The joy of a good cloth-bound or slowly matured Cheddar is as much in its texture as its taste. Those little crystal crunches between the teeth tell you it is a more interesting cheese than its industrially produced cousin. Slicing it thinly with a cheese-paring tool is one way to get that experience, rather than eating it in cubes. Softer fruits are a nice contrast to this. And these cheeses can take blowsier flavours, like ripe juicy plums, soft oozing figs or even cherries if you can get your hands on them.

○ Potatoes may be a cliché but they're a cliché that works: step forward cheese and onion crisps. A slow-roasted boulder of a potato that fluffs into steamy mounds when sliced needs two things – butter and a good grating of Gouda. Smoked or unsmoked. We're not fussy.

○ A good office snack or bowl of sustenance for a child is a mix of raisins, small chunks of Cheddar and nuts. Brazil nuts or toasted walnuts if you're feeling sophisticated; peanuts if you're not. On a cheeseboard, toasted or smoked almonds and Tomme de Savoie are a special pairing.

DRINKS WE LIKE WITH PRESSED UNCOOKED CHEESES

○ There are so many tastes and aromas in this category that it is impossible to give a definite wine match. Apart from Cheddar and claret, Goudas can do very well with a chunky Chardonnay, although mature ones can also pair with heavier reds. An interesting match for many harder styles of cheese are dry sherries, from Manzanilla types to Amontillados.

○ Cheddar and claret are a classic wine and cheese pairing but beers and ciders work well with these cheeses, too. Good ale is our favourite match – it has the depth but also the freshness to cut across the big, caramel flavours of a mature Gouda and to bring out the savoury flintiness of an English territorial.

○ For a non-alcoholic match try elderflower cordial. Make sure it is not too sweet and mix with sparkling water and fresh mint leaves.

SOME OF OUR FAVOURITE PRESSED UNCOOKED CHEESES

15 FIELDS

PRODUCER: Lonergan family
MADE: Waterford, Ireland
PRODUCTION: farmhouse, using their own milk
MILK: raw cows'
RENNET: traditional
TYPE: pressed uncooked, Cheddar

RIND: breathable coating with mould and yeast growth
RIPENING: 8 to 14 months
APPEARANCE: 2.5kg and 5kg wheels
TEXTURE: compact, firm, smooth
TASTE: sweet nuttiness together with savoury notes from the rind

NAMED AFTER the 15 fields that make up the Lonergan family farm, this cheese is a collaboration between the Lonergans and Sheridans Cheesemongers. Our objective is to produce an appealing cheese that comes from and reflects the unique aspects of a single family farm. It is made from April to October when the cattle are out on grass. The cheese is produced on the farm to a traditional Cheddar recipe then shipped the next day to our warehouse in Co. Meath. It is given a breathable coating and then matured on wooden shelves, where it is allowed to develop a coating of moulds and yeasts. The texture is compact but not too dry. The flavour is slightly sweet but with a full mouth and gentle acidity. We are particularly happy that there is a gentle, yeasty, mould flavour coming through the rind, something that would normally be associated with cloth-bound Cheddars.

CORLEGGY

PRODUCER: Croppe family
MADE: Co. Cavan, Ireland
PRODUCTION: farmhouse, using milk from a single herd
MILK: raw goats'
RENNET: vegetarian
TYPE: pressed uncooked

RIND: washed
RIPENING: 1 to 4 months
APPEARANCE: 500g and 2kg wheels
TEXTURE: firm, moist and a little crumbly with age
TASTE: sweet, nutty and herby

SILKE CROPPE has been producing cheese in Cavan for over 20 years. She is a true artisan producer who has never let the difficulties involved in small-scale farming and cheese-making stand in the way of retaining a real authenticity. Along with this, her most famous cheese, she also produces various other wonderful cheeses from raw goats', sheep's and cows' milk. As well as selling to independent retailers and restaurants, she runs the most wonderful cheese stalls that are packed with all shapes, sizes and flavours of cheeses, all from her own production. Silke also runs a small school where visitors can learn the many arts and crafts of cheesemaking. Her son, Tom, is now fully involved and the second generation of Corleggy looks to be in safe hands.

The basic recipe for Corleggy is similar to Cheddar but has evolved to suit the best aspects of the local raw milk and maturing environment of North Cavan Farm. One of the most unique and wonderful aspects of Silke's cheeses are the rinds. The delicate texture is imparted by the cloth used to shape the cheeses, a sea-salt bath hardens and protects the rind but humid maturing allows it to develop subtle moulds. When the cheeses are young, the rind is a delicious and delicate part of the cheese. Each cheese varies a little depending on season and the weather in the fields and conditions in the maturing rooms. The flavour is delicate and nutty, with lots of floral and grassy herbal notes.

WESTCOMBE CHEDDAR

PRODUCER: Westcombe Dairy
MADE: Somerset, England
PRODUCTION: farmhouse, using
their own milk
MILK: raw cows'
NAME PROTECTION: PDO
RENNET: traditional
TYPE: pressed uncooked, Cheddar

RIND: cloth and lard with mould
growth
RIPENING: 12 to 18 months
APPEARANCE: 24kg wheels
TEXTURE: firm and dense but with
a good creaminess
TASTE: some grassy notes with
nuts and caramel, along with a
lovely savoury influence from the
rind

WESTCOMBE DAIRY's journey over the last century has seen it move from traditional Somerset farming and cheesemaking, through pasteurisation and the mechanisation and production of block Cheddar back to raw milk traditional Cheddar. It reflects much of Somerset's relationship with the wonderful food it has given the world. It is only in the last 20 years that the world, and Somerset herself, began to realise that Cheddar is not just a cheesemaking technique to be utilised in the production of a food commodity, but a food that is of a place and a particular farming culture and tradition. Since we first visited the farm and tasted cheeses with the impossibly enthusiastic and energetic young Tom Calver, we have seen the cheese develop from decent but very inconsistent Cheddar into one of our favourite of all cheeses. Tom had just taken over responsibility for the cheesemaking from his father Richard, who continues to look after the farm and work with Tom to produce the quality of milk that is the basis of all great cheese. They have been relentless in their push to produce the best Somerset Cheddar possible.

APPLEBY'S CHESHIRE

PRODUCER: Appleby family
MADE: Shropshire, England
PRODUCTION: farmhouse, using
their own milk
MILK: raw cows'
RENNET: vegetarian
TYPE: pressed uncooked, English
territorial

RIND: cloth and lard
RIPENING: 12 to 18 months
APPEARANCE: 8kg wheels
TEXTURE: flaky and crumbly but
still moist
TASTE: mild, mellow, savoury
flavour and slightly acidic, salty
tang

CHESHIRE IS almost certainly the oldest cheese in the British Isles. Roman records of a hard cheese made on the salt plains of northwest England date back almost 2,000 years and the cheese is mentioned again in the Domesday Book (AD 1086). The sweet, salty tang associated with Cheshire is said to derive from the salty and mineral soils on which the cattle graze, giving a unique flavour to the milk. The Appleby family have been involved in cheesemaking for several generations. Their cheese is the last remaining raw milk farm in Cheshire. In the 1920s there were over 1,200 farmhouse Cheshire producers. The whole family are dedicated to making great Cheshire and they work almost as custodians of this tradition through their farming and cheesemaking. Cheshire has a reputation as a dry, crumbly, acidic cheese but when you open a wheel of Appleby's and take a chunk to your mouth, it is such a different experience. The texture is crumbly and flaky but melts in your mouth. The flavours are so gentle and balanced yet fill your whole mouth, leaving a mineral, lactic flavour. This is truly a great cheese.

BREBIS D'ESTIVE

PRODUCER: various farms
MADE: Béarn, France
PRODUCTION: single farms
MILK: raw sheep's
NAME PROTECTION: AOC, PDO
RENNET: traditional
TYPE: pressed uncooked

RIND: washed
RIPENING: 6 to 12 months
APPEARANCE: 4–5kg wheels
TEXTURE: firm, supple
TASTE: delicate, creamy, sweet, a
little caramel

THE OSSAU-IRATY-TYPE cheeses of the French Pyrenees have been one of our favourites for many years. The variety and range of quality available is daunting. Some years ago we sent our then Dublin shop manager (now a barrister) and Brebis obsessive, Dan Fennelly, to the great *affineur* of this region, Gabriel Bachelet, to find the best cheeses. This is some of what he wrote about his discoveries:

Master *affineur* Gabriel Bachelet introduced me to the *fermier* cheeses of the Vallée d'Ossau, Vallée d'Aspe and Vallée de Barétous in Béarn, south-west France. The Brebis d'Estive cheeses mark the absolute pinnacle of quality and are stamped with a special triangular symbol to distinguish them. This is a pressed, uncooked cheese produced from June to September when 80 shepherds take to huts in the high Pyrenees at 900 to 2,000 metres above sea level. Life is hard in the

mountains, but my conversation with the shepherds indicated that many of these men live for these summer months of solitude in the high pasture. The sheep graze on grass, wild flowers, clover and wild thyme, which give their milk, and ultimately the cheese, an inimitable floral aroma. They are milked by hand twice daily and the raw milk is made into cheese by the shepherd himself, generally in a saucepan over a gas burner. The cheeses are generally aged a minimum of four months, but can age for eight months and more. At five to six months the flavour is lactic and slightly tart but with intense floral aromas unlike any I have come across in any other cheese, and a slight nuttiness. There are also more savoury aromas of mushroom and cellar. For me this cheese is a remarkable testament to the region's ancient transhumance tradition of people moving with their livestock in an increasingly modern world.

COOLEA CHEESE

PRODUCER: Willems family
MADE: Co. Cork, Ireland
PRODUCTION: farmhouse using
milk from a single herd
MILK: cows'
RENNET: traditional

TYPE: pressed uncooked, Gouda
RIND: breathable wax coating
RIPENING: 12 to 24 months
APPEARANCE: 8kg wheels
TEXTURE: firm, smooth
TASTE: caramel, nutty, floral

COOLEA IS made in the hills of Coolea, near Macroom on the Cork/Kerry border in south-west Ireland. Together with Milleens, it was the starting point for modern Irish farmhouse cheese and is still one of the best. Helene Willems and her husband Dick had moved to remote and rural Ireland from urban Holland to pursue a quieter and more fulfilling lifestyle. All was good except for the intolerable quality of cheese available locally to a family used to having access to great quality Dutch Goudas. In 1979, Helene, tired of feeding her young children on processed cheese, decided to try to make some Gouda cheese with the milk from the family herd. Like so many of the pioneers of Irish farmhouse cheese, Helene began experimenting with simple equipment in the kitchen. It wasn't long before she was supplying friends, neighbours and local restaurants with her new creation. Nowadays, Coolea is made by their son Dick junior. Dicky grew up in the dairy playing around the vats and moulds and helping his mother.

His knowledge and instinct for cheesemaking is striking. Dick senior has retired from farming and the cheese is now made from the milk of two neighbouring herds. During the summer, the Willems use milk from a herd about two miles from their farm, whilst during the winter they use milk from a different herd, feeding on pasture which is drier than most others at that time. They never make cheese when the cattle aren't grazing. Dicky insists that all milk used comes from grass-fed animals, as he says that silage can taint the flavour of the cheese as it ages. We tend to go for quite mature cheeses between 12 and 18 months. At this age, the cheese develops a sweet, almost toffee-like flavour and a slight crystalline consistency, not unlike Parmigiano. What makes Coolea so special, even in comparison to the best farm Dutch Goudas, is that it can age and develop robust flavours yet retain a delicateness as well as some of the gentler floral aromas of younger Goudas.

KILLEEN

PRODUCER: Marion Roeleveld
MADE: Galway, Ireland
PRODUCTION: farmhouse, using milk from their own herd
MILK: goats'
RENNET: traditional
TYPE: pressed uncooked, Gouda

RIND: breathable wax coating
RIPENING: 3 to 12 months
APPEARANCE: 4kg wheels
TEXTURE: firm, smooth
TASTE: sweet, nutty, floral, developing a deep caramel flavour as it matures

DUTCH-BORN Marion Roeleveld has been making Killeen's goats' cheese at the Killeen Millhouse outside Ballinasloe, Co. Galway, since 2005. The Gouda-making technique works very well with goats' milk and Marion produces the best we have ever tasted. The rind has a breathable coating applied to the young cheeses. As they develop and age, a thin layer of yeast and mould builds on the rind, helping to develop the flavour. This cheese is at its most impressive when it has aged for eight to 12 months. It develops those classic big Gouda flavours of caramel and fudge. However, what is really special about Killeen is that it is so delicious when still a young cheese. It is mild but, unlike most young Gouda, it is never bland. There is a little sweetness and a lovely floral aroma. It is one of those wonderful cheeses that everyone enjoys: you can put it in children's sandwiches or on the cheeseboard of a Michelin-starred restaurant.

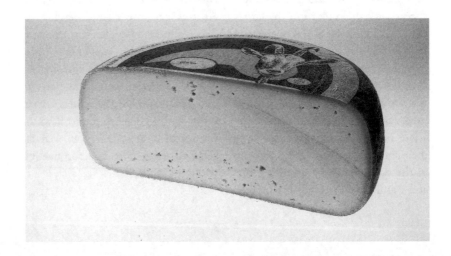

RASCHERA D'ALPEGGIO

PRODUCER: various small co-operatives and farms
MADE: Piedmont, Italy
PRODUCTION: small mountain co-ops or farms
MILK: raw cows', sometimes with a little goats' and sheep's milk
NAME PROTECTION: PDO
RENNET: traditional
TYPE: pressed uncooked

RIND: natural, brushed and washed
RIPENING: minimum 2 months
APPEARANCE: 5–9kg wheels and squares
TEXTURE: slightly elastic with irregular holes
TASTE: savoury and a little salty, with a delicate herbal and floral aroma

WE FIRST came across this cheese in the maturing caves of Beppino Occelli in the Maritime Alps of Cuneo and fell instantly in love with the delicate, nuanced flavours. These cellars built into the side of the mountain are a haven for the rare and wonderful cheeses of Cuneo, where they are matured and ripened with absolute dedication. Raschera is a type of mountain Tomme, typical of Piedmont, but it has a long reputation as being of particular quality. The Alpeggio cheeses are those that are made during the summer months in the high pastures when the cattle are brought up to graze. Raschera is a good cheese but Raschera d'Alpeggio aged well is a magnificent cheese. The rind is beige with speckles of yellow and rusty moulds. The paste is elastic but breaks, revealing some moisture, and the flavour is earthy and savoury with many delicate herbal and floral notes.

RED LEICESTER, SPARKENHOE

PRODUCER: Clarke family
MADE: Leicestershire, England
PRODUCTION: farmhouse, using
their own milk
MILK: raw cows'
RENNET: traditional

TYPE: pressed uncooked, English
territorial
RIND: cloth and lard
RIPENING: 6 to 9 months
APPEARANCE: 10kg wheels
TEXTURE: compact, firm but moist
TASTE: rich savoury with a little
sweetness and bite

WALK DOWN any supermarket dairy isle and you will no doubt see plenty of Red Leicester blocks, yet this is the first real Red Leicester to be made in Leicestershire for over 50 years. Sparkenhoe is named after the farm where David and Jo Clarke revived this great British territorial cheese in 2005. There had been a long tradition of cheesemaking on the farm stretching back to the mid eighteenth century, but this died out in 1875 when the Chapman family, who had made cheese there for over a century, retired from cheese-making. Local dairy farmers David and Jo Clarke took over Sparkenhoe Farm in the early 2000s. Having grown up with factory versions of Red Leicester, the couple were initially sceptical of the virtues of the cheese. However, after speaking to a number of older people in the area who remembered farmhouse versions of Red Leicester from their youth, they decided to give cheese-making a go. David and Jo have managed to wrestle Red Leicester from the grasp of factory producers and reinvent one of the great lost British territorial cheeses, a great achievement for a couple who have only recently become involved in cheesemaking. The cheese is beautiful to just look at. The cloth-bound rind is a mottled beige and grey and, when opened, there is a deep orange colour that comes from the addition of annatto, a natural dye. The paste is really compact yet not at all dry. The flavour is rich savoury and nutty and has a multilayered complexity which is very smooth.

MARYLAND CHEDDAR

PRODUCER: A. J. Barber
MADE: Somerset, England
PRODUCTION: farmhouse, using their own milk
MILK: cows'
RENNET: vegetarian

TYPE: pressed uncooked, block Cheddar
RIND: none, matured in plastic
RIPENING: 12 months
APPEARANCE: 20kg blocks
TEXTURE: compact and firm
TASTE: nutty with a tang

THE BARBERS have been making Cheddar on their farm in Shepton Mallet since the early 1800s. Block Cheddar is not a product we would normally promote but we have to be honest and say that we and our customers really like this cheese. This is despite it being made using modern techniques that don't allow for rind development and the additional flavours that brings, or the use of raw milk and the complexity of flavour that results. The Barbers do retain and protect many traditional aspects of West Country cheesemaking whilst producing their block Cheddar, though. All the milk used comes from the Barber's 3,000-acre farm, which is run to very high environmental and sustainable standards. Starter cultures are one of the most important but least discussed elements of cheesemaking. The Barbers are not only unique among block Cheddar makers in using traditional starter cultures rather than freeze-dried modern versions, they have actually revived traditional starter cultures in the region. The starters are used by the Barbers for their own Maryland Cheddar but are also used by some of the very top producers of artisan Cheddar in Somerset. The result is a really rich, tasty Cheddar.

KNOCKDRINNA MEADOW

PRODUCER: Helen Finnegan
MADE: Kilkenny, Ireland
PRODUCTION: farmhouse, using
  milk from a single herd
MILK: sheep's
RENNET: vegetarian

TYPE: pressed uncooked
RIND: washed
RIPENING: 2 to 4 months
APPEARANCE: 4kg wheels
TEXTURE: firm, moist and smooth
TASTE: sweet, nutty and lactic

HELEN IS one of those cheese-makers who is endlessly creative, always producing a new cheese. She makes bloomy, washed and hard cheeses from cows', goats' and sheep's milk. All the milk used in her sheep's milk cheeses comes from Henry Clifton Browne's herd of East Friesian ewes, which also provide the raw material for Crozier Blue made by the Grubb Family. Helen began making Knockdrinna Meadow in 2007 in response to the constant requests she received at her market stall for a hard sheep's milk cheese. It is somewhat similar to the French sheep's milk cheeses of the Pyrenees but has a little more moisture and the rind is a little more active. The flavour is quite mild and really pleasant, with a sweet nuttiness and a little lactic tang, combined with that rich, fatty flavour provided by the sheep's milk.

And here are some favourites from our friends around the world.

MACCAGNO

PRODUCER: Caseificio Pier Luigi Rosso
MADE: Piedmont, Italy
PRODUCTION: small dairy, using milk from neighbouring mountain farms
MILK: cows'
RENNET: traditional
TYPE: semi-hard pressed

RIND: medium consistency, brown colour, often with yellow mould – Maccagno printed on one side
RIPENING: 60 days
APPEARANCE: 2kg wheel
TEXTURE: firm dough, small holes might appear
TASTE: delicate and refined with hints of butter

UP IN THE mountains of the ever-busy Piedmont you can still find a piece of history left behind. So it is for Maccagno, one of the best-kept secrets in the Piedmont's gastronomical tradition. It is a classic Toma, traditionally produced directly in the *crotin*, the little building that in the summer was a shelter for the farmer and cellar for his cheese on the high green pastures (the name itself, Maccagno, comes from Alpe Maccagno, a pasture 2,000 metres high, located in front of Monte Rosa). It was made with freshly milked milk, and the average heating temperature of the curd never reached more than 36°C. This was due to the limitations of the *crotin* (there was not a lot of combustible material around, for example) but it ensured a uniquely genuine mountain cheese, still rich with all the mountain's green and flowery smells. It was then sold during the autumn/winter in the nearby cities, mostly Torino, where it enriched polenta (a traditional dish, like porridge but made with cornmeal, which is drowned in melted cheese, saucy meat and tomato). It is said that Quintino Sella, a notorious nineteenth-century Italian politician, used to keep a substantial reserve of Maccagno in his *cantina* for his personal use, and that he was particularly distressed when one day some thieves whisked all his wheels away. Nowadays the Rosso brothers (Enrico and

Riccardo) carry on this tradition with the utmost care: their Maccagno is raw milk and seasoned on white pine shelves, like it was in the *crotin*. *Karl-Heinz Berthold and Laura Gandolfi, gourm.it, Italy*

MANCHEGO PASAMONTES CURADO

PRODUCER: Maria Dolores Palomares Pasamontes
MADE: Castilla-La Mancha, Spain
PRODUCTION: small dairy, using milk from five herds
MILK: raw sheep's
NAME PROTECTION: DOP, PDO
RENNET: traditional
TYPE: pressed uncooked
RIND: breathable coating
RIPENING: 12 months
APPEARANCE: 2.5kg wheel

TEXTURE: crumbly, granulated in texture at the same time that the paste acquires a butterscotch, ivory-yellow colour
TASTE: firm and compact consistency – the paste has some scattered small 'eyes'; an intense and alluring aroma and its taste is intense, lingering and almost piquant, with a wonderful nutty hint that leaves an extremely pleasant aftertaste

THIS INCREDIBLE cheese has the honour of being made in one of the oldest dairies in Spain, inhabited by the same family since 1896. The dairy is in Moral de Calatrava in the province of Ciudad Real (Castilla-La Mancha). Ciudad Real is the province that has the oldest and biggest tradition of Manchego DOP. The Pasamontes family maintains the artisanal and handmade techniques but combines them with new technology to process the cheese. This year they have improved the rind a lot. It has a natural matte aspect and is edible, too, which is an exception in a Manchego cheese. The aged cheese is dark yellow and has the traditional pattern of the esparto creases on the sides and on the top and bottom of the cheese – the so-called 'flower' or pattern/mark traditionally made by the wooden press slats. The flavour and aromas of this product have always been my favourite. When I taste it, I can recall my childhood, so I can say it is part of my life: one of the best places in the world that I love to be is inside a Manchego maturing chamber. It is important to underline that this cheese was a pioneer in being exported abroad as it was soon 'discovered'. *Mar Sanz, Arca Gourmet, Spain*

MRS KIRKHAM'S LANCASHIRE

PRODUCER: Graham Kirkham
MADE: Goosnargh, Lancashire
PRODUCTION: farmhouse, single farm, using their own milk
MILK: raw cows'
RENNET: traditional
TYPE: pressed uncooked, English territorial
RIND: cloth-bound, buttered
RIPENING: 2 to 12 months

APPEARANCE: 8kg and 20kg truckles
TEXTURE: thought of as crumbly, though can be creamy, almost frothy
TASTE: round, warm and expressive of the milk; more buttery and milky when young, with full flavours similar to Salers as it ages

LANCASHIRE EXEMPLIFIES the British mesophilic tradition (using moderate-heat bacteria). It is very slow to make, using minimal starter. It is forgiving of time, in the same way that a sourdough starter is compared to commercial yeast when making bread. By the time the acidity begins to rise, all the mechanical work has been done; most of the whey has been worked out of the curd. The cheeses are made using curds that are one and two days old, adding depth to flavour and texture. I select batches for Neal's Yard Dairy every month and this involves tasting through every day's make.

Recently the cheeses have fit a warm, creamy, frothy style or a dry, more crumbly style. Both are delicious and can be said to have a characteristic buttery crumble. We will often choose some of each. Graham learned to make cheese from his mother and has been making it since the mid 1990s. Now his sons Shaun and Mike are involved as well. Mike makes cheese with Graham and Shaun runs the farm. I love this cheese year round. At home we eat it alone, with dinner, we cook with it and send it to school in my kid's lunches. It stays on the counter and never goes near the fridge. Once it has been warm for a few days, it seems to expand. I feel like I'm eating cheese cake. *David Lockwood, Neal's Yard Dairy, London*

MOUNTAIN COTIJA

PRODUCER: various farms
MADE: Michoacán, Mexico
PRODUCTION: farm
MILK: raw and pasteurised cows'
RENNET: vegetarian
TYPE: uncooked, hard

RIND: washed
RIPENING: 4 to 36 months
APPEARANCE: 28kg cylinder
TEXTURE: firm to granular
TASTE: rich, salty-sweet

A FARMSTEAD aged cheese made in the mountains of central Mexico, Cotija is made with raw cows' milk and aged for up to 36 months. The flavour is gamey, with notes of butter and rock salt. Perfect to eat alone with candied fruits or to sprinkle on top of Mexican corn dishes. Aged by Esteban Barragán and Rogelia Villa, it is better at 12 months when the small crystals start to develop. I pair it always with a good mezcal or tequila. *Carlos Yescas, Lactography, USA*

VERMONT SHEPHERD, VERANO

PRODUCER: Major Farm
MADE: Vermont, USA
PRODUCTION: farm, using their
   own milk
MILK: raw sheep's
RENNET: traditional

TYPE: pressed uncooked
RIND: washed
RIPENING: 3 to 5 months
APPEARANCE: 3kg wheels
TEXTURE: firm
TASTE: sweet hay, nutty, earthy

I WENT TO Vermont to see Cindy Major. She's a real pioneer lady in American cheese. Her farm took my breath away. There was a sheepdog chasing all the sheep, barking at them. It was a storybook scene and Cindy is a storybook innovator, really. She learned how to make Pyrenees mountain cheese in France, then brought that technique to Vermont and put her own unique spin on it. Her Vermont Shepherd cheese ranks highly among my all-time favourites. She's really an American treasure. *Rob Kaufelt, Murray's Cheese, New York, USA*

PYENGANA

PRODUCER: Pyengana Dairy Company
MADE: Tasmania, Australia
PRODUCTION: farmhouse, using milk from their own herd
MILK: cows'
RENNET: traditional
TYPE: pressed uncooked, Cheddar
RIND: cloth and lard, natural moulds
RIPENING: 8 to 12 months
APPEARANCE: traditional English cloth-bound Cheddar with speckled mould
TEXTURE: dense, firm when young and becomes more crumbly in texture with grainy crystalline crunchy flecks when matured
TASTE: rich, earthy, cellar-floor, musky flavours and aroma, with more caramelised flavours when aged

HAVING LIVED in the UK and having worked at Neal's Yard Dairy, one can't help but develop an immense appreciation for and love of English cloth-bound Cheddar. On returning to Australia, finding a quality Cheddar of similar integrity was of high priority. Cheesemaker Jon Healy, from Tasmania, is a fourth-generation dairy farmer and his family produce this traditional English style of cloth-bound Cheddar that rocks my world. Pyengana Cheddar is an impressive example of the Australian artisan cheese movement. Earthy, tangy, long-lasting, rich flavour profiles prevail throughout this crumbly farmhouse cheese experience. 'Pyengana' translates as 'meeting of two rivers' in the language of the first Australians and is the name of the

region in which the cheese is pro-
duced. *Claudia Bowman, McIntosh* & *Bowman Cheesemongers, Sydney, Australia*

SQUARE WHEEL

PRODUCER: Twig Farm, Michael
  Lee
MADE: Vermont, USA
PRODUCTION: farmhouse, using
  milk from their own herd
MILK: raw goats'
RENNET: traditional
TYPE: pressed uncooked
RIND: natural rind

RIPENING: 3 months
APPEARANCE: free-form square
  shape
TEXTURE: semi-firm and sliceable,
  yet toothsome with slight
  crumble
TASTE: rich buttermilk and cream,
  lemony, notes of hazelnut

ONE OF MY favourite cheeses from a man who went square 'because he was fed up with the circle shape', the Square Wheel is made by ladling curd into cheesecloth and squeezing until a non-conformist, four-sided form takes hold. His Goat Tomme is a similar recipe but cylindrical. The Square is left to develop its flavours in the cellar under the Lee family's home. The natural rind takes on the ambient yeasts and moulds of the region – sometimes grey, brown and white colours and a light fuzz – but the fresh flavour of the goats' milk always shines through. *Kirstin Jackson, It's Not You, It's Brie, California*

RECIPES

SPRING

Butternut Squash and Courgette Quiche with Pyrenees Brebis / Ossau-Iraty

You don't have to make the pastry for this but if you do you get to add the secret ingredient – that teaspoon of ground cumin gives a lovely background warmth to everything. This makes a gorgeous supper with a fresh spinach or fiery mizuna leaf salad.

SERVES 6

90g butter, plus extra for greasing

100g plain flour

100g wholemeal flour

½ teaspoon salt

1 teaspoon ground cumin

a splash of cold water

1 small butternut squash, or ½ large one

1 tablespoon olive oil

1 clove garlic

1 medium courgette, sliced into long ovals

4 eggs

200ml natural yoghurt

50ml milk

120g Brebis / Ossau-Iraty, grated

freshly ground black pepper

Preheat the oven to 180ºC and butter a large springform tin.

Put the flours, salt and cumin into a food processor and whizz to mix.

Cut the butter into small chunks and add them to the processor. Whizz to turn the mixture breadcrumby.

Add a splash of ice-cold water to the processor and mix slowly until the pastry forms a dough.

Turn the dough on to a floured surface and knead briefly before wrapping it in clingfilm and resting in the fridge. (Whisper it – if you're in a hurry you can skip this stage. The sky won't fall in. Your pastry case will just shrink a little.)

Roll the pastry out on to a sheet of parchment paper and use this to lift it into the prepared tin, flattening it into the corners with the paper still on the top and trimming the edges. Using dried beans or baking beans to weigh down your pastry, bake the pastry case blind for about 20 minutes or until it's golden brown.

Meanwhile, cut your butternut squash in two and spoon out the seeds and thready flesh. Peel off the hard skin and then slice into half moons. Put these in a bowl with the olive oil and coat them well with your hands. Tip the contents on to a baking tray and bake in the oven alongside the pastry case. (If you're in a hurry you can roast the squash in its skin and scoop out the flesh with a spoon.)

Chop or crush the garlic to a fine pulp and fry in a large pan with a little olive oil over a medium heat. Add the courgette slices and turn off the heat. You're just trying to coat the courgette with the garlicky oil and soften their outsides.

Mix the egg, yoghurt, milk and grated cheese together with a good grinding of black pepper. Arrange the squash segments on the bottom of the pastry case and put the courgette ovals on top. Pour the eggy cheese mixture over the vegetables and then bake the quiche in the oven for another 30 minutes, or until the middle no longer wobbles.

SUMMER

Rachel's Cheddar Biscuits

This is what we made as children if there weren't the ingredients for ginger snaps or buns. They were also more approved of by grown ups, since they have no sugar – we could get away with making them more often and eating them more quickly! We also thought they were kind of sophisticated.

MAKES ABOUT 12 DEPENDING ON THE SIZE OF YOUR CUTTER

100g butter, salted

100g good Cheddar cheese (Montgomery's is great), finely grated

1 egg yolk

½ teaspoon cayenne pepper, paprika, black pepper, mustard powder or whatever spice you like

100g flour, sifted

Preheat the oven to 220°C and grease a baking tray. Chase all dogs from the kitchen and wash your hands.

In a large bowl, cream the butter until fluffy. Gradually beat in the cheese, egg yolk and choice of spice. Fold in the flour to form a dough. Refrigerate for an hour or so.

Chase all dogs from the kitchen again. Take the dough out of the fridge and knead for 3 minutes. Roll out on to a lightly floured surface until it is 5mm thick. Cut into narrow rectangles or use pastry cutters to make whatever shape you fancy. The biscuits are quite crumbly, so simple shapes work best.

Place the biscuits on the prepared baking tray and bake in the preheated oven for about 10 minutes, or until slightly browned. Careful now – they are hot. Resist eating until they have cooled down!

AUTUMN

Kevin's Cheese and Onion Toastie

Cheese on toast may well be my favourite food. It's taken a long time to perfect my recipe. I think this nails it.

SERVES 1

1 slice white sourdough bread
butter
½ teaspoon English mustard
25g Sparkenhoe Red Leicester, thickly sliced
1 small onion, thinly sliced

Lightly toast your bread until it is barely crisp.

Butter it lightly and then spread over a scant hint of mustard.

Place the cheese slices on top. (If you're particularly hungry you could pop a thick slice of carved ham under the cheese.)

Scatter the slices of onion over the top of the cheese.

Place under a hot grill until the onion is cooked and the top layer of the cheese slice has melted. The trick is to remove the toastie from the grill when the top of the cheese has melted but the cheese underneath is just warmed.

WINTER

Smoked Knockanore and Gubbeen Chorizo Baked Potatoes

Potatoes and cheese are a brilliant combination but when you throw in the smokiness of Eamonn's cheese and Fingal Ferguson's chorizo you've got one of the tastiest supper dishes imaginable. These baked potatoes take a bit of time but most of it is oven time rather than slaving-over-a-hot-dish preparation time.

SERVES 4 AS A MAIN COURSE AND 8 AS AN ACCOMPANIMENT

4 large Rooster potatoes, cleaned but unpeeled

olive oil

salt

a knob of butter

120g Gubbeen chorizo, cut into small pieces

2 large shallots, peeled and finely sliced

100g crème fraîche

1 teaspoon Dijon mustard

200g Oakwood Smoked Knockanore

Preheat the oven to 180°C.

Rub the outsides of the Roosters with olive oil and a little salt. Slice them into oval halves. Place them on a roasting tray and bake them for up to an hour until the skins are crisp and the insides are soft.

While they're roasting, melt the butter in a frying pan over a medium heat and fry the chorizo until crispy. Remove the chorizo from the pan with a slotted spoon and set aside.

Turn the heat right down, add the shallots to the chorizo oil and butter in the pan and fry slowly until they are golden and melting, for up to 15 minutes.

Turn off the heat and return the chorizo to the pan. Stir in the crème fraîche and mustard and grate in 150g of the cheese.

When the potatoes are cooked, scoop out some of the flesh, leaving a good thick shell of skin and flesh behind. Mix the cooked potato with the chorizo and cheese mixture and then spoon it back into the potato skin shells.

Sprinkle the last of the cheese over the top of your stuffed shells, return to the oven and bake for 15–20 minutes, until the cheese is crispy and brown on top.

CHAPTER EIGHT

PRESSED COOKED CHEESES

FROM PARMIGIANO TO EMMENTAL – THE CHEESE VAULT AND CHEESE ON TRIAL

My sense with Ireland was that the raw materials here, the land and the milk, were extraordinary. They were super high quality. But they were all being turned into corporate-style agri-foods.

Bill Hogan, cheesemaker

These are the great cheeses of the Alps and Jura mountains; the giants in stature and in personality. They are the big cheeses that one man would struggle to carry; sturdy cheeses built to last. They are cheeses that are made and aged in a way that builds complex flavour profiles without losing delicate nuances. These are cheeses like Gruyère, Beaufort, Comté and Emmental and the Grana cheeses of the Po Valley in northern Italy, most famously Parmigiano-Reggiano and Grana Padano.

What separates these cheeses from the other hard and semi-hard cheeses is an additional step taken in their production: the cooking of the curd. This cooking expels more whey than is achieved through cutting and pressing. But it also encourages a different family of bacteria to take an active role in the cheese.

The cooking stage happens after the curd is cut and while it is swimming in the separated whey. This mass of soft solids and liquid is gently heated in the vat. The cheesemaker brings the temperature up to at least 40°C but often as high as 55°C, and then the temperature is held while the small curds are stirred, contracting and becoming drier as they are heated.

Bacteria naturally present in the milk and added by the cheesemaker can be divided into two types: thermophilic and mesophilic. Thermophilic bacteria love higher heats and are active in temperatures up to 55°C, while mesophilic bacteria prefer cooler conditions and are active only up to temperatures of 39°C. Cooking the curd at these high temperatures means that the thermophilic bacteria are given the upper hand. The curds and whey are colonised by these heat-loving bacteria, who digest lactose to create lactic acid, and different enzymes to those produced by their chillier mesophilic cousins. They create different kinds of flavours and textures as they interact with the proteins and fats in the cheese.

After they're cooked, the drier curds are squeezed under great pressure, making them perfectly suited to ageing for long periods. These cheeses are quite often (but not always) made in large wheels. The great cart wheels of Gruyères and Comtés weigh between 35 and 40kg, the weight of a large child. Parmigiano-Reggiano are heavy half barrels of 35–40kg and the super heavyweight champion is Swiss Emmental – a wheel of which weighs in at about 100kg.

The great heft and size of these cheeses contribute to their ability to age well. The larger the cheese, the less rind there is per kilo, therefore less surface through which they can lose moisture. If we see cheese as an invention to preserve the nutrition of milk, allowing it to be

stored for long periods and transported over great distances, then these are the perfect cheeses.

They make us wonder whether the cheesemongers of 100 years ago were a lot stronger than us. It just doesn't seem practical to make 100kg wheels of cheese to be transported across the Alps before decent roads and forklift trucks. But the explanation lies not in cheese-monger muscle but in taxation. Emmental wheels only grew to colossal proportions in the nineteenth century when Russia intro-duced import taxes on cheese not by weight but by unit. Canny cheesemakers realised that the bigger they made their cheeses the lower the taxes. New railway systems and large dairies in the Emme Valley also allowed the production and transportation of these giant, tax-wheeze cheeses.

Most people are familiar with the classic Gruyère and Grana-style cheeses in this category but there are many other wonderful varia-tions. Switzerland is really the home of these great cheeses. Apart from Gruyères and Emmentals there are also other fairly well-known

Swiss cheeses like Sbrintz, Appenzeller and Tilsiter along with numerous others, many made by single-family-owned dairies. Versions of Gruyère and Emmental are also produced in France – we have, of course, Comté, Emmental de Savoie and Beaufort. In Italy, Parmigiano-Reggiano and Grana Padano are accompanied by many similar variations produced by individual dairies.

But these are not just practical cheeses, they are also delicious. The unique production methods, together with long ageing, produce delicate aromas and complex flavours. There are so many flavours to be savoured when tasting these cheeses. In their base notes they remind us of comforting cooked foods like roasted nuts, browned butter and slow-cooked bone broths, then they have the sweet finish of the milk that made them.

Their home is the mountain slopes and valleys of the Alps. Wonderfully, very many of these great cheeses are still produced with raw milk, allowing the unique flavours and aromas of the pastures to be carried in the cheeses. Fundamental to the origin of these cheeses are the farming practices of the people who inhabit the mountain ranges that produce them. An obvious reality of farming in mountainous areas is that the pastures are revealed every summer by the melting snows, and the rich resource of these pastures is harnessed by farmers who move with their animals up into the mountains. Making cheese on the mountain slopes to preserve the nutritional and commercial value of this resource is inseparable to the farming culture. This culture of mountain cheesemaking is by no means limited to this cheese type, but no other one is so defined by the relationship of farmer and mountain. These cheeses also give us a sense of place, a kind of taste travel experience that we don't get with other cheeses. Handling and eating Swiss cheeses always takes us to the area in which they are produced – the Alpine pastures that are among the most spectacular landscapes on the planet.

Although the Alps and the mountainous landscapes that move from Switzerland into northern Italy and eastern France are the home of these cheeses, this most efficient way of preserving milk has spread across the world. Many industrial and farm cheesemakers have adapted the pressed cooked cheese method to produce countless varieties of cheese. It was the Romans who first brought rennet-coagulated cheese to Switzerland, and the Italians were producing hard, aged cheeses long before the Swiss – for 800 years or more the people of Parma and the surrounding Po Valley have been making probably the most successful and famous cheese in the world: Parmigiano-Reggiano.

PROTECTED LABELS

The French have been using state laws to protect the origin of traditional foods since 1411, when Roquefort was regulated by a parliamentary decree. In the early part of the twentieth century, regulations on the protection of traditional wines and foods began in earnest, with a French national institute set up in 1935. Wines, spirits and many foods including olives, peppers, meats and honeys as well as cheeses are granted an AOC (Appellation d'Origine Contrôlée) label, which translates as controlled designation of origin. Under the AOC system it is not only the geographical area that must be respected but also production and farming methods. The Italians followed suit and began to introduce their DOP (Denominazione di Origine Protetta) label in the 1950s. Spain operates a similar protection system under the label DO (Denominación de Origen) and the Portuguese have the DOP label (denominação de origem controlada) while the Swiss operate AOP (Appellation d'Origine Protégée) and IGP (Indication Géographique Protégée) labels.

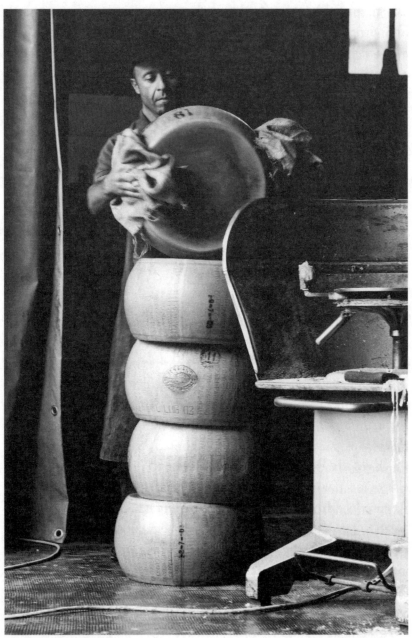

Sergio Peroli in the Craver warehouse.

In the early 1990s the EU brought in a three-tier system of origin and production control for traditional foods that could be applied across Europe. Two of them (PDO – Protected Designation of Origin – and PGI – Protected Geographical Indication) assign a geographical area to a product, with the PGI also regulating some of the production methods. A third category, Traditional Specialities Guaranteed (TSG), emphasises traditional ingredients and methods in a product that must have been made and sold for at least 25 years.

In an age when intellectual property protection can become a means for large pharmaceuticals, agri-food companies and technology giants to maximise profits and dumb down flavours, it is heartening to see a system that protects food and agricultural communities against the worst aspects of international trade. Critics say these rules suffocate traditions rather than allowing them to evolve and adapt. But in a food world dominated by globalisation we believe these systems have at their heart a respect for craft.

The protection by the French State of Comté cheese has had multilayered benefits for the farmers, cheese producers and *affineurs* in the production zone as well as for French agriculture and culture and the wider cheesemaking world. The regulations have not only protected high-quality cheese but have guaranteed a sustainable income for over 2,500 family farms.

Stipulating that Comté farms only farm traditional breeds of cattle on ample free grazing and without the use of GMO feed has protected the landscape and environment of the Jura region.

By having the use of raw milk written into the regulations, Comté along with Roquefort and Parmigiano Reggiano provide the best protection against the increasing pressure for raw milk cheese production to be regulated out of existence. Large retailers need to have these world-famous brands on their shelves, so they must accept the use of raw milk in their production. And the cheese sells like hot cakes. The regulation system has protected a food that people love.

THE CHEESE VAULT

When Seamus took off for Milan in 1998, he had one goal: to source the best Parmesan he could find. For the first few years we had been buying our Parmesan from wholesalers in London. The quality was good but we knew there was better out there and, as with every cheese, we yearned to get closer to the makers.

He was picked up at Milan airport by his Italian friend, Enrico Fantasia. Enrico was a French horn player who hated orchestras and had sought refuge in wine and cheese. He has since moved to Ireland, where he works in partnership with Sheridans, importing the best of Italian and other old-world wines. Enrico has an encyclopaedic knowledge of cheese and wine, and his father lived in Emilia-Romagna, the birth place of Parmesan cheese, or to give it its formal Italian name: Parmigiano-Reggiano.

Enrico had not seen his father for a while and Seamus had the feeling he wasn't looking forward to telling him he had given up his music to follow his dream and work in a wine bar, so they spent an hour cleaning the car to give a good impression. When they arrived, Seamus kept his head down until dinner.

The meal was in an old, rural, ramshackle restaurant with chicken pens in the car park and hens running around outside. Seamus was greeted by the restaurant's patron, Cesare. This old man was very close to Enrico. A few years earlier he had organised Enrico's mother's funeral in this very place. The visiting Irishman was ushered in and immediately given a huge lump of Parmesan and a half pint of

Lambrusco, the local red wine. This would be the ritual everywhere Seamus went on that trip – being presented with a hunk of cheese every place he visited.

Wherever he went, there seemed to be someone who knew a friend whose brother worked in a dairy that, for sure, was the best Parmesan producer in the entire region. This speech was always accompanied with Lambrusco and a hard stare as Seamus sampled the cheese in question. Then there was the food of Emilia-Romagna, which is not for wimps. First you get a version of pork crackling wrapped neatly in a white napkin. The next course is the region's other famous delicacy, prosciutto. This is cut at your table in slices so thin they fall quivering like skin on to the plate. It is a knife skill you know you will never have. Then comes a clear broth with pork-stuffed tortellini swimming below the surface – hot parcels of piggy flavour wrapped in soft, homemade pasta envelopes. You are now full and content and drinking soft red wine. Then out comes the trolley – the Carrello dei Bolliti. On one side is a selection of boiled meats and offal accompanied by boiled vegetables. On the other side is a selection of roasted meats. Being of a skinny disposition, Seamus was always given a good selection from both sides. Only the vegetables were optional.

They travelled around the area eating Parmesan and drinking Lambrusco. They visited a tiny ancient producer who made only two cheeses a day, watching as that day's 800 litres of milk were crafted into two wheels of Parmesan. These then joined the cheeses from the previous 24 days of production in a white sink that went the full way around three walls of the room in an unbroken line. The cheeses rested in this salty brine, which was older than the men who worked there. Once the cheese was made, ricotta was made from the whey – cooked in a tin pot over a camp stove. Free ricotta was a bonus for the cheesemakers.

Seamus and Giorgio.

The last place they visited was Quara, high in the mountains of Emilia. This seemed to be what Seamus had been seeking. They spent all day tasting and looking in awe at the massive storage rooms where the Parmesan wheels rested and turned golden brown. They visited the farms that supplied the milk. They even tasted the hay the cows were fed on, chewy threads of grassy sweetness. Numbers and details were exchanged. Seamus's job was done. Enrico dropped him at a train station and Seamus travelled north to seek out an organisation he had read about called Slow Food. It was in the little town of Bra where he found the birthplace of this food movement that went on to change the world. It was here that Seamus met his first Parmesan ager, Giorgio Cravero.

SLOW FOOD PRESIDIA CHEESES

ONE OF THE most important projects undertaken by Slow Food is their Presidia. Presidia are the instruments used internationally by Slow Food to protect high-quality foods in danger of extinction. They work to preserve the food, the species, communities and/or habitats that form the basis of the food production.

The first step in creating a Presidia is to record all of the elements that come together to make the production of the food possible and which make it unique and of great quality. Most importantly, the Presidia then work to protect these foods through promoting them as great foods for everyone, not museum pieces.

There are 70 Presidia dedicated to protecting unique cheeses, in 13 countries around the world. The first cheese Presidium was for Casizolu, a cows' milk cheese from Sardinia. Though now famous around Italy, it was once little known, a rarity from an island known mostly for sheep's milk cheeses. As well as working to protect little-known cheeses, Presidia have also been created to protect what seem like quite established cheeses. In these cases it is the smaller scale, more unique and original versions of a cheese, often pushed out of the market by more commercial versions, which the Presidia work to protect. The work of Slow Food internationally and the Presidia at local level is invaluable for the protection of cheese culture. The focus on taste quality in conjunction with the cheese's place in the community works in a much more detailed and nuanced way than the national and international protection schemes such as AOC and PDO.

Giorgio is the sixth G. Cravero and is the same age as Seamus. When you meet someone with so much knowledge and so much history behind them, there can be a feeling of almost awe. Giorgio never let that feeling stand. Neither did he come across as a suave northern Italian foodie. In fact, he looks quite Irish with a reddish tinge to his hair and glasses that don't hide his open, kind and immediately welcoming face.

Giorgio isn't small but looks it when standing beside his father, who even in his eighties stands proudly, shoulders back and reaching well over six feet. The conversation immediately jumped to Ireland and Giorgio's love of the country where he had holidayed a couple of times. Then they walked down a laneway and into a magical yard, one of the most wondrous places Seamus had ever seen or smelled. Walking through the big wooden doors, you are immediately struck by the oily sweet smell of Parmigiano. Then you look around trying to take in the scale of the place. There is row after row of floor-to-ceiling shelves full of neatly placed wheels of cheese. Giorgio explained his family history and their connection with the cheese. He told how his great-great-great-grandfather left Bra one day and came back with a cart of selected cheese for the market in Turin. Then they built up a trade in the fabulous but quite rare Bra cheese, which is made in the hills and mountains surrounding the town after which it was named. Over the years, the family focused more and more on the selection and maturation of Parmigiano-Reggiano.

He cautioned Seamus about buying direct from the producer. We would not get a constant supply of quality, he told him. We would not get cheese properly aged. We should trust him and his family and leave the selection to them. It was a big promise. And a cynic might see it as the sales spiel of a Parmesan agent but we felt that a business doesn't last six generations unless it delivers on its promises. We trusted his word and we've never regretted it. Every year Giorgio selects and buys cheese at 12 months, then ages it for a further 12 months before sending it on to us.

The 150-year-old family business is called G. Cravero Affineurs. Giorgio's father is called Giacomo and his grandfather was called

Giorgio. His great-grandfather was called – yes, you've guessed it, Giacomo. And, of course, Giorgio Cravero's son is called Giacomo. So G. Cravero Affineurs continues. Giorgio deals with just three of the 300 Parmigiano-Reggiano producers because he believes these three farms produce the best Parmesan in Italy. Pinned down, he finds it difficult to explain exactly why each of his dairies produces the best cheese. It is not one or two stark differences but a continuous dedication to producing Parmigiano of outstanding taste and texture. Giorgio points out that under the regulations governing the production of Parmigiano, feed for the cattle cannot be brought in from outside of the production zone but this rule is often ignored. He insists that the hay for feeding the cattle in his dairies is locally grown and believes this is one of the important details.

The strictly regulated production of Parmigiano starts, as with all cheese, with the milk. If you drive through the Po Valley around the countryside that produces this cheese, the most valuable aspect of the Italian agriculture industry, you may be surprised that you will see almost no cows. This is because the cattle are kept indoors all year round. The fields that surround these giant sheds are more efficiently put to use to grow grass converted to hay to feed the animals. Unlike many of the protected French cheeses of this stature there are no regulations on the breed of cattle that can be used and so 99 per cent of them are Friesian, bred for their yields, or their capability to produce vast quantities of milk.

A typical day in a Parmesan dairy starts around 5am with the delivery of fresh morning milk. The evening milk from the day before has been left on steel trays, skimmed of its cream. The cream is often sold to make butter.

This skimmed evening milk is mixed with fresh whole morning milk. The mixture of milks is measured into copper-lined steel vats. Several litres of whey (the run-off from the previous day's cheese ferment) is added to each vat. This is the most traditional method of introducing the cultures needed to get the cheeses started.

The milk is warmed to around 30°C to encourage the bacteria to begin to work. Rennet is then added and, after about ten minutes, the curd is ready to be cut. As the curd is cut, the whey separates, the curds are broken down into rice-shaped pieces with a special long-handled whisk. The whole soup is then cooked for about 12 minutes, up to 55°C. This heat causes the curds to contract and expel more whey; it also kills off many of the bacteria in the milk but allows particular heat-loving ones to thrive. These bacteria will continue to be active as the cheese matures. The whey is drained and the curd sinks to the bottom of the vat. Now one large spongy block, it is sliced by hand with a sword-length knife into two blocks, each weighing about 50kg. Each block of curd is pressed into a mould that embosses the famous Parmigiano-Reggiano name on to the sides of the cheese.

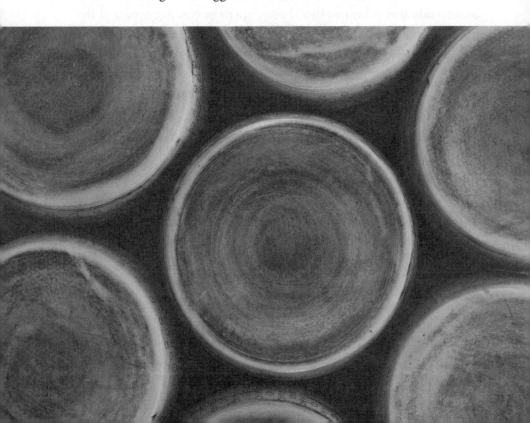

After four days of being pressed to squeeze out even more moisture, these giant cheeses are immersed in huge baths of warm brine, where they gently bob for about three weeks, absorbing the salt as they begin to form a protective skin. After salting, they go on to wooden shelves to begin their long, silent journey towards maturation. The caves of many Parmesan dairies house thousands of wheels of cheese, worth millions of euros, stacked floor to ceiling on high shelves. They are disturbed intermittently by a small machine that runs up and down each row clamping the cheeses, gently turning them and brushing them to keep moisture even and rinds clean.

Long-aged cheeses aren't just left to their own devices for months or years at a time, not least because of the financial investment they represent. A cheese cave filled with cheese is a multimillion-euro bank vault. Cheeses need to be sampled at different points after they are made but before they are opened, so cheese maturers have devised tools that allow them to take a sample without opening the whole cheese. The tool is called a cheese-iron. It consists of a half cylinder steel blade, sharp and slightly narrower at one end and attached to a handle at the other. The length and gauge can vary but they are generally no longer than 15cm and no wider than 2cm. The iron is pushed into the cheese with a little twist and then gently withdrawn. The iron brings with it a long cylinder out of the depths of the cheese. This sample can then be examined, smelled and tasted to reveal how the cheese is developing. Only a small piece is tasted from the tip of the core and the remainder is pushed back into the cheese and the small cut in the rind is sealed over with a small amount of the cheese.

This sampling of a maturing cheese is essential to determine how the cheese is developing and then being able to gauge how long to let the cheese mature. If the flavours are quiet and coherent, lactic, tangy tastes knitted together with no single note out of balance, then the cheese can be matured on. But if something more jarring is developing, a bitterness or sharpness or a tiny bit of fizz on the tongue, that's a warning that the cheese may need to be sold younger. Ageing will almost definitely exaggerate any of these less desirable flavours, so tasting is essential to catch them before they overpower what we expect from a pressed cooked cheese. It is also useful in gathering information on how changes made in production are developing without having to wait until the cheese reaches its full maturity. Most long-aged, cooked curd cheeses are graded as they age. These grades determine which label they will carry or how long they will be allowed to mature.

In some cases an expert grader does not bore the cheese but merely listens to it. For Parmigiano-Reggiano, after one year of ageing an independent expert called a *battitore* (which loosely translates as batsman or beater) arrives to evaluate each wheel. The *battitore* taps each wheel of cheese with a special hammer, listening for tones indicating whether the cheese has developed holes. It's a bit like tapping a wall to see if there are hollow spots inside. Holes or hollow spots are the most common defects in long-aged cheeses. They're caused by a bacteria that produces gases in a process called late-blowing.

If the *battitore* isn't sure about something he or she has heard in the cheese, they use a second tool, a long, thin needle probe called an *ago*. This is spiked into the cheese and then sniffed to check the condition. If it smells almost putrid or sulphurous, like rotten eggs, then the *battitore* knows there's a problem. The hammering and listening method is also used by many graders and *affineurs* of hard cheeses. Tapping is a blunt tool really, designed to catch one particular but common defect. It will not determine the subtle development of flavours in the cheese but it's a good way to weed out cheeses that have serious problems and ensure only the soundest cheeses remain on the maturing room shelves.

ADDED FLAVOURS

WE AT SHERIDANS are not the greatest fans of adding flavours to cheeses. This is mostly because many flavoured cheeses use the additives to hide a very mediocre cheese, and good cheeses have plenty of flavour of their own. The idea of mixing in dried fruit, chillies or even chocolate doesn't really fit with our idea of great cheese; if you like these flavours with your cheese, have them with them, not in them. There are however two strong arguments in favour of cheeses with added flavour. The first is that if people enjoy eating them, then that in itself is enough – there is no room for gastro-snobbery in the search for great food. The second is that there are some additives that really do work when used sensitively to enhance an already good cheese. Seaweed and smoke are two that can work in harmony with the cheese flavours and also function as additional preserving agents. The use of cumin and fenugreek in Goudas works particularly well, as the cheeses age and gain that rich caramelly flavour which plays off the aromatic spices.

SEASONALITY

The importance of seasonality in cheeses has diminished as animal husbandry has developed over the last few decades; however, it is still an important element in the quality of cheeses available at a particular time of year. I think one of the richest qualities of farmhouse foods is their relationship with the seasons – in a world where 'the consumer' must have anything at any time, it is refreshing to find foods that change over the year and some which we can only find at particular times.

When we speak of seasonality in cheese, really there are three main components: animal feed, lactation cycle and curing conditions.

Most modern dairy farmers work hard to produce consistent milk all year round through feed supplement and staggered calving/lambing, etc. This minimises the impact on the cheese, as they are able to deliver more consistent milk, which means more consistent cheese. Modern temperature- and humidity-controlled curing rooms lessen the impact that weather changes have on the curing of cheeses. However, for many cheeses the seasons still have a very real impact on production and in some cases are integral to the nature of the cheese.

Milk is of course produced by a mammal to feed its young and so is produced from birth up until the young are able to eat solid food. Most animals also produce young at a particular time of year to maximise the well-being of their offspring. So naturally animals will not produce milk all year round but usually from giving birth in spring until sometime in autumn. The modern demand for year-round milk and cheese production has resulted in many dairy farmers having staggered birthing in their herd. This is easier to achieve with cattle and also needs a reasonably sized herd. For most producers of sheep's and goats' milk, and many smaller farmers of dairy cattle, it is easier and more productive to stick with the natural lactation cycle, which mostly also coincides with a plentiful feed supply. When producing mature cheese, this does not cause much of a problem, as the cheeses can all be made at a particular time of year but sold at slightly different ages all year round. For fresher cheeses the simple answer is to sell the cheese only for a portion of the year and allow your customers to wait for the new season. The classic example of such a cheese is Mont d'Or, which is only made, conversely, when the cattle are down from summer pastures and feeding on hay. Rather than this being to the commercial disadvantage of the cheese, the contrary is the case, with customers around the world waiting for the first cheeses of the season to arrive in October. Traditionally, most fresh goats' milk cheeses are only available from spring to autumn; however, only a few smaller producers remain true to this seasonality and even small producers have autumn kidding or freeze curd in the summer for use in the winter.

Apart from influencing the actual production cycle of cheese, seasons also influence the qualities of the cheeses being produced. Even in Ireland, where we have our cattle out on fresh grass for up to ten months of the year, the animals need feed supplement right through the winter months when there is little grass growth. This feed can be fermented grass, hay or other dried or fermented feeds. From spring to autumn, grass growth changes and the protein levels of the grass change, while there can also be different foliage growing in the fields. In dairy-farming cultures in mountainous areas the animals are often moved up in the summer to take advantage of receding snow and abundant pastures. The lower fields in the valley are then generally used to harvest hay to feed the animals when the snow returns. All of these changes in feed for the dairy animals affect the protein and fat levels in the milk but also the flavours that are transferred through the various seasonal foliages such as wild flowers and herbs. So even though a cheese may be made all year round it will change slightly as it goes through the seasons. This is compounded in the production of cheeses that have active mould and culture rinds. Different fungi are active at different times of year and so the mix changes on the surface of the cheese, in turn changing the flavour development of the cheese.

There are no hard and fast rules about which cheeses are better when. We might think that washed-rind cheese made in December would be of lower quality than one made from spring milk; for certain cheeses this is true but some producers manage to make really good winter cheese. In general, fresher softer cheeses tend not to be as good in winter; however, winter can always be brightened by the goodness and flavour of matured summer milk cheeses. The important thing is to enjoy the different flavours and cheese that the changing seasons bring us.

SPLITTING A WHEEL

Receiving a full wheel of Parmigiano into a shop is a great occasion. The scale and beauty is breathtaking. Of course our job is not to display beautiful cheeses but to sell them cut into pieces for our customers. Cutting is the wrong word. Parmesan isn't cut, it's split. When we received our first full wheel, we had briefly witnessed Parmesan being opened and we had acquired the right tools. These were the days before YouTube, so we were on our own, no expert demonstrations at our fingertips.

No cheesemonger ever forgets splitting their first wheel of Parmesan. We had ordered a set of short, wooden-handled knives and they had duly arrived by post. Our first full wheel lay in wait. We looked at the knives. We guessed the hooked one was for scoring the hard rind. We took it from there. We scored the rind across the top and down each side. Then flipping the heavy wheel over we scored across what was now the top. There were two dagger-shaped knives and another with a longer blade like a wide chisel. We drove the chisel into the centre of each scored side and the daggers into the corners, pulling them out with some difficulty. The cheese remained whole. With a dagger in the centre of each side score and the chisel hilt deep in the centre of the top face we used three of our four hands to twist and wriggle the blades. Despite our fuss and commotion the cheese opened slowly and quietly. The sweet salty smell wafted up and a few shards of golden cheese dropped on to the table. With some practice and confidence the job becomes mush easier. A wheel of Parmesan is a huge, heavy and unwieldy thing, but when you've seen someone open a wheel by hand you realise that it is not about muscle strength and force. You work with the cheese's own weight and structure. It's almost like it wants to be opened. You are just there to help it along.

We took a lot of time and care over that first wheel. As young cheesemongers we could not afford to make a mistake. We had a lot of turnover invested in our lump of gold. Now cheesemongers can look up the art online. We recommend everyone does. Our favourite clip is cheesemaster Carlo Guffanti cracking open a wheel of Parmigiano.

Walking down almost any supermarket aisle in the world we can see Parmigiano-Reggiano in value packets or in fancy premium packaging. These cheeses are all made and aged in pretty much the same way, so why should we bother bringing in full wheels from Giorgio Cravero when we could buy Parmesan already nicely pre-cut and packed for far less per kilo? Or why should you as a customer go to the extra hassle of visiting a specialty shop and most likely paying more money for your Parmesan? The answer is very simple – buy a piece of pre-packed Parmesan and buy a freshly cut chunk from a good cheesemonger, taste and compare. We guarantee you will never want to buy pre-packed again. It is not only the effect of the cheese spending months wrapped in plastic rather than its natural breathing skin – we used to have our Cravero Parmesan pre-packed into 2kg and 4kg pieces for wholesaling to restaurants and small shops. But after sitting down and really comparing the two versions we stopped and now only sell freshly cut. Plastic wrapping kills what's brilliant about Parmesan. In addition, most of the pre-packed Parmesan comes from producers who are much more focused on producing cheese at the cheapest price rather than with the best flavour. Small short cuts and little differences add up to quite a different cheese.

The greatest rewards from opening a wheel of Parmigiano-Reggiano are the small chunks that drop to the table as the cheese first opens. Your nose is already full of sweet butter and hay aroma but then when you bite into a small chunk there is a crystallised crunch that, at the same time, melts slightly in your mouth. The taste is so rich – all of that milk condensed and transformed through long fermentation. You are given a burst of perfectly intermingled flavours – caramel, roasted hazelnuts, pineapple, butter and a little spice. All hail Parmigiano-Reggiano, the king of cheeses.

CHEESE ON TRIAL

If things had gone differently Bill Hogan might have been, in his own words, a 'wise old fart' by now. He might be pottering around a dairy casting an expert eye on the curds of a young cheesemaker. But Bill's story doesn't end so happily for Ireland's food scene. An articulate, patrician American with a sparse white beard and glasses, he looks like a retired lawyer. If you look more closely you'll see the jutting outline where a prosthetic limb joins his leg. He lost the lower half of his right leg to long-term illness four years ago. He is a veteran of a war on ideas about what constitutes good food.

First the back story. And it's a humdinger. Bill grew up in New York State in the 1950s, the son of Irish parents. He went from high school to the offices of Martin Luther King in Atlanta, where he worked in the post room as an office boy. Bill was given a book by Dr King about rural life and agriculture that had been written by Ghandi. It had been one of the many items that arrived in the post room. It was a signpost for his next step in life. In June 1968, after Martin Luther King's assassination, he moved to Costa Rica to escape America, a country in which he no longer felt at home. There he studied at university, bought a farm and met Swiss cheesemaker José Dubach, his first teacher. Twelve years later Bill came to Ireland with

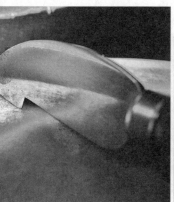

a friend to sell wholesale coffee in the 1970s. Two years in the coffee business made him enough money to buy a small farm in Donegal and follow his dream to make cheese.

A neighbour Sean Ferry began helping him to make cheese on the farm. In the summer of 1986 they worked in the Alpine cheese factory of Josef Enz, a friend of José Dubach. Bill wanted to bring a Swiss-mountain-style cheese to West Cork, where they moved after returning from Switzerland. It was a plan he believes was viewed at best with indifference and at worst with suspicion.

Bill was told by two former government ministers, Peter Barry and Justin Keating, that a political decision was made in the 1960s to take Irish agriculture down the New Zealand road of large-scale butter and beef production with American corporate management practices. West Cork cheesemakers making cheese with raw milk represented a throwback that tarnished this new agricultural image.

But Bill and Sean were determined. They bought a small farmhouse outside Schull, sourced milk from two local farms, formed the West Cork Natural Cheese Company and in 1987 they started making two pressed cooked cheeses called Desmond and Gabriel.

Both cheeses were a resounding hit. The World Cheese Guide awarded both a star and described Gabriel as 'a rock hard cheese which nevertheless melts in the mouth . . . a deep fruity flavour and mellow aftertaste'.

By 2002 Bill and Sean were making about eight tonnes of Gabriel and Desmond a year with unpasteurised or raw milk from four local herds. They had an arrangement with the Department of Agriculture that each herd would be tested for TB before the cheese-making started. Despite a phone call to the Department to request a test, one of the herds wasn't tested until August, and when it was tested TB was found. It was a catastrophe for the West Cork Natural Cheese Company. In September two tonnes of cheese, made between July and August, were deemed by the Department of Agriculture to be unfit for human consumption. We got a phone call from Bill telling us the disastrous news. Bill decided to fight the order. At the time, we realised how unique Bill's case was – no cheesemaker had taken on the State. And this was a battle in which history played a huge part. There was a strong legacy of fear in Ireland about TB. But we knew instinctively that the cheese was safe. Gabriel and Desmond were made with curds heated to 47°C and 52°C respec-tively, and then aged for more than a year. The science backed up our gut instinct.

When Bill, Sean and their supporters walked into the District Court in Skibbereen that day, they had cleared the court of the usual small-beer traffic offences and fines in order to hear Bill's challenge to the State. A long bitter battle ensued. But eventually Bill and Sean won. In April 2004 Judge Terence Finn ruled that the cheese was safe and fit to be eaten. Then the State reacted swiftly and with full force. Within days the Food Safety Authority of Ireland issued a prohibition order on the cheese. This was challenged in the District Court and defeated. It was a second victory for the cheesemakers.

And still the State hadn't finished fighting. They appealed the original District Court ruling that the cheese was safe. Bill and Sean won the appeal. In his judgment in December 2004, Circuit Court Judge Sean O'Donnabhain lambasted the State from the bench for what he called its 'conviction to which all science must bend'.

Bill and Sean had won three victories but ultimately they lost. Despite lengthy negotiations with the Department of Agriculture over compensation, they got nothing. Their last option was to take a High Court action for damages but by then Bill was losing his leg and his will to keep fighting.

Gabriel and Desmond continued to be made under Sean's super-vision by Newmarket Co-op in North Cork. Then the economic crash hit the Co-op hard and it was taken over by the dairy giant, the Kerry Group. And that was the end of Gabriel and Desmond cheeses.

After he talks about how his Irish cheese story ended, we wander around Cork's English Market and find a chunk of Gabriel at a cheese stall. It's five years old, at least, he tells the cheese seller. 'It's probably a bit funky, by now. It's Mummy cheese,' he jokes. The rind has turned to a woody bark in parts. The crumbling cheese still tastes of milk and herbs but there is a strong back note. There are no young Gabriels with which to compare it, in order to get the mellow aftertaste that Bill loved. This is the last of it.

Bill's and Sean's cheeses were some of the most beautiful cheeses in Ireland. Their battle was an attempt to keep that from being lost. Their legacy is that small cheesemakers refused to accept the heavy-handed treatment of the TB threat. The State had to re-examine its position on TB and cheese. But Bill would like to have been able to leave something more delicious behind. He would love to see another thermophilic cheese being made in Ireland. Glebe Brethan, a Comté-style cheese made from a pedigree Montbéliarde herd, was that cheese for a number of years but since the death of its maker, David Tiernan, it hasn't been replaced.

COMTÉ

When we're asked what's our bestselling cheese, the answer is simple: Comté. We are not alone in having Comté as our top seller. There are almost a million kilos of Comté eaten every week around the world. It is such an easy cheese to sell. The wheels are impressive sitting on the counter at 40kg. It looks beautiful and presents no challenges to people new to shopping in a cheesemongers. There is no mould. The rind is clean and even, the cheese smooth and uniform. It is easy to handle, store and keep in good condition. It isn't that sensitive to temperature or humidity. It can take a knock or two and is an all-round sturdy cheese.

Comté is a cheese in which you can taste the cooking that went into making it. It has a rounded, baked flavour, like a warm, oniony broth, with a nuttier more animal flavour than younger cheeses. It also has a sweetness to it.

Comté's robustness comes from the way it is produced. And this is shaped by the landscape from which it originated. It's another story of how cheesemakers figured out the best way to preserve, store and transport milk. The production of Comté dates back almost a thousand years and is based around the plateaus of the high Jura mountains and the rich grazing they provide.

The Jura cheesemakers discovered that finely cutting the curds, then cooking and pressing them into large wheels of cheese was the best means of expelling moisture and producing a cheese that would last the journey from the mountainous regions to the more populated towns and cities like Lyon and on to Paris and beyond.

Then we come to flavour. Comté has a subtle sweetness, a broad, savoury, brothy taste. It is a long experience, a flavour that develops in your mouth and up through your nose, always leaving lingering aromas.

Comté is produced to many levels of quality. Much of it is produced and matured to bring the flavours out early, allowing it to be sold as young as four months and to keep costs down. There are also many *affineurs* who select cheeses that will age gently and slowly up to 24 months and sometimes even longer. All of our Comté comes from Marcel Petite, a cheese company in the Jura mountains near the border between France and Switzerland that dates back to the 1840s. They age their Comtés in a converted military fort 1,100 metres above sea level. The solid stone walls and cool mountain air make it an ideal ageing chamber for these enormous cheeses. They also practise the art of listening to the cheese by tapping the wheels with a wooden hammer to determine their ageing potential.

Comté is not only beautiful to sell and to eat, it is also a shining example of what can be achieved when a State decides that it is in the interest of the country to protect its traditional produce. Comté was the second French cheese after Roquefort to receive AOC recognition in 1958, with full regulations introduced in 1976. In order to be called Comté, the cheese must be made with the milk of two stipulated breeds of Comté cows, Montbéliarde (95 per cent) and Simmental (5 per cent), in the high Alpine area of the Doubs, Jura and Ain regions between Lyon in France and Basel in Switzerland. Each cow must have at least 2.5 acres of natural pasture and any feed must be natural and free of fermented products and GMOs. The cheese must be made with fresh milk, within 24 hours of milking. Wheels must be aged for a minimum of four months on spruce boards. The stipulation around the use of GM, and some other revisions, were added in 2007 to ensure that modern technologies and practices were not used to get around the spirit of the protection order.

The Comté rules also surround the *fruitière* system. *Fruitière* is a term that has been used in the region since the thirteenth century to describe the cheesemaking centres where farmers bring their milk. The origin of the word is hotly disputed but it may have been linked to the idea of the milk 'bearing fruit'.

After being made, every cheese must be graded. Marks are given out of 24 for appearance, taste and texture. Any cheese scoring 15 or above gets a green label, indicating that it is the best. A mark of between 12 and 15 gets a brown label. Less than 12 and the cheese can't be called Comté. Instead it is sold as Gruyère.

GLEBE BRETHAN

When artisan cheese production began again in Ireland in the late 1970s and 80s, there was no script. We didn't have generations of traditional makers handing down their rules and ideas. We just had land, milk and some people with a notion to make cheese. These cheesemakers broke new ground with experimentation and massive creativity. Those first Irish cheesemakers either came from traditional European cheesemaking backgrounds or looked to them for influence. There was no attempt to copy. The cheeses that resulted and lasted have their origins in the traditional European recipes but have been adapted to their Irish setting and have adapted themselves to the landscape and traditions of Irish farming.

In the early 1990s Irish dairy farmer David Tiernan was not fully convinced of the agricultural advice that had led him, and almost all of his contemporaries, to concentrate on farming the modern Holstein-Friesians. It's a breed that gives high milk yields but can be difficult to farm. After some research and a trip to the Jura mountain region, he decided to purchase two Montbéliarde cows: Maggie and Katie. David was more comfortable with this older breed, who seemed more at home in the fields. They calved more easily and their off-spring were more valuable as beef cattle.

Over a decade, he converted his whole herd to Montbéliardes. In his trips over to the Jura to look for animals and learn more about the breed, David became fond of Comté cheese. After a little research, he decided that it would make sense to try to make a similar cheese on his farm. With the help of a French cheesemaker, he produced his first wheels of Glebe Brethan in 2004. The cheese's name combines Glebe Farmhouse and Baothan or Brethan, an Irish monk who founded the monastic settlement at Lannleire, now Dunleer, in the smallest county in Ireland, Louth on the north-east coast.

David knew very little about cheesemaking when he began and always shrugged off the title of artisan producer. He preferred to think of himself as a good dairy farmer who turned his wonderful milk into a food that did justice to its quality. The care and consideration that he put into his farming was translated into how he went about cheesemaking.

He made cheese for just two to three months in the summer when the quality was at its best. He would get up at 4.30–5.00am to milk his herd and then pump the warm raw milk into the copper vat he had brought over from Jura. He made two wheels of cheese, seven days a week, all on his own – from separating and cooking the curd, to pressing the giant wheels, to salting and then minding them, turning and brushing them as they quietly aged. The cheese developed slowly and only reached its best at about 24 months.

Tragically, David died in early 2013. Though Glebe Brethan had its origins in the traditions of Comté, over its short life it developed into a unique cheese, a product of David's own personality and the land and animals he farmed. The last batch was made in the summer of 2012. It was, of course, the best he had made. It was less sweet than its French cousin and not as instantly pleasing, but the length and depth of the flavour were outstanding.

David Tiernan.

RIGHT: Triskel Farmhouse 'kids'.

BELOW: Derrick Gordon, St Tola goats' cheese.

SHERIDANS IRISH FOOD FESTIVAL

LEFT: Kevin, Elisabeth Ryan, Giana Ferguson, Freddie Sheridan.

BOTTOM: Paddy Furey (**left**), Ed Hick (**right**).

OPPOSITE: (**left to right**) Children in the brown bread competition; Flood's butchers; Silke Cropp; Maura Sheridan, brown bread competition.

LEFT: Jeffa Gill and Veronica Steele.

ABOVE: Mary Burns and Helene Willems.

BELOW: Kevin, Catherine and Seamus.

EMMENTAL'S HOLES

EMMENTAL IS FAMOUS for the large holes that are spread throughout this great cheese, and they are there by design. One of the starter cultures used in Emmental is *Propionibacterium freudenreichii*. When this bacteria consumes lactose during maturing, it produces CO_2 as well as other compounds that contribute to the distinctive sweet nutty flavour of this cheese. Other similar bacteria that also feed off lactose can be present in cheese but these unwanted bacteria are mostly active later in maturation and produce gas which causes unwelcome holes or cracking in the cheese and also quite putrid off flavours.

You may see an allergy warning on the label of your cheese which says 'Contains egg'. This isn't because it gives another flavour dimension or a shiny rind. Small amounts of Lysozyme, an enzyme extracted from egg white, is added to the milk when making some hard cheeses, most particularly Grana Padano but also many Manchego and other hard cheeses. It is there to limit the activity of these gas-producing bacteria.

HOW TO CHOOSE PRESSED COOKED CHEESE

It's rare to find these cheeses in bad condition. Their sturdy nature means that it is quite hard to do them much damage. When choosing, you should try to determine the quality of the cheese. Seeing Parmesan pre-packed can be an indicator that the cheese is being produced for a mass market and will not have the quality and breadth of flavour found in cheeses sold in a specialist store. Parmesan is certainly a stable cheese and one would think vacuum packing it would make no difference but, although the difference is subtle, a whole cheese opened and cut on the counter always tastes better than pieces that have been vacuum packed.

HOW TO STORE PRESSED COOKED CHEESE

Once a cheese is aged it becomes more stable and sturdy, so how it is stored when you bring it home is not quite as important as with younger cheeses. This category of cheese is the most sturdy of all. It was made to travel and last. They can be tightly wrapped to help avoid moisture loss. We still recommend wax paper or kitchen parchment paper rather than clingfilm, but it is not essential. The cheeses do not need to be kept too cold and, as with all cheeses, they are better served at just under room temperature. So it is really handy to have a chunk on a plate in a cool cupboard in order to be able to take a piece for a snack without having to worry about letting it warm up. The main risk with storing these cheeses at a higher temperature is that you might get a bit of surface mould growth. Don't worry about this. The smooth texture allows you to scrape it off without losing too much of the cheese.

FOOD WE LIKE WITH PRESSED COOKED CHEESE

We love to see Parmesan on a cheeseboard. It is a must when Seamus is asked to do a special board for something like a wedding. In the wine bar any small broken pieces from the splitting of a wheel are used as a treat for customers.

○ Most of these cheeses have a concentrated sweetness and you might expect that adding more sweet foods would be too much, but it actually works very well. This is the category of cheese that can take sticky fruit preserves – figs roasted till they're jammy, poached plums and pears slick with their sugary poaching liquor. Likewise honey works very well drizzled over a well-aged Gruyère or Grana. In summer these cheeses are gorgeous shaved over a roughly smashed hummus of broad beans and fresh peas.

○ Kale crisps or sprouting broccoli teamed with toasted almonds are beautifully finished with some pared Gruyère.

○ These are the cheeses that love pasta, whether it's in our Domini Kemp recipe for Mac and Cheese or just shaved over a bowl of lightly oiled pasta with some anchovy-butter-drenched croûtons stirred through at the end.

DRINKS WE LIKE WITH PRESSED COOKED CHEESE

○ When we think of the big brothy flavours of these cheeses, we might think of matching them with equally big reds wines; however, the best matches are whites. Some of our favourite pairings are Parmesan and Champagne, or Comte and Vin de Paille. Full-bodied Chardonnay will take on any of the bigger flavours in this category. Other good matches are Pinot Grigio, Soave and reasonably dry sherry.

○ Beers of all types work pretty well with these cheeses. For the big flavours of the more mature cheeses look for an IPA with rich malt and a little caramel.

○ Pear juice is a good non-alcoholic partner to these cheeses, served with ice to dilute its soupiness and stirred with a sprig of fresh rosemary. Strange but good.

SOME OF OUR FAVOURITE PRESSED COOKED CHEESES

GRUYÈRE VIEUX

PRODUCER: Dairy Le Crêt
MADE: Canton of Fribourg, Switzerland
PRODUCTION: dairy, using milk from a small number of herds
MILK: raw cows'
NAME PROTECTION: AOC, PDO
RENNET: traditional

TYPE: cooked curd, pressed
RIND: washed
RIPENING: 15 to 17 months
APPEARANCE: 35kg wheel
TEXTURE: firm but still creamy
TASTE: light broth, grass and hay notes; light fudge notes

JEAN-MARIE DUNAND runs the Dairy Le Crêt situated at about 900 meters above sea level, in the very heart of the Gruyère AOC area. The dairy is supplied by eight local farms, which deliver milk daily to produce 18–20 wheels. The cheeses are matured in cellars 10km away, the only maturing rooms still in the Gruyère production zone. The salt used in production is exclusively Sel des Alpes, a 200-million-year-old salt deposit that is continually rinsed with glacial water. The flavour of this Gruyère is finely balanced: it avoids being dominated by the big salt and caramel flavours that are typical in aged Gruyères and allows more subtle, earthy, fruity and herbal notes to come through.

COMTÉ FORT SAINT ANTOINE

PRODUCER: Affinage Marcel Petite
MADE: Franche-Comté, France
PRODUCTION: various small
    dairies
MILK: raw cows'
NAME PROTECTION: AOC, PDO
RENNET: traditional

TYPE: cooked curd, pressed
RIND: washed
RIPENING: 10 to 24 months
APPEARANCE: 34kg wheel
TEXTURE: firm, smooth
TASTE: onion broth, roasted nuts,
    light caramel

COMTÉ IS always one of our most popular cheeses and all our Comté comes from the most celebrated *affineurs* in Franche-Comté, Marcel Petite. This company has been making cheese in the region since the 1840s, and ageing other farmers' cheeses since 1932. We generally sell two Comtés, both of which are aged in the renowned Fort Saint Antoine in Franche-Comté, some 1,100 metres above sea level. Originally constructed for military purposes in the 1870s, Marcel Petite have been ageing cheese here since 1965. The solid stone walls and cool mountain air of the Fort Saint Antoine make it an ideal place in which to age these enormous cheeses. In terms of flavour, the 10–14 month Comté (which we often sell up to 16 months) is livelier on the palate due to the higher moisture content in the cheese. By contrast, the Extra Mature Comté at 16 months and beyond – we generally sell it up to 22 months or so – is drier and more crystalline due to proteolysis and has a longer finish. Conversely, it tends to be a little less lively on the palate. Both are superb cheeses, and preference is really down to personal taste.

BEAUFORT CHALET D'ALPAGE

PRODUCER: Affineur Denis
  Provent
MADE: Savoie and Rhône-Alpes,
  France
PRODUCTION: small *fruitières*
MILK: raw cows'
NAME PROTECTION: AOC, PDO

RENNET: traditional
TYPE: cooked curd, pressed
RIND: natural
RIPENING: 24 months
APPEARANCE: 40kg wheel
TEXTURE: firm and smooth
TASTE: sweet, rich, cooked nuts

BEAUFORT IS a wonderful mountain cheese. It brings us the brothy, caramel and nutty flavours of the best cooked-curd cheeses but it also has another layer of sweet pungency reminiscent of pressed washed-rind cheeses. Only raw milk from Tarentaise and Abondance cattle are used to make Beaufort. For Beaufort Chalet d'Alpage, the milk must only come from cows grazing the high pastures of the Haute-Savoie Alps during the summer months. The giant wheels have a lovely distinct concave circumference that is caused by a wooden loop which is tightened around the wheel when the cheese is formed. For the first weeks of maturing, the cheeses are washed with brine every day and then with a *morge*, which is a mix of brine, whey and old cheese rinds. This mix ensures that the same ancient bacteria continue to colonise the rinds of the new cheeses. The rind of the mature cheese is dry and has a mottled beige colour but with a pinkish glow; the compact smooth paste is deep yellow ochre under the rind becoming pale yellow towards the centre.

PARMIGIANO-REGGIANO CRAVERO

PRODUCER: Caseificio Fontana, *affinage* Giorgio Cravero
MADE: Reggio Emilia, Italy
PRODUCTION: small dairy
MILK: raw cows'
NAME PROTECTION: DOC, PDO
RENNET: traditional

TYPE: cooked curd, pressed
RIND: natural
RIPENING: 24 months
APPEARANCE: 36kg wheel
TEXTURE: firm, granular but with a softness
TASTE: light fudge, roasted nuts, cooked fruit

OUR PARMIGIANO-REGGIANO comes from master *affineur* Giorgio Cravero of Bra in Piedmont. Giorgio reckons there are about 300 producers of Parmigiano-Reggiano within the permitted production area of Parma, Reggio Emilia and Modena. He says that, of these, about 10 per cent are genuinely interested in the quality of their product. Of this 10 per cent, Giorgio deals with just three producers. Each producer of Parmigiano has a unique number that is always embossed on the side of the cheese. Since we began sourcing our Parmigiano from Giorgio, we have always used the cheeses from dairy 841. This is the producer Caseificio Fontana, from the town of Rubiera in Reggio Emilia. The dairy is located in the most valuable area of Reggio Emilia's production – the high plane, close to the Apennines – and it is famous for its *prati stabili*,

the most traditional way to produce fodder for Parmigiano-Reggiano milk. This ancient method provides for the growth of *erba medica* or lucerne. The fields are rested for a year after three years of producing fodder to allow the soil to recover. The milk is supplied to the 841 dairy by six local farms, plus a pretty large 'co-operative cowshed', which is supplied just for local grass and hay by many small, sometimes tiny, other local farms. In total, around 1,000 cows produce around 90,000 litres of milk a year to make around 40 wheels a day at the dairy. This is not a small producer but their focus is on the quality of the cheese, using the best feed for the animals and cheesemaking craft. Giorgio visits the dairy every month to select his cheeses. They have worked together for 30 years; they know the cheeses that Giorgio likes and the relationship is built on friendship and trust.

In turn, we trust Giorgio to provide the best Parmigiano for us. And it seems to work, as our customers love it.

L'ETIVAZ

MADE: Vaud Alps, Switzerland
PRODUCTION: small *fruitières*
MILK: raw cows'
NAME PROTECTION: AOC, PDO
RENNET: traditional
TYPE: cooked curd, pressed

RIND: natural
RIPENING: 5 to 18 months
APPEARANCE: 30kg wheel
TEXTURE: firm to granular
TASTE: intense fudge, roasted nuts and cooked onion

L'ETIVAZ IS a seasonal, Gruyère-style cheese from the Vaud Alps in western Switzerland. This wonderful cheese is only made between 10 May and 10 October, when the milk and pasture are at their very best. All L'Etivaz is made in copper vats over wood fires by 80 families in the region. All production takes place at altitudes between 1,000 and 2,000m above sea level, and is made exclusively using raw milk from the herds that graze the rich Alpine pastures during these months. Production is small: between 320 and 330 tonnes, or 12,000 and 14,000 wheels, are produced annually. The AOC requires that the wheels be aged for between five and 13 months before release. When aged for 12 months or more, this cheese offers an incredibly rich flavour. It combines deep savoury broth and cooked-milk flavours with an undercurrent of herbs and grasses. It is a very special cheese that we generally only stock for a few months every winter when these rich flavours work best.

GRAN KINARA

PRODUCER: Le Fattorie Fiandino
MADE: Piedmont, Italy
PRODUCTION: single farm
MILK: raw cows'
RENNET: cardoon thistle
TYPE: cooked curd, pressed

RIND: natural
RIPENING: 24 months
APPEARANCE: 36kg wheel
TEXTURE: firm and granular
TASTE: sweet milk, roasted nuts
and cooked fruit

THIS GRANA cheese is similar to its cousins Grana Padano and Parmigiano-Reggiano but also very unique. It is made exclusively by the Fiandino family on their farm and they use artichoke thistle as rennet, instead of the traditional animal rennet or more modern microbial rennet. Another very unique and interesting characteristic of this cheese is that it is naturally lactose free. Normally a cheese would need to be aged for at least 30 months before all of the lactose is converted into lactic acid but because of the action of this flower rennet, the lactose has all been converted by 18 months. Aside from these differences, the cheese is as good as the best Parmigiano and better than many. It has a rich and floral flavour with all the depth you would expect from good Parmesan and a firm texture without being dry.

ST GALL

PRODUCER: Shinnick family
MADE: Co. Cork, Ireland
PRODUCTION: farmhouse, using
their own milk
MILK: raw cows'
RENNET: traditional
TYPE: cooked, pressed

RIND: washed
RIPENING: 3 to 9 months
APPEARANCE: 4kg wheel
TEXTURE: smooth, slightly elastic
TASTE: cooked onions and herbs
with a little sharpness

FRANK SHINNICK is a passionate dairy farmer who believes strongly in the benefits of raw milk and raw milk cheeses, not only for their great flavour but also for their health benefits. His wife Gudrun is an accomplished cheesemaker who produces a variety of cheeses from the family's herd. St Gall is named in homage to St Gallen, the Irish saint who reputedly brought cheese-making knowledge to the Swiss region of Appenzell. The recipe for St Gall is based on Swiss Appenzell cheese. When ripening their cheese, the Shinnicks use a similar method to that of producers of washed-rind cheeses: encouraging the growth of certain strains of bacteria on the rind to help the cheese develop its own unique flavour. Although this is a cooked-curd cheese, we like it quite young, between four and six months. The paste is still quite moist and the flavour retains a milky sweetness as well as rich cooked onions and a little spice.

And here are some favourites from our friends around the world.

TUADA

PRODUCER: Verano Bertagni
MADE: Tuscany, Italy
PRODUCTION: dairy farm, using milk from neighbouring mountain farms
MILK: sheep's
RENNET: traditional
TYPE: cooked, pressed

RIND: hard, straw yellow, with wood-board signs
RIPENING: 5 months
APPEARANCE: 2kg wheel
TEXTURE: firm, grainy with flakes
TASTE: exceptionally sweet, considering the long ageing process, with an earthy flavour

IT IS NOT easy to reach, but I recommend it to you: if you pass by Tuscany, make a stop at Verano's dairy farm. Again really not easy to reach, but after you've done two hours of driving your car around impossible winding mountain streets, more twisted than your garden path, and losing yourself up and down the Emilian-Tuscan Apennines, you'll reach Caseificio Bertagni seasick, tired and two years older. But you'll be happy, as we were when we got there. It is a small operation, passed from father to son for almost a century now. There is a small dairy farm and a smaller shop, always full of hungry and savvy locals and a few lucky tourists. Tuada means 'cellar', and a lot of this cheese's precious taste comes from the seasoning process. The cheese is rubbed with olive oil and lightly dusted with vegetable ash yielding a dry yet edible rind, and is left to rest in a cellar on beech boards for five months. But Tuada's richness is also in the milk. Collected from small farms in the immediate vicinity of the dairy, it is sheep's milk from ancient breeds like Massese and Garfagnina – which are incredibly ugly-looking beasts, believe you me, but are also strong animals, with a rich and scented milk. What you get is an exceptionally sweet cheese, considering the long ageing process, with an earthy flavour. A pecorino Toscano, sure, but not your everyday pecorino Toscano. *Karl-Heinz Berthold and Laura Gandolfi, gourm. it, Italy*

GLARNER ALPKÄSE

PRODUCER: Margrit Streiff
MADE: Glarnerland, Switzerland
PRODUCTION: farmhouse, using
milk from their own herd and
neighbouring farms
MILK: cows'
RENNET: traditional
TYPE: cooked, pressed

RIND: washed but dry
RIPENING: 4 to 12 months, sea-
sonally available
APPEARANCE: 4.5kg
TEXTURE: firm, creamy dough,
small holes might appear
TASTE: nutty, with plenty of herb
flavours

LOCATED IN the Canton of Glarus in eastern Switzerland, the little village of Braunwald can only be reached by funicular. Up there, the family Streiff runs a little farm with 20 cows. During the summer, they go up on to the Alps with their cows and more animals from other farmers – in total 50 cows. There, Margrit Streiff produces the 'Braunwalder Alp Cheese', a 4kg piece of washed-rind cheese. At the beginning, the cheese has a very milky flavour. During the winter, the cheese stays in the cellar in the Alps and has a very slow maturing process. In early summer of the following year, the cheese has turned into a hard cheese with aromas of all the herbs of the Alps remaining in the cheese. It is very unusual to find a 4kg Alp cheese in Switzerland that can be aged for one year. The dry and cold cellar in the mountains allows the cheese to mature slowly. It might be good for us humans also to spend some time up there in order to get away from all the speedy life in the cities, as the whole area of Braunwald is free from private traffic. *Konrad Heusser, Mundig Cheese, Switzerland*

NUFENEN

PRODUCER: Sennerei Nufenen
MADE: Canton of Graubünden, Switzerland
PRODUCTION: village dairy, milk from 22 farms
MILK: raw cows'
RENNET: traditional
TYPE: cooked curd, pressed
RIND: washed

RIPENING: 9 months
APPEARANCE: 4.5kg wheel
TEXTURE: firm with light, crunchy, crystalline development
TASTE: prevalent toasty notes (toasted bread and walnuts), with occasional tropical flavours of pineapple and lemon

THIS CHEESE comes from one of the most beautiful places I have ever visited. There are two fascinating things about this cheese. Firstly, it comes from a true co-operative. Every member of the co-op had a hand in building their own *affinage* facility. They built it together. And secondly, when they built the milking parlour for Pastoral Transhumance they created a milk pipeline so the milk actually travels back down the Alps to the dairy for production. It's one of the coolest things I have ever seen. *Adam Moskowitz, Colombia Cheese, New York, USA*

PLEASANT RIDGE RESERVE

PRODUCER: Uplands Cheese
  Company
MADE: Wisconsin, USA
PRODUCTION: farm, using their
  own milk
MILK: raw cows'
RENNET: traditional

TYPE: pressed cooked
RIND: washed
RIPENING: 6 to 12 months
APPEARANCE: 5kg wheels
TEXTURE: firm
TASTE: roasted nuts, sweet vege-
  table broth

I WAS A judge the year Mike Gingrich entered Pleasant Ridge Reserve in a contest for the first time. We judged it best in show. No one ever wins in their first year, but Mike did. He has a great story. He went to Europe and fell in love with Beaufort. His Pleasant Ridge was a way of tipping his hat to Beaufort, while also peeking into the future at what's next in American cheesemaking. When I tasted Pleasant Ridge at that contest, I knew I wanted more of it. Those were struggling years for me, but it didn't matter. I needed the cheese and Mike needed the cash to continue his craft at his Uplands farm. So I paid him in advance. Later, of course, we started buying more and more wheels of Pleasant Ridge and ageing them ourselves. Each bite has lingering notes of salt and pineapple. It's a truly wonderful cheese.

Years ago I was at Gabrielle Hamilton's restaurant, Prune, on 1st and 1st in downtown Manhattan. I was sitting with a few other cheese fanatics, including Mike Gingrich. Across the way, I saw Alice Waters having dinner with her daughter. I knew Alice; she blurbed my book. She's also a goddess in the modern food movement. When she got up to leave, she walked over to our table. Mike extended his hand and said, perhaps with a slight bit of trepidation, 'It's an honour to meet you, I'm Mike—,' and before he could finish, she said in a cool tone, 'I know who you are.' That made Mike's day. And that's when we knew Pleasant Ridge Reserve had arrived. Today, it stands as a remarkable testament to the power and innovation of American cheesemaking. *Rob Kaufelt, Murray's Cheese, New York, USA*

CHALLERHOCKER

PRODUCER: Walter Rass, Kaserei
  Tufertschwil
MADE: Canton of St Gallen,
  Switzerland
PRODUCTION: village dairy, milk
  from 11 farms within 2km
MILK: raw cows'
RENNET: traditional
TYPE: pressed cooked

RIND: washed
RIPENING: 10 months
APPEARANCE: 7kg wheel
TEXTURE: firm but fudgy texture
  with light, crunchy, crystalline
  development
TASTE: slightly smoky with notes
  of sweet cream and peanut butter

AS A THIRD-GENERATION cheese importer, Challerhocker is one of the best cheeses I have ever eaten. It is a perfect cheese. Edible at every meal, on its own and as an ingredient. Everyone who tries it tells me they love it. Walter Rass is a master of his craft. *Adam Moskowitz, Colombia Cheese, New York, USA*

RECIPES

SPRING

Baked Parmesan and Gruyère Savoury Custard

This is a delicious and simple starter or lunch that combines the luxury of two great cheeses with the comfort of cream and eggs. It is not very difficult, particularly for those who make their own sweet custard. You are simply replacing the vanilla and sugar with garlic, thyme and grated cheese. Remember you need an hour or two gap between step one and two to allow the first stage of the sauce to chill.

SERVES 8

100ml milk

350ml cream

2 cloves garlic, peeled and cut in large pieces

sprig of thyme

100g grated Parmesan

100g grated Gruyère

pinch of salt

pinch of white pepper

4 eggs

3 egg yolks

Preheat the oven to 160°C and very lightly butter 8 ramekins.

In a heavy saucepan, warm the milk, cream, garlic and thyme over a gentle heat. As it warms up, add the grated cheeses slowly and keep stirring until they have melted. Season with the salt and white pepper. Do not let the mixture boil but rather keep heating it gently. When finished, pass the sauce through a sieve to take out the thyme and garlic. Place in the fridge to cool down.

In a large bowl whisk the eggs and egg yolks. Add the cooled cheese sauce slowly and keep whisking until combined. I always pass the custard through a sieve again to ensure there are no hidden lumps.

The custard is now ready to bake. Divide the mixture into the ramekins and place in a deep oven tray. Pour water into the tray around the ramekins – it should come 2–3cm up the sides. It is very important to cook the custards in water like this – it is called a bain-marie. Bake the custards for an hour or until set.

When they are ready, either let them rest for a few minutes before unmoulding them from their ramekins or sprinkle them with leftover cheese, brown them under a grill and serve in the ramekins. Serve with a green salad or, if in season, they are wonderful with fresh asparagus.

SUMMER

Parmesan Ice Cream

This unusual ice cream taps into the same sweet-salt flavour vein we love in salted caramel or salted chocolate. A perfect sweet alternative to the cheeseboard, served with a few amaretti biscuits crumbled on top.

SERVES 6

6 eggs
250ml maple syrup
450ml cream
100g Parmesan, grated

Beat the eggs and then gently stir in the syrup and cream.

Pour into a heavy-bottomed saucepan and bring gently to the boil, stirring until it thickens to the consistency of yoghurt. This should take about 10 minutes. Take the mixture off the heat.

Stir in the Parmesan, mixing well.

Strain the mixture through a sieve and then spoon into a freezer-proof dish. Place in the freezer, giving it a stir every hour or so as it freezes (or let your ice-cream machine churn it, if you own such a gadget). It should take about three hours for the ice cream to be frozen, depending on your freezer.

Let the ice cream soften in the fridge for half an hour or so before serving.

AUTUMN

Domini Kemp's Bad Bitch Mac and Cheese

This is one of the Irish Times' *food writer's wickedest recipes. At every point in the cooking she cranks up the flavour. It is a fiendish dish perfect to thump down in front of a famished family or a gathering of friends.*

SERVES 8–10

750g lardons

250g butter

1 tablespoon brown sugar

1kg macaroni

100ml olive oil, plus extra for the pasta water

salt and freshly ground black pepper

6 egg yolks

100ml white wine

750g crème fraîche

200g Parmesan, grated

300g Gruyère, grated

1 large Spanish onion, peeled and thinly sliced

200g flower sprouts (a cross between kale and brussel sprouts) or kale

4 cloves garlic

Preheat the oven to 180ºC and butter 1 or 2 gratin dishes, depending on the size.

Start by cooking the lardons in a large frying pan with 50g butter over a medium heat. Once the lardon juices have evaporated, add the brown sugar and cook until starting to caramelise and become crisp. This takes about 15 minutes. Set the lardons aside and try not to nibble on them.

Cook the pasta in plenty of boiling water, to which you have added a glug of olive oil. Cook until al dente – less is more, as it will get more cooking later. Ladle out 500ml of the pasta water and set this aside. Now drain the pasta and add a good 150g butter and some olive oil to stop it sticking. Season very well with plenty of salt and black pepper.

Whisk the egg yolks with the wine and add about 300ml of the pasta water. Stir this into the cooked macaroni, along with the crème fraîche and three quarters of the cheeses and mix really well. You want it to be a reasonably wet mixture – if it feels too stodgy, add more pasta water. Taste and make sure it is well seasoned. It should taste evilly good.

Meanwhile, sauté the onion in 50g butter over a low heat. Cook very slowly until starting to caramelise naturally. Season well and set aside.

Very briefly blanch the flower sprouts or kale and then drain and refresh. Finally sauté in the remaining butter with the garlic until soft. Season well.

Add the lardons and the sprouts or kale to the pasta and mix well. Check the seasoning again and then pour the pasta into the prepared gratin dish or dishes. Top with the caramelised onions and the remaining cheeses.

Bake in the preheated oven for around 30 minutes until piping hot and golden brown on top.

WINTER

Harriet's Cheese Soufflé

A soufflé might seem like a scary dish to pull off. Will it rise? And, if it rises, will it flop before you get it to the table? But this recipe from Harriet Leander makes individual one-pot dishes that are a lot more robust than a big flouncy chef's toque version. They're less likely to lose the wind from their sails and they're such a cinch to make you can knock one up for a single supper, eliminating any risk of audience anxiety entirely.

SERVES 1

1 egg
25g Parmesan, grated
a good pinch of flour
a good pinch of cayenne pepper

Preheat the oven to 180°C.

Separate the egg, putting the white to one side.

Mix the egg yolk, grated cheese, flour and cayenne pepper together to a smooth paste.

Whisk the egg white until stiff. A good test is to turn the bowl upside down – if it doesn't fall out, it's done!

Gently fold the yolk mixture and the whisked egg white together, trying to keep as much air in the mixture as possible.

Pour the fluffy soufflé mixture into an individual ramekin, filling to just below the rim.

Put an inch of water into the bottom of a roasting tray and place your ramekin into the tray and then the tray into the oven.

Bake for 20–25 minutes, until it has puffed up and is brown and toasty on top.

Serve immediately with a fresh green salad.

CHAPTER NINE

THE BLUES

FROM CASHEL BLUE TO STILTON – THE FAMILY BEHIND THE CHEESE AND PREPARING TO FEAST

Unfermented, or cream cheese, when quite fresh, is good for subjects with whom milk does not disagree; but cheese, in its commonest shape, is only fit for sedentary people as an after-dinner stimulant, and in very small quantity. Bread and cheese, as a meal, is only fit for soldiers on march or labourers in the open air, who like it because it holds the stomach a long time.

Mrs Beeton (1836–65) from her *Book of Household Management*

So far we have divided cheeses into those ripened slowly from the inside out, like the Cheddars and Gruyères, and those ripened from the outside in like Camemberts and washed-rind cheeses. Blue cheese fits into neither box. It's a kind of inside-out cheese. The blue mould that spreads through these cheeses acts like the outer rinds we've seen in bloomy- and washed-rind cheeses. It doesn't just provide flavour but works on the curd within the cheese, breaking it down in the same way that an active rind does: softening it and unlocking additional flavours.

Theoretically, any cheese could be turned into a blue cheese by introducing spores of blue mould and having cracks or holes in the paste to allow oxygen into the cheese to feed that mould. And many blue cheeses could be quite nice cheeses without the addition of blue mould. There are some examples where a non-blue version is made, such as white Stilton. But the addition of internal blue moulds adds another dimension. Typically the spores of the blue moulds, either *Penicillium roqueforti* or *Penicillium glaucum*, are added to the milk as part of the starter culture at the beginning of the cheesemaking process. These spores lie dormant until the cheesemaker pierces the cheese with metal spikes, allowing oxygen in to awaken them. The more loose and open textured the cheese, the more the mould can spread. When the curd of the cheese is not packed tightly when the cheese is first made, there are plenty of gaps and fissures throughout the cheese, leaving space and air for the blue mould to grow in its own random pathways. In more modern 'hybrid' blues, such as blue Brie, there is no open texture and so the blue mould only spreads along the punctures left by piercing needles.

There are a few different legends as to how cheesemakers first began to encourage the growth of blue mould through cheeses intentionally. If a cheese has cracks and fissures running from the rind through the cheese, the cracks will allow moulds present in the environment to spread and grow through the cheese. No doubt there were many accidental blue cheeses of this type. We still get the odd example. Perhaps some became appreciated for their distinctive flavour and so the cheesemaker repeated the faults by design. Cabrales from the north of Spain and Castelmagno from Piedmont are two famous cheeses where the blue mould enters the cheese from the environment rather than being added to the milk. In these cheeses the spread of blue mould tends to be more haphazard and the cheeses can vary greatly from one wheel to the next.

The most famous legend, though, is that of Roquefort, where it is said a shepherd sheltering from a storm in the now famous caves at Roquefort-sur-Soulzon discovered an old curd sandwich left there months before. The rye bread had disintegrated into a mouldy dust, which had spread through the sheep's milk curd. The reluctant (and presumably hungry) shepherd ate the mouldy curd anyway and was surprised by how delicious it was. Roquefort was created.

Regardless of how we stumbled upon this wonderful combination, blue cheeses like Gorgonzola, Roquefort, Cabrales and Stilton are amongst the most revered gastronomic delights of our food cultures. We have a natural suspicion of, if not repulsion towards, mouldy food, whether taught to us from our parents or innate, but if we overcome our instinct and eat one of the wonderful blue cheeses, we are rewarded with an eating experience found in no other food. A blue cheese gives us a basic combination of sweet and salt, along with a third sharp or tart acid flavour. These form the background to an array of flavours and aromas that are present, depending on the individual cheese type. In a good blue cheese these hefty flavours act to bring out the more subtle tones, from floral to caramel, toasted nuts to spicy notes.

Blue cheese, more than any other type, encapsulates the paradoxes present in this ancient food. The practical purpose of cheese is preserving the nutrients of milk, in order to prevent it from spoiling, yet cheesemakers harness the agents of spoilage and decay to provide sensory pleasure.

HOW MUCH MILK GOES INTO A CHEESE?

CHEESE IS MADE from the solids that are suspended in liquid milk. The amount of milk it takes to make a cheese depends on how much moisture is left in the cheese and the amount of solids that were there in the first place. So it takes more milk to make a harder cheese than a softer one. As a very general rule it takes ten litres of cows' milk to make 1kg of hard cheese and seven litres of cows' milk to make 1kg of soft cheese. Goats' cheese takes a little more milk than cows' to produce the same amount of cheese. However, sheep's milk will produce about double the quantity of cheese because of its higher concentration of solids.

THE FAMILY BEHIND THE CHEESE

It is mid morning and we're watching a batch of Ireland's famous Cashel Blue cheese being made in a large open vat. We are standing on a raised steel walkway overlooking the vats, which look like giant shiny baths. There is a very organised and orderly sense to the large room, and a sterile look. Yet the feeling is not cold. The whole atmosphere is softened by the enthusiastic chat of the cheesemakers and the homely aroma of yoghurt and fresh milk. In the big vats yellow liquid swirls and clumps of soft, creamy curd breach the surface, gently turning and tumbling. This is the secret, Sarah Furno explains, scooping a handful of curd from the vat. It is the softness of the curd that makes Cashel Blue the cheese that it is.

Despite all the technology and noise here, the impression that you leave with is how simple – beautifully and deliciously simple – this cheese remains. This is despite the great transformation in the three decades since Jane Grubb (Sarah's mother) first ladled soft curd into the sections of Wavin drain pipe she used as her first cheese moulds. Cashel Blue is sometimes seen by the Irish farmhouse cheese fraternity as almost too large and industrial to be still considered 'farmhouse'. This is compounded by the Grubb family's sensible business acumen and professionalism.

In many ways Cashel Blue is a true farmhouse cheese, though, more so than many smaller more haphazard operations. Scale does not necessarily lead to dehumanised or denatured food production, nor does small guarantee integrity. Sarah and her family are adamant that they remain part of and will continue in the farmhouse tradition. The mechanisation of the production process has been done with

Sarah Furno and her mother Jane Grubb.

care and sensitivity to the cheese. Where the human touch brings benefit to the cheese it has been kept and where technology can be used to ease backache and improve quality it has been integrated. The family and their head cheesemaker, Geurt van den Dikkenberg, insist on retaining open vats and the curd is still cut and stirred by hand to retain its softness.

Milk from their own herd makes up almost half of production and the remainder comes from five local farms. Family members are employed in many positions and preference is always given to members of the small rural community when new jobs are available.

Penicillium roqueforti, the blue mould that gives Cashel its 'blue', is the first addition to the milk as part of the starter culture early in the morning. For the moment, though, it remains dormant, invisible. After an hour, rennet is added and the milk slowly transforms into a semi-solid mass. The curd is cut with a gentle sweep back and forward with a cheese harp strung with taut fishing line. The large clumps of curd separate and swim in the deep yellow whey, where they are allowed to rest for about half an hour while the silent army of cultures continue to do their work.

A second cutting releases more whey and the curd is kept moving with a long-handled tool like a giant child's beach spade. Then they're ready for the next stage. The liquid in the last vat starts to disappear, draining into stainless steel pipes underneath which separate curds from whey. The soft curds are piped on to a conveyor belt that loads them noisily into box moulds.

With the cheeses in their moulds, more of the whey needs to be gently drained. The box moulds are held in huge stainless steel frames. With a switch, the cages lift and spin the moulds up and over, turning the cheese and releasing more whey on to the floor as the weight of the curd presses out a fresh gush of liquid. Sarah grins. 'This is "so Dad".' It's a typical Louis Grubb contraption, she explains, referring to her botanist, amateur engineer, farmer father who designed the system with an engineer friend.

After four more turns, the cheeses are taken out of the moulds and brined for 24 hours in the original brine Sarah's mother used when they moved from hand-salting the cheeses to brining them. The brine bath is a step in cheesemaking which is often overlooked by the outsider but which cheesemakers can feel very passionately about. Almost every cheese requires the addition of salt – it acts as a preservative and it pulls moisture from the curd. It can be added directly to the curd, rubbed on dry to the newly formed cheese or introduced by bathing the cheese in a brine bath. Brine baths are the most popular method, as this system ensures an even absorption of salt. The proportion of salt in water is always enough to ensure that it is inhospitable to any fungi but not so much that the solution becomes saturated.

An outsider and many food hygiene auditors question why a cheesemaker would not create new brine every day or week, ensuring it is clean. However, cheesemakers tend to be very keen to top up the original mixture with extra salt and water as needed, rather than replacing the whole bath. On many occasions we have heard of cheesemakers blaming problems they are having with their cheese on having had to start a new brine.

As the cheeses floating in the brine absorb the salty solution, they also release whey, which then becomes part of the brine. Over time this action creates a brine with a pH or acidity level the same as the cheese and so does not reduce the acidity of the soaking cheeses. There may also be other subtle actions taking place. A solution is created over time that carries the imprint of the cheeses that have gone before it and it somehow imparts this history back into the next generation of cheeses. It's little wonder that cheesemakers can be as precious about their brine's personality as breadmakers are about their starters.

The final step in turning Cashel Blue blue is to spike the cheeses with a tool that looks like a stout steel brush. It's a round piece of plastic stuck with stainless steel needles. Two are used, one on each side of the cheese, to punch holes at regular spaces into the cheese to let oxygen flow through it and allow those silent blue mould spores to begin to awaken. Sarah remembers her mother hunting down the right-sized knitting needles to do the job originally. The knitting needles had bottle corks skewered on at a certain level to indicate how far they should be pushed into the cheese.

The blueness of Cashel Blue was born the moment the starter culture, with its parcel of spores, hit the milk. All the cheesemakers have to do after that is manage the cheeses' natural environment to encourage the blue mould to grow. And initially there will be nothing blue about it. It is funny to see the familiar cheeses sitting in the first maturing room, the size and shape of Cashel Blues, but naked and new, without their distinctive blue blush and the speckled golden-yellow natural rind that will colonise them over the coming weeks. Although the blue isn't visible, you can smell it in a tangy fresh scent that prickles the nose, spiking the milky sweetness of the cheeses in the air. As the chilly air in the ageing rooms circulates around and

PJ Ryan stirring the Cashel Blue curd.

through the cheeses, feeding the spores with oxygen, the mould will colonise its host and the cheeses begin to bloom.

In a packing area, around a quarter of the cheeses are selected to be sliced by hand into ten half-moon pieces and packed in breathable packaging for supermarkets. This portion is perfect for households where only one person likes blue cheese, a very common scenario, Sarah explains. Not all of the cheeses that are selected to be portioned are the same. Some customers prefer a milder, younger cheese and others a more developed flavour. Overall, though, the cheeses sold as half-moon chunks tend to be a little younger and milder than the cheeses sold as full wheels.

The other cheeses are wrapped in gold foil, like chocolate wrapping only heavier, and packed into crates in a cold room. Twenty-five thousand wheels are here today. The smell at the end of the room is a more pungent version of that first delicate whiff of blue in the new cheeses. The high fizzy notes have deepened into a mushroomy blast.

Sarah and her husband Sergio Furno came into the family business in 2003 after ten years of doing their own thing, having met at university. Sarah is instantly recognisable from her photograph in the entrance lobby. It is a picture of her as a ten-year-old holding a round of cheese up to the camera. She has the same serious brown eyes that shine when she talks or breaks into her infectious laugh. They now have their own ten year old, who is the eldest of their three children, all growing up on the family farm near the tiny Tipperary village of Fethard.

Sarah and Sergio didn't just join the business to allow the first generation to retire and take over the work that was being done; they added a new dimension. They brought new experiences, particularly their knowledge of flavour compounds and tastes learned while studying and working in the world of wine.

This morning we're selecting a batch of cheeses that we are going to take with us to the warehouse. Sarah knows the kind of cheese we like. She and Sergio have focused more than anything else on improving the maturing of their cheese. They taste every batch, selecting the ones that are ready, depending on how long they need to be matured, picking the ones that are right for their many different customers' needs and tastes.

Sarah takes three wheels to taste. Using a cheese iron to take a sample from the middle of the cheese, she first looks at the back of the tool to check the texture. Creaminess is a word that keeps coming up. No cream is added to the cheese but the effect of the blue mould on the milk has been to turn up its creaminess. The cheeses have developed quite differently across a similar band of flavours. Raw mushrooms, sometimes lettuce, a touch of caramel and that uncooked vegetable sweetness are all there against the creamy, salty cheese. The ideal is when everything comes together in a circle, Sarah explains, to start with one taste, go through some others and then return to that first taste impression. We select the batch with the more subtle first impression for Sheridans. We like how the flavour comes on more gently and builds slowly, coming together in harmony, rather than the slightly more aggressive flavour of another wheel.

Cashel Blue didn't start in its current factory setting but in a quirky, three-storey farmhouse that dates back to 1780 with its cool earth-floored cellar where the cheeses used to mature. Over the years, the cheese operation moved from the apple store to the calf shed, to the haybarn, until the cheese got its own building where it's made now.

In the farmhouse across an ancient, cobbled stable yard, the kitchen smells of just-baked brown bread from the Aga. Over lunch of roast beef, potatoes and sinus-clearing horseradish sauce we hear the history of the family and their cheese, which are both intertwined in this farmhouse. The new plant opened in 2011 and recently the

Sergio Furno.

business phone number was transferred there, so the house is quiet in a way that it hasn't been for decades.

Jane started making cheese in the 1980s, not blues at first. She made Caerphilly- and Cheshire-style cheeses to sell at their local country market – 'Not farmers' market,' she says firmly, her tone leaving you in no doubt that there's a difference between the two, with the impression that a country market is more of a real deal than many farmers' markets. The Tipperary village of Fethard got its country market in 1947 thanks to a group of local women, including Hannah Leahy, mother of the Dublin-based homeless campaigner Alice Leahy. Hannah is now in her nineties and still baking for the country market. In the early 1980s it was just eggs, veg and apple tarts produced by locals who had a can-do approach to rural life.

Jane approached the biggest creamery in the area, Avonmore, and they told her they'd buy a soft blue cheese if she began to make it. She went to another Irish creamery, Mitchelstown, where a version of Danish Blue was being made and marketed as 'Irish Blue'. Jane managed to get the basic recipe from them. Then she made the lucky mistake of getting the temperatures wrong, leading to a softer curd blue cheese than the one she was aiming for. It became Cashel Blue.

In the end, Avonmore didn't buy Cashel Blue but Jane started selling it to food shops and chefs. Having worked in Ireland's most famous kitchen at Ballymaloe House, Jane approached the chef patron Myrtle Allen, who became one of her first customers. Myrtle still talks about the 'elephant's foot' Cashel Blue, the cheeses that bulged slightly at the bottom in the days before they were as uniformly produced as they are today.

Since Jane made her happy mistake, the family has concentrated on keeping the cheese as good as it can be. The change over to pasteurisation wasn't a big deal for them. They began using raw milk and introduced a pasteurised version to satisfy a large UK supermarket. For some years they produced the two alongside each other. It was at this point we began buying Cashel Blue and we always had the raw milk cheese. After a few years, Louis decided that they needed to focus on improving and perfecting the cheesemaking system as a whole and the raw milk version was dropped. In our early days of selling Cashel Blue the whole process was a little more haphazard. We would receive the cheeses too young for our liking, so we would mature the wheels in their boxes in a cold press under one of our fridges. We would rotate the boxes, turning them every few days until the cheeses were quite oozy. There was always a lovely, sweet, salty smell in that fridge. The resulting raw milk Cashel was more inconsistent but we certainly look back fondly on some very delicious, extremely creamy cheeses.

The move from the dairy that had been built into the yard at the farmhouse to a custom-built unit on the farm was a very big step for the family. Sarah's eldest son often reminds people not to use the 'f' word when they refer to the new Cashel Blue plant – factory is a word that makes Sarah wince. They were focused on creating a production facility that was efficient and would be able to cope with ever-increasing demand for the cheese. But they weren't willing to sacrifice the quality of the cheese, looking only for improvements. This proved quite a traumatic process. Dealing with the large dairy companies who supply the equipment for cheesemaking facilities, they found that there was a culture where efficiency and systems took precedence over the quality of the cheese. A Spanish system to get the curd out of the whey and into the moulds was installed. The expensive new machinery didn't make the Cashel Blue they liked, so they took a deep breath, pulled it out and got a French company to install the one that is there today. In a very real sense the cheese is in charge. Everything else has been built around it.

How does Sarah feel about being the second generation in a cheesemaking family? She says it's a simple decision. If she went out to try to find a job that is 'so tangible and gives you so many ups and downs', she's not sure she'd find it.

'Then there's a colder way of thinking about it. Why go through the really hard graft of starting something from scratch when you can take what's already there and reinforce it? Everything needs new waves of energy.'

Crozier sheep.

Louis agrees. He likes the idea of young people being in charge, especially of something as demanding as a cheesemaking operation.

Even on a grey February morning, the hot autumn weather of 2014 is still making its presence felt in the Grubb family milk. Their winter cheeses are typically paler, the milk slightly lighter in colour, but this year the animals were out on grass until early November and the sunny autumn days were concentrated into the hay they're now eating, so they're not producing the typically paler winter-coloured cheese. It's still a creamier, lighter yellow colour. The cows will be out soon on spring grass and the cheese will shift another notch.

This latest wave of family energy has produced impressive developments on the Grubb farm but it hasn't taken away from the simplicity of what's involved: turning great milk into a very special cheese. The recipe for Cashel Blue is different now to the one that Jane followed three decades earlier but that has happened very slowly over the years and in incremental steps. You only make one change at a time, Sarah explains, and that way you can judge how that change is affecting the cheese. Sheridans and our customers are very happy with the Cashel Blue that has evolved over the 20 years that we have been selling it. The quality is more consistent – Sarah and Sergio are committed to getting us the cheese that our customers love. Driving away with our batch of cheese, we are sure that Cashel Blue still deserves its place as a genuine Irish farmhouse cheese, shaped by the family and the farm.

CALCIUM CHLORIDE

You MAY SEE this as an added ingredient in your cheese. It is generally not used in traditional cheesemaking, where the process is more gentle than in mechanised production. Calcium chloride (CaCI$_2$) is a salt solution, which is used in cheesemaking to restore the calcium balance in pasteurised milk. The heating and rapid cooling of the milk decreases the amount of calcium and can affect the coagulation process.

When making hard cheese from goats' or sheep's milk, calcium chloride can also be of benefit, as the milk goes through a natural homogenisation process in the animal's body and without added calcium it may produce a curd that is too weak to cut properly. Sometimes it is used in raw cows' milk cheeses when the animals have been on a feed that reduces the calcium levels of the milk.

PREPARING TO FEAST

Christmas in a cheese shop is a special time. In the two weeks before Christmas we see what it would be like to be selling a mainstream product. Every day from early December we sell as much cheese as we would normally sell in a week. On peak days as it gets closer to Christmas, and finally, on Christmas Eve, we sell the same volume of cheese we sell in a fortnight of normal business in a single day. Our shops can't be designed for this short period, so queues form and often stretch down the street. We love selling cheese in the shops at this time, not just because of the extra business but because it's such a joy to serve customers who normally shop in a supermarket or who eat very little 'special' cheese during the year.

One of the proudest moments Kevin had as a cheesemonger was

Christmas queue, South Anne St, Dublin.

when he overheard a young woman, in her early twenties, say to someone else in the South Anne Street shop queue, 'I always come here for my cheese at Christmas. I remember queuing here every year with my dad when I was little.' It is such an honour to be part of a personal Christmas ritual. Naturally, we wish that all these Christmas cheese shoppers would come every week, but that just isn't the way it works. For most people the type of cheese we sell is a special treat, something to be eaten as part of a feast or a celebration.

Blue cheese is a part of almost everyone's Christmas cheese selection and Stilton is certainly the most popular choice. Stilton probably became the traditional Christmas cheese because it's at its best around the end of the year. It's made with late autumn milk and by Christmas it's in perfect shape for eating. We also believe the popularity of Stilton relates to the idea of serving the best food at a feast. We can see this from many of the foods eaten at Christmas. They are not always what we would eat from week to week but they do represent the very best available.

We have only ever sold Colston Bassett Stilton for the simple reason that it is the best Stilton by far and one of the best cheeses of any kind. The Stilton story is a model of artisan pride and business astuteness. The Stilton Makers' Association was set up in 1910 to protect Stilton makers from competitors trying to copy the cheese. As a result, today only eight dairies are legally permitted to make Stilton. The Colston Bassett Dairy is universally recognised as the best of these. This 100-year-old dairy has been making Stilton with the same techniques for three generations, the only difference being the intro-duction of pasteurisation in 1990.

More recently we have sold the wonderful new raw milk Stichelton. It can't be called Stilton because it is made with raw milk but in every other way it fits the criteria. And, in spirit, it is a more true Stilton than most of the overly salty, overly sharp, perfectly veined industrial cheeses which are churned out by the thousands of tonnes.

We can understand the logic behind producing cheese in the most cost-effective manner when it is to be eaten as a staple, but we disagree that quality of taste should be sacrificed to reduce costs and make a cheese more suitable for the mass market. It seems almost perverse to us to produce cheese, which is being consumed for the pleasure of eating, in the cheapest possible way. Cheaper food means bigger profits for the large retailers, and many people really like blue cheese but have only ever had the opportunity to experience a mediocre ver-sion. We still encounter customers who ask for 'a piece of Danish Blue'. They do this because that is what their local supermarket has been offering them for the last 40 years. When we explain we don't have any but offer a taste of several others, they always leave happy with at least one piece of a new favourite and hopefully they will be back for more.

LEFTOVER CHEESE

As with all food, it is terrible to see good cheese go to waste, especially when we consider the effort and resources that have gone into producing it. It is totally unnecessary to ever be in a position where cheese is being thrown in the bin. The first step is to buy small and often if possible, as this not only cuts down on leftovers but also keeps the cheese in good condition. Unwanted mould on the surface of the cheese is the most common reason why people discard it. Surface mould is actually a sign that the cheese is being kept in good condition, not too cold and not too dry. Simply scrape the mould from the surface with the face of a sharp knife; there's no need to even cut a thick slice off. Softer cheeses with an active rind can develop off flavours if kept in the wrong conditions or for too long; the only solution is to use them up before this happens. Always trust your nose and tastebuds: they have been developed over millions of years of evolution to tell you what is good to eat.

Cooking with dried-up spare pieces is a great way to use up small amounts of cheese left over in the fridge. These can be great in a sauce or on a pizza. As a last resort you can freeze cheese but on defrosting its texture can suffer badly. A great solution is to grate the cheese before freezing and then use it in cooking when defrosted, where the texture is less important.

THE CHEESE COURSE

We are great proponents of eating cheese at all times for all occasions – breakfast, lunch and dinner, sandwiches, snacks and meals. The after-dinner cheeseboard can, however, be a great way to finish off a meal and also to take the time in company to really enjoy great cheeses.

A variety of textures, flavours and strengths should be the foundation of the cheeseboard. However, one great cheese is better than many mediocre cheeses. If you are trying to work out quantities, we generally say a ¼ pound or 110g per person. So if you are having six guests and serving five cheeses then you need about 130g of each cheese. Make sure that you serve the cheese at room temperature. If you take them straight from the fridge just before you serve, the flavours and aromas will be inhibited and the textures too firm. This does not mean that the cheese should be really warm. Avoid leaving them in a hot kitchen for hours, as this will be particularly damaging to the textures. Serving individual plates of cheese can be a bit precious; the conviviality of sharing a board of cheeses in the centre of the table is one of the nicest aspects of this after-dinner course. A shared board also allows everyone to go for an extra piece of their favourite and perhaps avoid one they dislike. Take the opportunity to serve some unusual cheeses with distinctive flavours that you don't normally experience but also include a couple of more subtle cheeses. Some cheese on a good board should be mild, rich and unctuous. A wonderful local goats' cheese tasting of fresh herbs and grass. An aged hard unpasteurised cheese with all its subtle and long flavours. A blue in good condition served at room temperature and just a morsel of something wild and strong.

Most importantly seek out great cheeses. If you do this and serve them from a paper bag straight from the fridge, they will still provide a fantastic course.

If you are drinking wine with your meal it is more than likely that you have at the latter end of the meal moved on to a relatively robust red wine. This is the main reason why most people associate eating cheese with drinking red wine. However, we find the softer, rounder flavours offered by white wines in general offer a better accompaniment to cheese than the more tannic red wines. A bottle of sweet wine or a fortified wine like port or sherry can also be a wonderful accompaniment to this course and will work well if you continue drinking them with a sweet dessert after the cheese.

HOW TO CHOOSE BLUE CHEESE

Many of the blues do surprisingly well in pre-pack, especially in foil wrap. It is more often the fact that the cheeses are being produced for a pre-pack market than the packaging itself that should ring alarm bells about the quality of the cheese inside. When producing a blue cheese for the pre-pack market, the main focus is very often on getting an even spread of blue veining through the cheese. When we cannot depend on a cheesemonger to offer a taste or some advice, all we are left with is our eyes and so the smart people in the retail business put more emphasis on the look than the taste. As with all cheese, blues will always be much better cut freshly from the wheel. The most common fault with blue cheese bought over the counter is that it has become overripe. Watch out for cheeses in which the paste next to the rind has begun to brown. Overripe blue cheeses have a tendency to look tired, the paste is a little dull and the blue and green mould and paste have begun to merge.

HOW TO STORE BLUE CHEESE

With the exception of Stilton and some firmer blues, such as Cabrales, blue cheeses really need to be kept cold. If the temperature is too high they will ooze moisture and lose their structure. Aluminium foil is often used to wrap these cheeses and it seems to work very well, allowing a little air circulation but also stopping them from drying out. Once wrapped well and in the fridge they keep very well. If you get a piece of blue cheese which you find too young, with a lack of flavour and an overly firm texture, leaving it wrapped in foil at the back of the fridge for a week or so can mature it nicely. As these cheeses mature they get more blue mould spreading across the cheese, adding to its flavour, and the body continues to break down and get softer. Then at a certain point the cheeses will begin to dry out, so be careful not to leave it too long!

FOOD WE LIKE WITH BLUE CHEESE

○ Walnuts work so well with blue cheese that they've become a food cliché. You can add a bit of jazz to the combination by stirring some olive, maple syrup, smoked paprika and salt together and then tossing your walnuts in the sticky oil before roasting them in the oven to caramelise them. Or do the same with pecans just to mix it up a bit. These sticky nuts make a perfect partner to a blue cheese on a cheeseboard.

○ Blue cheeses tend to be soft and crumbly, so a bit of crunch works well with them. Keep a jar of toasted sunflower, pumpkin and linseeds in your cupboard (just toast them on a tray with a drizzle of olive oil and some salt) and some blue cheese in your fridge, and you're never stuck for a snack. Cut up any fruit you have – apples, pears, even oranges – put them in a bowl and crumble over a little blue cheese and then sprinkle with the toasted seeds.

○ Like pressed cooked cheeses, the blues are big enough to take on sweeter jams and chutneys. A cherry and port compote works a treat spooned on to a plate beside a wedge of Stilton.

○ Gnocchi, homemade or shop bought, are delicious with a blue cheese sauce.

○ Brassicas love blue cheese, so for an Irish-inspired meal, try stirring some blue cheese into your colcannon mix of kale and potatoes at Hallowe'en.

○ Sweet potato wedges dusted with paprika and roasted in olive oil are delicious with some blue cheese dressing drizzled over the top. You can make this by warming a chunk of blue cheese with a little natural yoghurt.

○ Crusty, yeasty or sourdough breads work with all cheeses and blues are not an exception. We think our rye and linseed crackers offer a crunch and nuttiness that complements creamy blues.

DRINKS WE LIKE WITH BLUE CHEESES

○ Debates over pairing cheese and wine will continue for eternity, but the one combination that everyone agrees on is the pairing of blue cheese and dessert wine. Yes, Port and Stilton works. Like all food traditions it's traditional because it's good. Mould plays a role in sweet wines, too, which might explain why they're a match made in microbe heaven. After all, sweet wines like Sauternes are made from grapes that have begun to rot on the vines through fermentation by *Botrytis cinerea*, a fungus that shrivels and sweetens the grapes. The result is a syrupy fragrant wine that works brilliantly with the salty fizz of a good blue cheese. Other sweet wine such as aged Riesling, Grunerveltliner, Reciotos and icewines are also excellent. Paired with crackers it's the perfect end to a meal.

○ Blue cheese and porter is as close to a perfect match as you will get. The chocolaty rich tones of Irish stout porter roll over the sweet and salty creaminess of blue cheese faultlessly. Both are improved by the pairing, which is what we are always after. This combination works for milder, sweeter blues and the tangier spicy ones.

○ For a non-alcoholic drink, try a strong, fizzy kombucha, a fermented tea, often homemade but also now widely available commercially.

SOME OF OUR FAVOURITE BLUE CHEESES

VALDEÓN BLUE

PRODUCER: various dairies
MADE: León, Spain
PRODUCTION: small to medium
dairies
MILK: cows' and goats' mix
RENNET: traditional
TYPE: blue

RIND: natural, wrapped in syca-
more leaves
RIPENING: minimum 45 days,
cool damp cellars
APPEARANCE: 4kg wheels
TEXTURE: firm but moist
TASTE: intense, sweet and spicy

VALDEÓN IS instantly recognisable because of its rind, which is wrapped in sycamore leaves. Before the availability of plastic wrap or foil, this was a handy way to help protect the cheese from drying out too fast. The leaves are also credited with encouraging particular cultures to develop and penetrate the rind. The cheeses are made and matured in the Valdeón valley in León on the southern side of the Picos de Europa. This is quite a robust blue but, despite its strength, Valdeón is milder than other blues produced in the area, most notably Cabrales. The paste when the cheese is not too mature retains a lovely creaminess. It has a dense veining of blue mould and a resulting sharp tang but not so much as to overpower some of the more subtle, sweeter flavours.

BELLINGHAM BLUE

PRODUCER: Peter Thomas
MADE: Co. Louth, Ireland
PRODUCTION: small dairy, using
  milk from a single herd
MILK: raw cows'
RENNET: vegetarian
TYPE: blue

RIND: natural
RIPENING: 12 to 24 weeks
APPEARANCE: 3kg wheel
TEXTURE: firm but moist
TASTE: sharp and peppery with a
  little sweetness and pungency

PETER HAS been making his blue cheese since 2000. Production is quite small and Peter can easily be described as a real artisan producer dedicated to using raw milk and producing a unique product. The cheese is quite firm for a blue but the paste holds moisture so it does not feel dry in the mouth. The large, well-spread openings in the paste allow a strong growth of blue through the cheese. Its flavour can be initially harsh but it has length and depth and you will get lots of fruity, peppery and even floral flavours and aromas to follow. Peter likes his cheese well aged, when the flavour has really become robust – we persuade him to sell it to us a little younger, to keep those more subtle flavours.

CROZIER BLUE

PRODUCER: Grubb family
MADE: Fethard, Co. Tipperary,
  Ireland
PRODUCTION: farm, using milk
  from a single herd
MILK: sheep's
RENNET: vegetarian

TYPE: blue
RIND: natural
RIPENING: 8 to 16 weeks
APPEARANCE: 1.5kg wheel
TEXTURE: soft and buttery
TASTE: sweet and sharp, with a
  rich, fermented herb aroma

CROZIER BLUE is a sister cheese of Cashel Blue, and is made in the same production facility. The same cheese moulds are used to shape both cheeses, so they look almost exactly the same. On the counter it can be difficult to distinguish between them but the sheep's milk of Crozier gives the paste a much paler colour and the rind tends to be green blue to Cashel's dusty blue. The Crozier can also take a longer maturing period than Cashel and we would sell it up to two weeks older than Cashel. The resulting cheese is rich and well rounded with a decent salty bite.

ROQUEFORT PETITE CAVE

PRODUCER: Gabriel Coulet
MADE: Aveyron, France
PRODUCTION: dairy
MILK: raw sheep's
NAME PROTECTION: AOC, PDO
RENNET: traditional
TYPE: blue

RIND: natural
RIPENING: 3 months
APPEARANCE: 3kg wheel
TEXTURE: soft and buttery
TASTE: sweet and sharp with a rich fermented herb aroma

THE USE OF mouldy bread in the making of Roquefort reinforces the point that cheese was made by instinct well before anyone knew the science behind it. The mould *Penicillium roqueforti* was originally created from bread left in the caves. Over several months the loaves become totally shrouded in blue mould, which is then powdered and used to create the blue mould in the cheese. While most of the Penicillin is now produced in labs, some Roquefort makers still use the old method. The mould is added to the milk before it sets and grows happily through the natural holes of the cheese. All Roquefort cheese must be aged in the natural caves at Roquefort-sur-Soulzon. France's dairy giant Lactalis now owns the majority of the caves, producing more than 60 per cent of the world's Roquefort under its Société brand name. We recently found our favourite in Gabriel Coulet's Roquefort Petite Cave. Gabriel's cheese spends three weeks in the *fleurines* or caves of Mont Combalou, a week longer than the minimum two weeks other cheesemakers give it, which adds a deeper flavour. We find that many of the Roqueforts that are commonly available are quite one dimensional, the sharp flavour of the blue so dominant that the more gentle flavours and aromas of this great sheep's milk cheese do not get a chance to come through. Roquefort Petite Cave does have a pronounced blue tang but there are also notes of sweet butter, caramel and gentle wood smoke.

CASHEL BLUE

PRODUCER: Grubb family
MADE: Fethard, Co. Tipperary, Ireland
PRODUCTION: farm, using milk from five farms
MILK: cow's
RENNET: vegetarian

TYPE: blue
RIND: natural
RIPENING: 8 to 14 weeks
APPEARANCE: 1.5kg wheel
TEXTURE: soft and buttery
TASTE: sweet and gently sharp, with a rich, fermented herb aroma

CASHEL IS such a pleasure to sell; its creamy texture and sweet salty flavour are appealing even to customers who would normally be a little scared of blue cheeses. When matured to the right age, the texture is buttery and almost spreadable, and under the rind it is bulging. In Ireland you can buy Cashel Blue in pretty much every supermarket. It is great to see a farmhouse cheese and relatively new creation enter into popular food culture in the way this cheese has. However, the reaction from our customers when they taste and buy Cashel off our counter reinforces the often doubted theory that pretty much the same cheese from a specialist shop is of better quality. If customers are used to buying from a supermarket they will often comment on how different our Cashel is, and other customers comment that they made the mistake of buying Cashel in a supermarket recently and it was a very different cheese. It is hard to pin down what makes the Cashel we sell so much more appealing. We believe it is a combination of a few differences – cutting fresh from the whole wheel, the Grubbs selecting particular wheels for us and generally a longer maturing time.

SHROPSHIRE BLUE, COLSTON BASSETT

PRODUCER: Colston Bassett Dairy
MADE: Nottinghamshire, England
PRODUCTION: small dairy, four
  farms
MILK: cows'
RENNET: vegetarian
TYPE: blue

RIND: natural
RIPENING: 6 to 8 weeks
APPEARANCE: 8kg cylinder, paste
  coloured orange red with annatto
TEXTURE: firm, creamy
TASTE: fruity, sweet, gentle
  sharpness

THIS RELATIVELY modern cheese was invented in Inverness in the 1970s, presumably as a means of producing a Stilton-style cheese that was not subject to the same stringent geographical restrictions. Colston Bassett Dairy make the cheese in the same-sized cheese moulds as Stilton and before the cheeses are opened they look very similar indeed. However, the orange annatto dye used in Shropshire Blue ensures that the visual similarity between the two stops as soon as the wheel is opened. Stilton and Shropshire are quite similar in taste. In equivalent conditions, Shropshire Blue is the milder of the two, with a slightly fruitier flavour and less bitterness and richness than their Stilton.

FOURME D'AMBERT

PRODUCER: Fromageries Morin
MADE: Auvergne, France
PRODUCTION: small dairy
MILK: cows'
NAME PROTECTION: AOC, PDO
RENNET: traditional
TYPE: blue

RIND: natural
RIPENING: 8 to 12 weeks
Appearance: 2kg cylinder
TEXTURE: firm, creamy
TASTE: gentle sharpness with
  sweet, creamy background

FOURME D'AMBERT is among the most ancient cheeses in France and can trace its origins back at least as far as the eleventh century. Some sources indicate that the cheese existed in the mountains of Forez even prior to the formation of the Roman Empire. It is made in a lovely, tall cylinder with a crusty but moist bluey-grey rind. Within, the paste is quite open and has large pockets lined with blue mould. Despite the abundant distribution of blue throughout the cheese, the flavour is surprisingly mild. The aroma is sweet leaf mould and cellar, and the flavour is quite fruity and round. Much of the delicacy of our Fourme d'Ambert is down to the excellent selection and ripening by Xavier Morin of Aurillac. We are often surprised when tasting other Fourme d'Ambert how much drier the paste is and how harsh the flavour in comparison.

STICHELTON

PRODUCER: Joe Schneider
MADE: Nottinghamshire, England
PRODUCTION: small dairy, milk from a single herd
MILK: raw cows'
RENNET: traditional
TYPE: blue

RIND: natural
RIPENING: 8 to 12 weeks
APPEARANCE: 8kg cylinder
TEXTURE: firm, creamy
TASTE: savoury and nutty with a spicy, sweet, blue tang

STICHELTON WAS born out of the desire for Randolph Hodgson of Neal's Yard to revisit the flavours of raw milk Stilton that he had experienced in the early 1980s. It became possible with the partnership of Welbeck Estate and cheesemaker Joe Schneider. This cheese cannot be called Stilton because the use of raw milk rules it out, even though it ticks every other box in terms of production and geography. One of the regulations that govern the use of the name Stilton is that the cheese must be made from pasteurised milk. This rule was added just after Colston Bassett had begun to use pasteurised milk in the 1980s and the atmosphere was one of mistrust for raw milk and a view that pasteurisation was the future for successful cheeses. The use of raw milk is not the only difference between Stichelton and other Stiltons. The make is much slower, allowing the natural cultures and added starters time to develop in the milk and create the right acidity for coagulation without using too much rennet. This produces a much more delicate curd that must be handled with care and results in a creamy texture in the mature cheese. Looking at the open cheese on the counter, it often looks a little less attractive than a well-marbled Stilton but the mouth feel and flavour are rich and very rewarding.

And here are some favourites from our friends around the world.

BLAUROTER

PRODUCER: Bio-Käserei Zurwies
MADE: Allgäu, Germany
PRODUCTION: small dairy, using milk from neighbouring farms
MILK: cows'
RENNET: traditional
TYPE: blue
RIND: washed

RIPENING: 3 weeks
APPEARANCE: 500g brick shape
TEXTURE: soft, tacky and gooey texture
TASTE: intensely savoury and rich; funky and dank, but balanced with tremendous butterfat

THIS CHEESEMAKER, Anton Holzinger, is a cheese poet, revolutionary and philosopher. Everything he makes is special. This cheese delivers a Gorgonzola dolce vibe with a barnyard kiss. *Adam Moskowitz, Colombia Cheese, New York, USA*

CHIRIBOGA BLUE

PRODUCER: Käserei Obere Mühle
MADE: Bavaria, Germany
PRODUCTION: farm, using their own milk
MILK: cows'
RENNET: traditional
TYPE: blue with added cream
RIND: natural

RIPENING: 6 weeks
APPEARANCE: 2kg wheel
TEXTURE: semi-soft but dense, buttery texture; softer, wetter texture when aged longer
TASTE: bright, lactic (sour creamy) front, ending with rich cream and butter

MADE BY an Ecuadorian cheesemaker, Arturo Chiriboga, who married a German woman, this cheese is made entirely off-grid.

Eight per cent of their power comes from hydro and 20 per cent from solar. It is blue butter. *Adam Moskowitz, Colombia Cheese, New York, USA*

JAMBEROO BLUE

PRODUCER: Pecora Dairy
MADE: Robertson, NSW, Australia
PRODUCTION: farmhouse, single origin, single herd
MILK: sheep's
RENNET: vegetarian
TYPE: blue
RIND: natural moulds

RIPENING: 8 to 12 weeks
APPEARANCE: wheel
TEXTURE: semi-firm, dense
TASTE: dynamic combination of classic sweetness of sheep's milk and a jammy, yeasty, musky, savoury and piquant blue mould flavour profile

A BACKGROUND sweetness, a classic of sheep's milk, breaks through the salty, metallic mould profiles of this farmhouse blue, giving way to an earthier palate and then back again to a sweetness – a fruity, long, lingering flavour profile. Boring it ain't! This cheese earned 'city-corporate-turned-country-farmer-cheesemakers' Michael and his wife Cressida McNamara a gold medal in its very first year of commercial production. It's a fine example of Australia's fledgling artisan cheese movement. *Claudia Bowman, McIntosh & Bowman Cheesemongers, Sydney, Australia*

RECIPES

SPRING

—

Pancetta and Gorgonzola Gnocchi

This is one of the tastiest and fastest cheese dinners. It is also a dish where you have a good chance of finding all the ingredients under one roof in a good deli.

SERVES 4

1 onion, finely chopped

20g butter

100g pancetta, sliced

50ml white wine

150ml cream

100g creamy Gorgonzola

100g spinach, washed and chopped, or baby spinach, washed

500g gnocchi

freshly ground black pepper

Parmesan, grated

Have a large pot of boiling water ready for the gnocchi.

Fry the onions with the butter in a large frying pan over a low heat until soft. Add the pancetta and turn up the heat a little to give it a sizzle. When the pancetta starts to crisp, add the white wine and reduce the liquid to a slick of moisture.

Add the cream and Gorgonzola, and stir the two together as the cheese melts. Slowly reduce this creamy mix until it starts to thicken and form a sauce.

Tip in the spinach and let it wilt. Turn the heat down very low.

Cook and drain the gnocchi, then add them to your rich, tasty, creamy sauce. Stir carefully so they are all coated.

Serve immediately with a twist of black pepper and shavings of Parmesan.

SUMMER

Cashel Blue, Broad Bean, Pea, Mint, Coriander and Flaked Almond Salad

If your broad beans and peas are small and fresh enough you can make this salad without even cooking them. Just pod and peel them, splitting the broad beans in two with a thumbnail. Or mix raw and slightly blanched beans and peas for a variety of texture. It's a celebration of bounty in the garden, best made at the height of summer.

SERVES 4

300g broad beans

250g peas

a good handful of fresh mint leaves

a good handful of fresh coriander leaves

1 lime

2 tablespoons olive oil

200g Cashel Blue

100g flaked almonds

Briefly blanch the broad beans and peas in boiling water, drain them and slip the broad beans out of their individual skins.

Tear the mint and coriander leaves off their stems and mix them together in a large serving bowl with the peas and beans.

Zest and juice the lime. Add the zest to the salad and combine the juice with the olive oil in a small jug or bowl. Blend 1 tablespoon of the cheese into the lime juice and oil to make a light dressing. Use this to dress the herbs, beans and peas.

Toast the flaked almonds under a grill or in a dry frying pan, being careful not to let them burn. (This can happen in a split second, so watch carefully.)

Crumble the remainder of the cheese into small chunks over the salad and top with the toasted almonds. Drizzle with the dressing and serve.

AUTUMN

Kale Crisps with Stilton Cream

This is a great recipe for using up any leftover Stilton. The spreadable Stilton cream will keep in a tub and can be used as a dipping sauce or loosened with a little more oil and lemon juice to make a blue cheese salad dressing.

MAKES 500G

200g Greek yoghurt
2 tablespoons light tahini
250g Stilton
a large handful of black kale, or cavolo nero
olive oil

Preheat the oven to 160ºC.

Gently warm the yoghurt, tahini and crumbled Stilton in a saucepan over a low heat, stirring until it is smooth and creamy.

Remove the stalks from the kale but leave the tongue-shaped

leaves whole. Coat your hands with olive oil and rub it into the leaves until they're glistening.

Put the kale on a roasting tray and cook in the oven for 10–15 minutes, until the leaves are browned slightly but not blackened. Allow the kale to cool on the tray to a crispy finish.

Using a knife, spread each kale crisp with a thin layer of the Stilton cream. Serve immediately.

WINTER

Kefir and Walnut Scones

Using einkorn flour, an ancient grain that is smaller than hybrid modern grains, adds a great nutty flavour to these almost-savoury scones. It also makes them extremely light. But if you can't get einkorn flour, any wholewheat flour will do. We like to eat them hot out of the oven, butter melting on top and with a hefty slice of Cashel Blue.

MAKES 6

210g einkorn flour (or any wholewheat flour)

1 teaspoon baking powder

½ teaspoon baking soda

½ teaspoon salt

30g raw cane sugar

110g butter

90ml kefir milk or buttermilk

50g walnuts, finely chopped

Preheat the oven to 180°C.

Mix all the dry ingredients together and then rub in the butter until the mixture looks like breadcrumbs.

Make a well in the centre and pour in the kefir milk or buttermilk. Bring the mixture together to form a sticky dough.

Add the finely chopped walnuts and press them into the dough. You may need to add some more flour if your dough is too sticky.

Lightly flour a surface and turn out the dough. Pat it into a round about 4cm deep and then cut into circles using a scone cutter or a floured glass.

Place the scones on a baking sheet and bake them in the pre-heated oven for 20 minutes, turning the sheet around after 10 minutes to let them brown evenly.

Serve hot with butter and your favourite blue cheese.

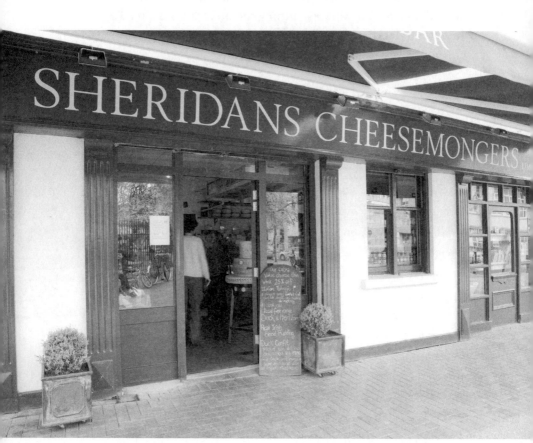

AFTERWORD

THOUGHTS FROM BEHIND
THE COUNTER

The origin of the initial concept is fading in the mists of time. Hunger and shame. There was nothing to eat; nothing interesting. The old shop in Castletownbere with its saucepans and shovels and Goulding's Manures clock wagging away the time, and smoked hams hanging from hooks in the ceiling and huge truckles of Cheddar on the wooden counter with their mouldy bandages. The crumbs of the cheese strewn around, scrumptious, tempting, melt-in-the-mouth crumbs which you could nibble at as you queued to be served with your message list. And then she would cut a fine, big chunk, golden or white, and what I miss the most is the way it crumbled. So they closed the shop and gutted it and extended it and re-opened it. Enter the trolley. Spotless, sterile, pre-packed portions sweating in their plastic. Tidy piles. Electronic scales. Keep moving. Don't block the aisles. No idle chatter. Big Brother is watching you. Don't ask for credit. Oh boy!

And then one day in a different shop that jolly French pair of geriatrics asked for the local cheese and were given Calvita. And then we bought a farm and a cow. Her name was Brisket and she only had one horn. She lost the other one gadding down a hill, tail-waving, full of the joys of spring. Her brakes must have failed. We had to put Stockholm tar on the hole right through the hot summer. And all the milk she had. At least three gallons a day. Wonder of wonders and what to do with it all.

345

And then remembering those marvellous Cheddars. So, for two years I made Cheddar. They were never as good as the ones in Castletownbere had been, but they were infinitely better than the sweaty vac-packed bits.

There was very little control at first but each failed batch spurred me on to achieve. I was hooked. Once I had four little Cheddars on a sunny windowsill outside, airing themselves, and Prince, the dog, stole them and buried them in the garden. They were nasty and sour and over-salted anyway. Those were the days.

So, one day Norman said, 'Why don't you try making a soft cheese for a change?' So I did. It was a quare hawk all right. Wild, weird and wonderful. Never to be repeated. You can never step twice into the same stream.

So there was this soft cheese beginning to run. We wrapped up about 12 oz of it and away it went with the vegetables and the pies and all the other good things to Sneem and The Blue Bull Restaurant, where it made its debut. The first, the one and only, Irish Farmhouse Cheese. At last, the real thing after so long. Rumour has it that there was a full eclipse of the sun and earth tremors when the first Milleens was presented on an Irish cheeseboard.

Milleens is no longer lonely as a cloud but forms a nucleus for the whole new industry in both farmhouse and, dare I say it, factory cheeses. A generation of new cheeses has developed in its wake. A dream is being realised.

A serious market-research study might well have had negative results. In those early days we were quite accustomed to hearing, 'It'll never sell.'

We have supplied the Dorchester Hotel in London with two cheeses a week for over five years without fail. Their cheese board is considered one of the greatest in the world. They have never once returned a cheese or made any complaint. Quite the contrary. We are proud of Milleens in *terms of quality, consistency and orderly improvement, and perhaps, above all, the way in which it has contributed to the opening up of delicatessen counters in every corner of Ireland where heretofore it had been considered impossible.*

Veronica Steele, Milleens Cheese, 1986

It is almost 30 years since Veronica wrote this and 20 years since we first began selling her cheese. So many great things have happened in the story of Irish cheese in that short time. We do not have the weight of cheesemaking heritage behind us. There is no long tradition of respect, verging on reverence, for cheese and the cheesemaker that can be found in the great cheesemaking nations of Europe. We do not have an established gastronomic culture and all the support that brings. There are no statutes protecting the integrity of our foods. But what was realised by Veronica and those who followed is that we have a blank page on which to draw something new and beautiful. Those same protections and traditions can inhibit as much as defend. Irish milk and dairying does have a long tradition. It is a part of our legends and our language; it has shaped our landscape. We have had the freedom to reach across Europe to gather the best of their great traditions and mix them with our own dairying culture to create new traditions of our own.

There are now well over 40 Irish farmhouse cheesemakers dotted around our small island making a living from producing cheese. There have been many great cheesemakers who have come and gone, but every year there are new producers renewing and reinvigorating the community. It is a tiny industry with a minuscule monetary value when compared with the multibillion Euro-Irish agri-food sector but its impact on Irish food culture has been enormous. The more famous cheeses are household names, found not only in specialist shops but in every large food store across the country. They have come to symbolise the potential of Irish food, presented at state functions and offered to visiting dignitaries and trade visitors. Not only is Irish farmhouse cheese a success in itself but the cheesemakers have created a culture of pride in Irish food that has led to a flourish in artisan and farmhouse producers of all kinds across the country. As a nation we no longer look to France or Italy for our culinary inspiration but instead take pride in what we very recently thought of as a basic and impoverished food heritage. There has been a realisation of the potential of Irish farming and farming people.

This new culture is, however, a delicate one, held together by the determination and inspiration of a small number of people. It exists despite, rather than because of, the country's agriculture and rural development policies. Standing behind the cheese counter we are proud of the Irish cheeses we have gathered and we are honoured to bring our customers some of the best cheeses in the world. But we cannot ignore what feels like an unstoppable force rushing across our world. When Norman and Veronica first arrived in 1974, there were 600 farmers on the Beara Peninsula milking small dairy herds. Today there are six. In 1975 there were 144,000 dairy farms across Ireland; now there are just 17,000.

You can start on the Steele's farm on the south-west tip of Ireland and go around the world to see the same story replicated – in Swiss Alpine valleys and in the Italian, Spanish, American and French countryside. There has been a massive consolidation process across the

farming world and this is the case in dairy farming more than in any other sector. Thousands of dairy farmers leave the land every year across Europe, selling small farms which are swallowed up by larger holdings. Large-scale farming is becoming the only viable option as farming methods become more intensified and productive. Dairy cows are producing more milk, helped by ever-more selective breeding and focused feeding regimes.

Small is not always better and big is not always bad. The commercial benefits are obvious. The new bigger farms typically need fewer people to work them. They produce a single product, a commodity with no variance from farm to farm, country to country. It is sold to a conglomerate skilled at finding new markets anywhere on the planet once existing ones are saturated. The great question is, who is reaping the benefits? Farmers' margins are decreasing as the cost of running the farms, particularly the cost of using increasing amounts of fertiliser needed to drive efficiencies, swells. The consumer has seen little decrease in cost, the price of milk products has, in general, tracked the overall increased costs of living. Milk processing has come to be dominated by fewer and fewer super conglomerates, with the top 20 companies representing almost 50 per cent of the total global turnover.

The cost of this increasingly detached production system can be seen very clearly in its impact on our environment. Ireland's agricultural emissions are our largest single-sector contributor to greenhouse gas emissions, accounting for a third of our total planet-heating emissions. The bacteria in a cow's stomach produces methane as they break down the grass and feed into nutrients. Methane is more than 30 times more powerful than carbon dioxide at trapping heat. In short, our cows pollute more than our cars. Despite the obvious environmental implications, Irish agricultural policy is to expand our dairy herd by 300,000 cows with the aim of increasing our already-phenomenal milk production by another 50 per cent by the year 2020. The policy makers who wrote these targets hold up New Zealand's dairy industry as the model for our success. But the New Zealand dairy story comes with a painful sting in the tail. The costs of cleaning waters, paying for agricultural emissions and fixing the soil were estimated by a Massey University economic study in April 2015 to be over $14 billion, more than the entire annual revenue of the dairy industry of $11.6 billion.*

The impact on our environment from the growing intensification of dairy farming is not restricted to greenhouse gas emissions and pollutants. The focus on increased production will inevitably have an impact on our physical landscape. As farms merge, smaller fields give way to larger ones, breaking down hedgerows and traditional field boundaries that have been part of our landscape for millennia. Biodiversity is heavily impacted through the destruction of mature grazing meadows, which are replaced by newly sown, more-productive but less-diverse grasses. Wildlife that has existed in the traditional farming landscape runs out of suitable habitat.

As competition for cheaper milk and protein commodities increases, every barrier to cheaper production must inevitably fall. It cannot be long before the sight of dairy cows roaming through the Irish countryside becomes rare. The production of arable feed, measured and balanced for optimum return, will replace traditional grass feeding. Animals will be housed in large sheds, not needing to waste valuable energy travelling to and from milking parlours. No need for farmers to walk out in the early morning or evening to gather the cattle in.

Perhaps the least spoken about but the most serious impact is on

* K. J. Foote, M. K. Joy and R. G. Death, 'New Zealand Dairy Farming: Milking Our Environment for All It's Worth', *Environmental Management*, April 2015.

the social fabric of our rural communities. More and more families are migrating from farming life to live and work around the giant processing plants that are feeding off the increased milk production. This brings a fundamental shift in our relationship with land and food production. The thousands of families who are leaving farming life mean thousands of children no longer grow up with a direct connection with land and food. The sharp divergence between the production of milk and dairy foods as a part of our culture, intrinsic to and interdependent on the farming heritage and environment of its origins, is growing ever wider.

Where does our cheese fit into this new landscape? Cheese is no longer a necessary transporter and preserver of nutrients; it has become obsolete as a functional food, easily replaced by modern preservation and speedy transport systems. As a people we love cheese, though; we love the taste of it, we love to cook with it, it brings us

Seamus and Manus Sheridan.

pleasure. Science's catch up on the traditional cheesemaker means that most of these properties can be achieved by efficient industrial production without the craft hand of the cheesemaker or the unique ecology of particular landscapes. We can satisfy our requirement for a thousand flavours and textures with handily packaged products at just the right price. We are no longer dependent on the restrictions of people or place. Across the world the demand for specialty cheese is growing. There are rapid improvements in technology that deliver a wider variety of tastebud-tingling flavours to a hungry market. The marketers move rapidly to wrap and package cheeses in a way that satisfies the growing appetite of consumers for a feeling of authenticity and a connection to a disappearing landscape. Is it more gluttony than gastronomy when we demand to have our appetite for taste and texture satisfied, focused only on that final hit of pleasure? Can we separate that final gratification from the steps that were taken to bring the food to our mouths? Are we satisfied with the soothing messages of the marketing departments of the giant food corps, telling us the selected stories we want to hear?

Genuine farmhouse cheese is one of the few products where the link between real people and real places is intrinsic to its value. It allows us to taste, to eat and to share food, to be a part of a process, the last link in a long chain. The full pleasure built into the atoms of the cheese carries the story of the fields, the animals, the hands and the history that brought it to our mouth. To share in this is a real pleasure.

We are not saying that farmhouse cheese is the answer to the world's agri-food problems but it is one small way in which we, as consumers and traders in food, can keep this link alive. Seeking out cheeses that retain this link is not an altruistic effort; it brings us so much pleasure and fulfilment.

Whether we enjoy cheese on a board in a cosmopolitan wine bar, or in a toasted sandwich in front of the TV, we have the opportunity not just to enjoy that taste sensation but to choose a food that supports our landscape, our heritage and our diversity of plant, animal and human life.

Standing behind the stall on the Galway market, opening those first boxes of cheese, we never imagined we would gain so much from our life in cheese. We have been blessed with a place in an amazing community. It is a community of customers, employees, food producers, farmers, chefs and the fraternity of cheesemongers in Ireland and across the world. In the grand scheme of things, cheese may seem like such an insignificant thing. It could be a food we might easily live without. The cheeses that carry the resonance within them of the authentic interaction of people with the land are more than just foods we eat or commodities to be traded. They carry within them the stories of human survival for thousands of years and hold one of the small threads of hope for the survival of the human connection to our land. We should not only seek to protect the cheeses and cultures, new and old, that provide this connection but look to nurture them so that they grow and become stronger. They can provide us not only with gastronomic delight but with a counter culture to a greedy and destructive ideology that sees land only as a resource to be exploited.

GLOSSARY OF TERMS

ACID COAGULATION: the method of splitting milk into curds and whey without using rennet. By lowering the pH of milk, the curds clump together when the protein molecules collide. Paneer, cottage cheese and queso blanco are all made using acid coagulation.

AFFINEUR: the French term used to describe an expert in the ageing and ripening of cheese.

AOC: Appellation d'Origine Contrôlée. This is the French system of regulating how and where cheeses must be made in order to call themselves by certain names. The Italian version is DOP, or Denominazione di Origine Protetta, and Spain operates a DO system, or Denominación de Origen.

ARTISANAL: French term defined under AOC regulations as a cheese produced in relatively small quantities using milk from the producer's own farm, though they may also purchase milk from local farms.

CARDOON THISTLE: the cardoon thistle (*Cynara cardunculus*) or artichoke thistle is a thistle-like plant in the sunflower family. It is native to the western and central Mediterranean. Cardoons are used as a source of enzymes for the coagulation of milk instead of animal rennet. It uses cardosin as its coagulating enzyme rather than chymosin and pepsin. The part of the plant used to coagulate milk for cheesemaking is the stamens that appear when the plant is in bloom. The stamens are plucked and can be used fresh but are normally dried and then soaked in water; the strained liquid is then added to the milk as another rennet. It is especially effective with the high fat and protein milk of sheep. It produces a softer curd and some distinct flavours in the cheese, particularly herbal and bitter.

CASEIN: the particular protein found in milk.

COAGULATION: the transformation of milk from liquid to solid by means of binding the proteins and trapping the fat within this structure.

Co-opérative: the French term defined under AOC regulations as a cheese that is made in an establishment run by local milk producers who pool their milk.

CURD: the part of milk that contains most of its protein solids and forms when the milk is split into curds and whey.

DO: Denominación de Origen. This is the Spanish system of regulating how and where cheeses must be made in order to call themselves by certain names.

DOP: Denominazione di Origine Protetta. This is the Italian system of regulating how and where cheeses must be made in order to call themselves by certain names.

ENGLISH TERRITORIALS: these are traditional cheeses that developed in distinct regions of England. Many but not all are bound in cloth and lard to protect them during maturing. Adding salt directly to the curd rather than through the rind along with milling the curd to help extract moisture are common production methods in these cheeses.

FERMIER: the French term defined under AOC regulations as a cheese which is produced on the farm where the milk is produced.

FPC: Fermentation Produced Chymosin – this version of microbial rennet is made by taking the enzyme-producing gene out of the mammal's cell's DNA string and introducing it into a host fungi's DNA string. This enables the fungi to produce the chymosin enzyme. This fungi can then be cultivated in a lab and fermented, ready to be used as rennet.

FRESH: when we use the word fresh to refer to a cheese, we mean a young, unaged cheese that is typically softer and moister than other types of cheese.

FUNGI: the plural of fungus. A fungus is any member of the group of organisms that includes unicellular microorganisms such as yeasts and moulds, as well as multicellular fungi that produce familiar fruiting forms known as mushrooms. They are mostly present on the rinds of cheeses or through the paste in blue cheeses.

INDUSTRIEL: French term defined under AOC regulations as a cheese that is made in a factory using milk from local, regional or national sources depending on the particular AOC regulations for the specific cheese.

LACTIC ACID: acid produced by the bacterial action on lactose within milk.

MOULDS: there are two kinds of entirely different moulds referred to in the cheese world. The first are the physical moulds: typically perforated plastic containers into which cheeses are put to be pressed into shape. The shape and size of the mould determines the shape and size of the cheese. The second type of moulds are the fungi that form living colonies on the surface rinds of cheeses, like bloomy rinds or the blue moulds used to make blue cheeses.

NSLABs: non-starter lactic acid bacteria – these are bacteria that are generally only found in small numbers in fresh curd but multiply during the maturation of the cheese. They are able to survive the relatively hostile environment of maturing cheese, including low moisture levels, high salt levels and high acidity. These bacteria strongly influence the biochemistry of curd maturation, contributing to the development of the final flavour and texture characteristics of the cheese. These essential bacteria are not added intentionally by the cheesemaker but come into the curd through the milk and environment. Even within industrial production systems these bacteria manage to infiltrate the curd, having survived pasteurisation, entered through the air or having managed to colonise parts of the apparatus.

PASTE: the word used to describe the interior part of a cheese to distinguish it from the rind.

PASTEURISED MILK: milk which has been heated to 71.7°C for at least 15 seconds or to 63°C for 30 minutes in order to kill any microorganisms which may be present.

PDO/PGI/TSG: A European system for the protection of the geographical names of certain foods. Since 1992, the European Union has developed a scheme to identify and protect the names of quality as PDO (Protected Designation of Origin) for products with a strong link to the defined geographical area where they are produced, or as PGI (Protected

Geographical Indication) for agricultural products and foods linked to a geographical area where at least one production step has taken place. Traditional Specialities Guaranteed (TSG) emphasise the products' traditional composition and traditional mode of production (proven usage on the domestic market for at least 25 years).

RAW MILK: milk that has not been heat-treated to more than 40°C.

RENNET: the ingredient added at the start of cheesemaking to coagulate milk into curds. Rennet works when its enzyme chymosin shaves the stabilising 'hairs' from the outside of the milk proteins, causing them to clump together to form curd. Rennet is made from the stomachs of young animals: calves, kids or lambs, depending on the kind of milk you're using to make cheese. Vegetarian rennet is derived from plants or made through genetic modification by injecting rennet-producing genes into bacteria fungi or yeasts to get them to produce chymosin during fermentation.

RIND: this is the covering of the cheese and it comes in many forms and plays many roles in how a cheese looks, tastes and feels. Rinds can be natural or nurtured. They can form when the outside of the cheese reacts with the air around it, be smeared on by the cheesemaker in the form of rind cultures or brine washes to encourage certain communities of microbes, and they can also be painted on in the form of inedible breathable waxes that prevent the cheese from drying out too quickly and seal in the textures and flavours. Rinds break down roughly into three categories: bloomy, washed and natural.

Silage: grasses and legumes preserved through air-tight storage and fermentation.

Spore: the seed of mould that will develop into a mould given the right conditions.

Thermalised milk: milk which has been heated to 63–65 °C for 15 seconds. Thermalising is similar to pasteurisation but a gentler process which is said not to damage the structure of the milk as severely as pasteurisation and so allow for better flavour development in cheeses.

Truckle: the term used in England to describe a cylindrical or barrel shaped cheese. This is the traditional shape of cloth-bound English territorial cheeses.

Vacuum packing: Vacuum packing is a method of packaging in plastic that removes all air prior to sealing. Modern cheeses are often matured in this type of sealed packaging, which by removing the air inhibits the growth of fungi on the surface of the cheese. The sealed pack also prevents moisture loss during maturation. Vacuum packing can also be used to seal pieces of cut cheese, preserving them quite well; however, if the rind of the cheese is made up of moulds or cultures the smothering effect can produce off flavours.

Whey: a by-product of the cheesemaking process, whey is the yellow liquid part of the milk that's left when the curds are removed. Once flushed away into rivers and seas, whey is now a lucrative dairy product sold to bodybuilders in the form of whey protein and used as a bulking agent and thickener in the processed foods and pharmaceutical industries.

PICTURE ACKNOWLEDGEMENTS

All images have been supplied courtesy of the authors and are the copyright of Sheridans Cheese Ltd unless otherwise stated. Every effort has been made to trace copyright holders. We apologise for any omissions in this respect and will be pleased to make the appropriate acknowledgements in future editions.

Text photographs
Page 11: courtesy of Harriet Leander. *Page 30:* courtesy of Mélanie Roffet-Salque/University of Bristol. Page 36: courtesy of Steve Rogers. Page 39: courtesy of the Kerry Cattle Society of England. Pages 40, 42, 45, 254 and 258: courtesy of Alberto Peroli. Pages 69, 71, 74, 75 and 76: courtesy of Anna L'Eveque. Pages 104, 106, 109, 113 and 119: courtesy of Cooleeney Farmhouse Cheese. Pages 151, 152, 154, 156 and 349: courtesy of Durrus Farmhouse Cheese. Pages 208 and 210: courtesy of Knockanore Farmhouse Cheese. Pages 308, 311, 314, 316 and 337: courtesy of J&L Grubb. Pages 323 and 347: courtesy of Bord Bia.

Colour
Page 5: courtesy of Durrus Farmhouse Cheese. Page 12: top, courtesy of Anna Leveque; bottom, courtesy of Bord Bia. Page 15: top right, courtesy of McKenna Guides.

INDEX

ABOUT THE AUTHORS

Seamus and **Kevin Sheridan** established Sheridans Cheesemongers in 1995 with a cheese stall at the Galway Saturday market in the west of Ireland. Since then the company has grown to include four cheese shops and a thriving wholesale business and now exports Irish food around the world. The brothers' food and business ethos is still firmly rooted in the simplicity of their first market stall. Their passion for food and respect for those who produce it has led them to be at the forefront of an exciting revival in Ireland's culinary heritage. Seamus and Kevin are tireless advocates for sustainable food and farming. They are both supporters of the Slow Food movement. Seamus is currently spokesperson on agriculture and food for the Irish Green Party and Kevin is chair of the Irish Taste Council.

Catherine Cleary is a journalist, author and broadcaster. She began her career as a news reporter with the *Irish Times* and became the paper's drugs and crime correspondent before joining the *Sunday Tribune* as its security correspondent. She started writing about food over a decade ago and now writes a weekly restaurant column for the *Irish Times*. Working with historian Juliana Adelman, Catherine co-wrote and presented *History on a Plate*, an RTE radio series on Irish food history. Her last book, *A Month of Somedays*, was an account of trying to take a gap year from the daily routine without leaving home.